SNOOPY

Titan Facsimile Editions by Charles M. Schulz

On sale now:
Peanuts
More Peanuts
Good Grief, More Peanuts!
Good Ol' Charlie Brown
You're Out of Your Mind, Charlie Brown!

Coming soon:
But We Love You, Charlie Brown
Peanuts Revisited
Go Fly a Kite, Charlie Brown
Peanuts Every Sunday

A NEW  BOOK

FEATURING

SNOOPY

by Charles M. Schulz

TITAN COMICS

SNOOPY

ISBN: 9781782761594

PUBLISHED BY TITAN COMICS, A DIVISION OF TITAN PUBLISHING GROUP LTD,

144 SOUTHWARK ST, LONDON SE1 0UP. TCN 304.

COPYRIGHT © 2015 BY PEANUTS WORLDWIDE LLC.

PRINTED IN INDIA.

10 9 8 7 6 5 4 3 2 1

WWW.TITAN-COMICS.COM

WWW.PEANUTS.COM

ORIGINALLY PUBLISHED IN 1957 BY RHINEHART & CO. INCORPORATED

NEW YORK & TORONTO

A CIP CATALOGUE RECORD FOR THIS TITLE

IS AVAILABLE FROM THE BRITISH LIBRARY.

THIS EDITION FIRST PUBLISHED: OCTOBER 2015

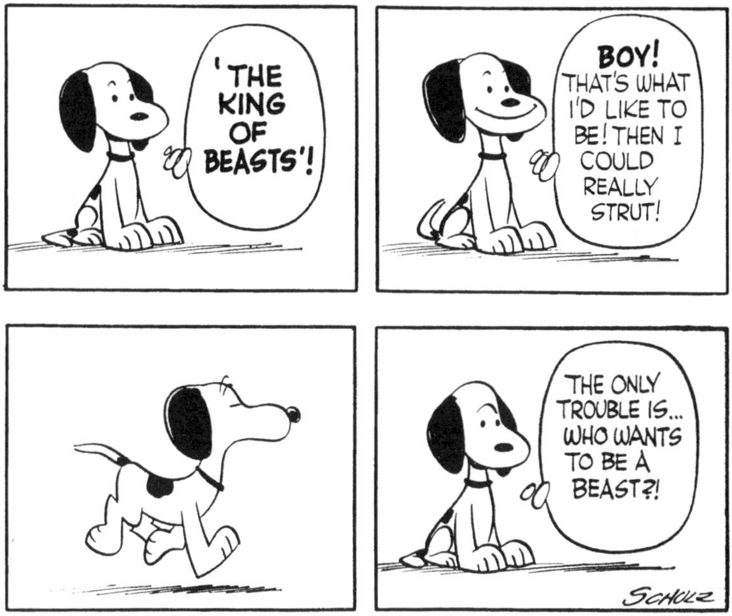
'THE KING OF BEASTS'!
BOY! THAT'S WHAT I'D LIKE TO BE! THEN I COULD REALLY STRUT!
THE ONLY TROUBLE IS... WHO WANTS TO BE A BEAST?!
SCHULZ

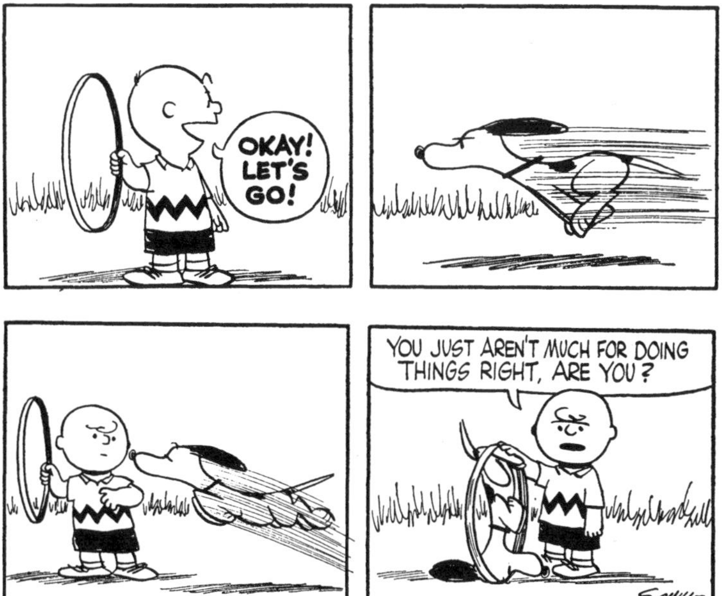
OKAY! LET'S GO!
YOU JUST AREN'T MUCH FOR DOING THINGS RIGHT, ARE YOU?
SCHULZ

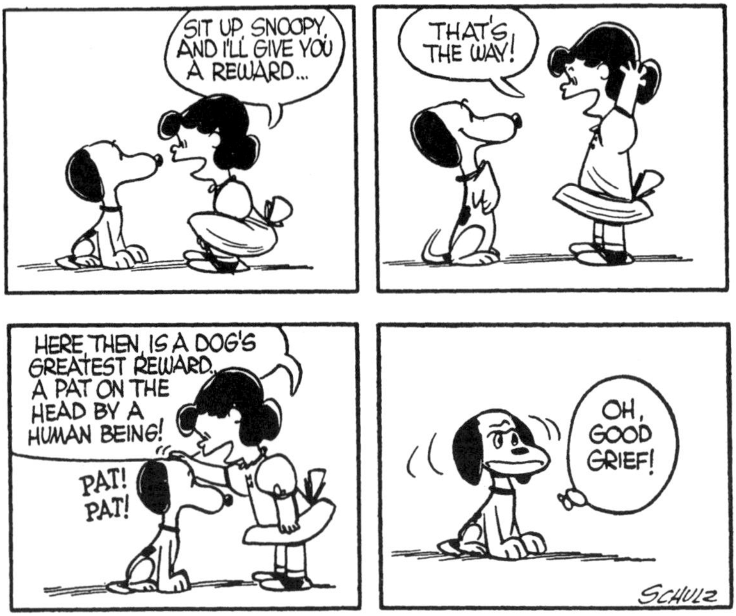
SIT UP, SNOOPY, AND I'LL GIVE YOU A REWARD...
THAT'S THE WAY!
HERE, THEN, IS A DOG'S GREATEST REWARD... A PAT ON THE HEAD BY A HUMAN BEING!
PAT! PAT!
OH, GOOD GRIEF!
SCHULZ

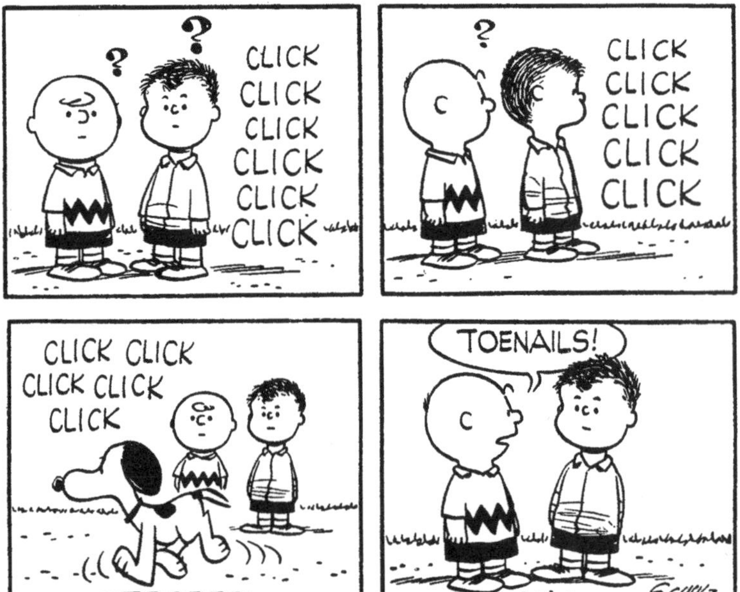
CLICK CLICK CLICK CLICK CLICK CLICK
CLICK CLICK CLICK CLICK CLICK
CLICK CLICK CLICK CLICK CLICK
TOENAILS!
SCHULZ

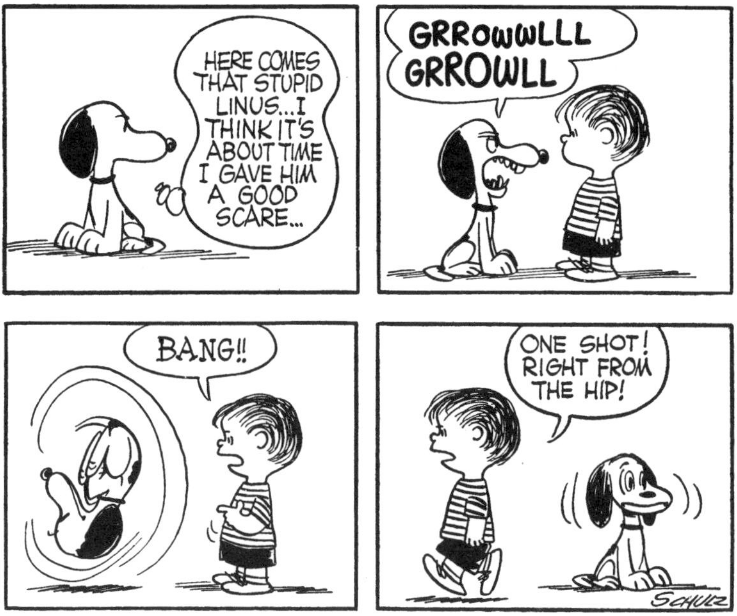
HERE COMES THAT STUPID LINUS...I THINK IT'S ABOUT TIME I GAVE HIM A GOOD SCARE...
GRROWWLLL GRROWLL
BANG!!
ONE SHOT! RIGHT FROM THE HIP!
SCHULZ

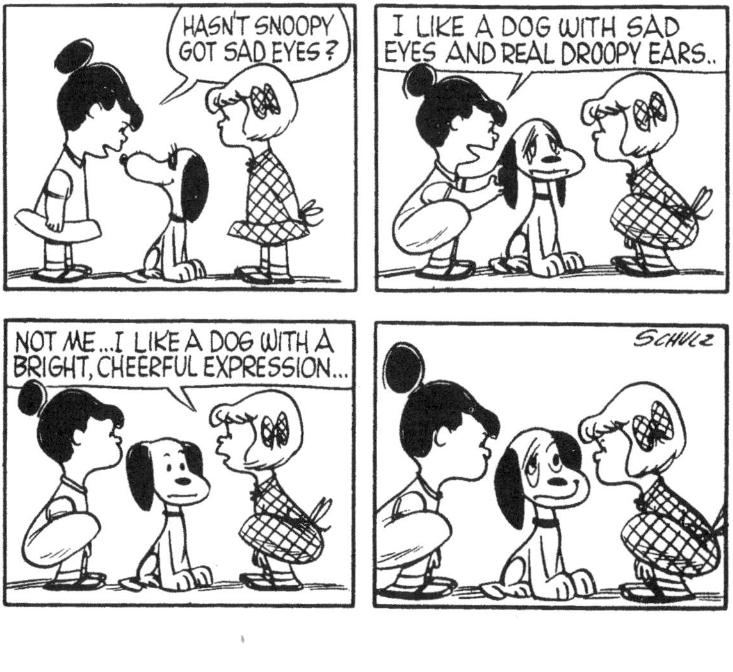
HASN'T SNOOPY GOT SAD EYES?
I LIKE A DOG WITH SAD EYES AND REAL DROOPY EARS..
NOT ME...I LIKE A DOG WITH A BRIGHT, CHEERFUL EXPRESSION...
SCHULZ

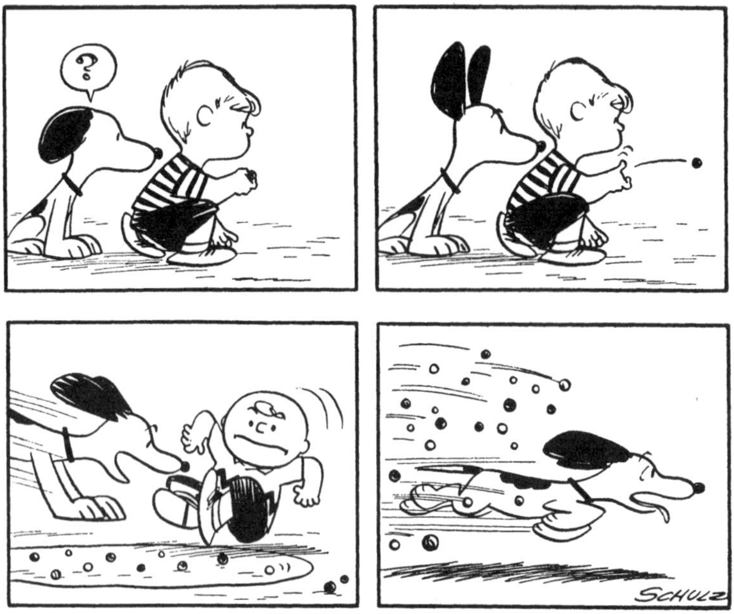
?
SCHULZ

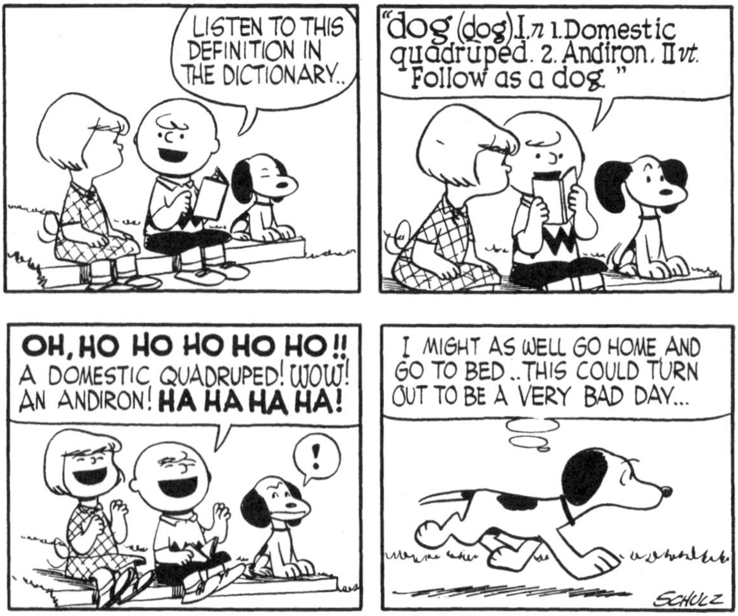
LISTEN TO THIS DEFINITION IN THE DICTIONARY..
"dog (dog) I. n 1. Domestic quadruped. 2. Andiron. II vt. Follow as a dog."
OH, HO HO HO HO HO!! A DOMESTIC QUADRUPED! WOW! AN ANDIRON! HA HA HA HA!
!
I MIGHT AS WELL GO HOME AND GO TO BED.. THIS COULD TURN OUT TO BE A VERY BAD DAY...
SCHULZ

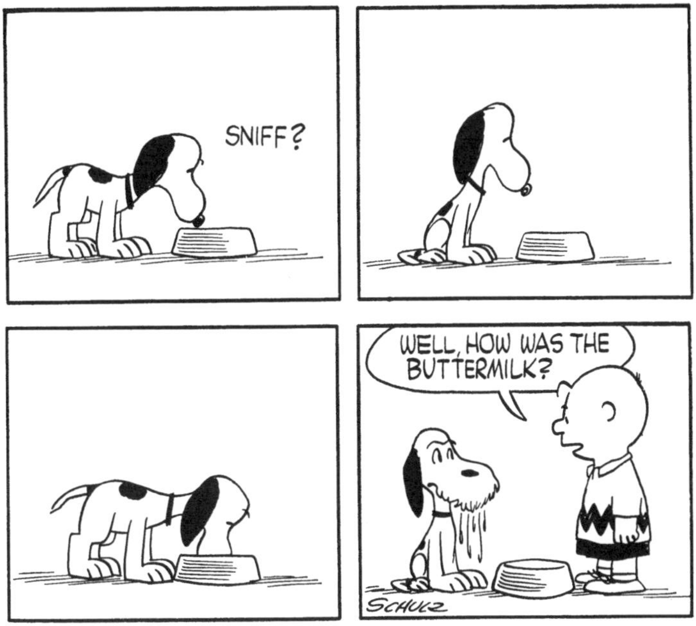
SNIFF?
WELL, HOW WAS THE BUTTERMILK?
SCHULZ

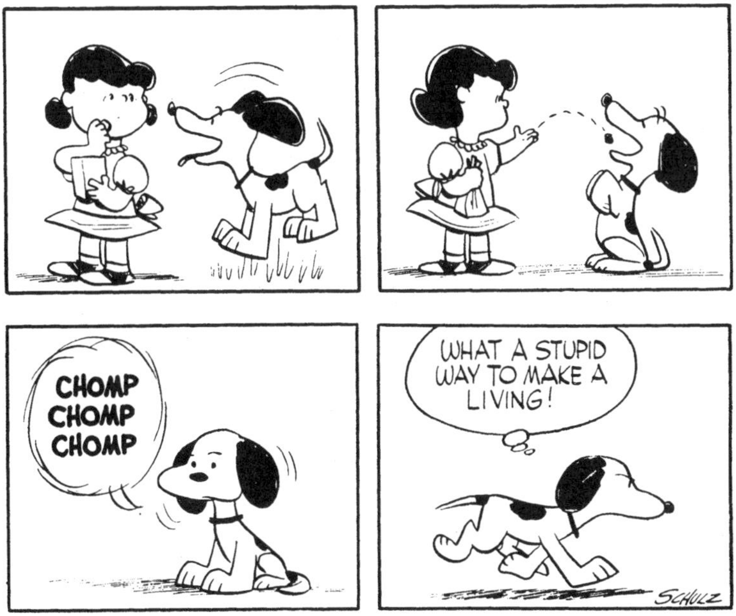
CHOMP CHOMP CHOMP
WHAT A STUPID WAY TO MAKE A LIVING!
SCHULZ

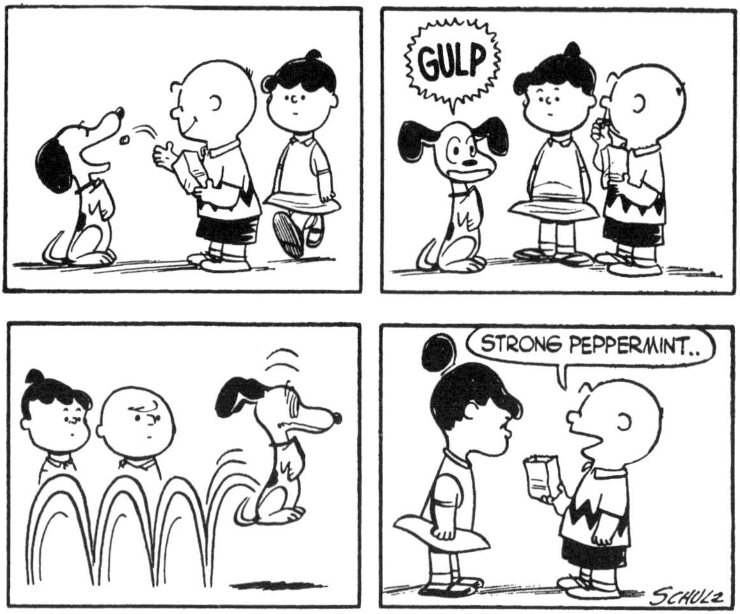
GULP
STRONG PEPPERMINT..
SCHULZ

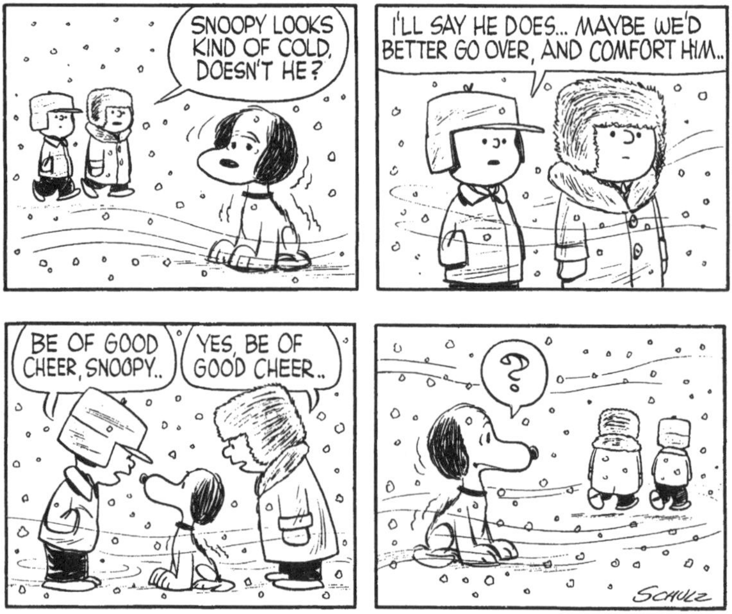
SNOOPY LOOKS KIND OF COLD, DOESN'T HE?
I'LL SAY HE DOES... MAYBE WE'D BETTER GO OVER, AND COMFORT HIM..
BE OF GOOD CHEER, SNOOPY..
YES, BE OF GOOD CHEER..
?
SCHULZ

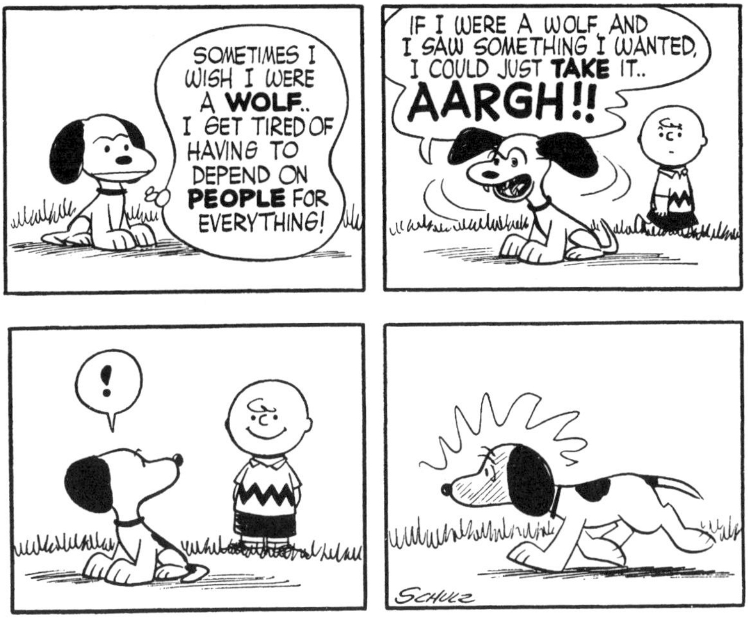
SOMETIMES I WISH I WERE A **WOLF**.. I GET TIRED OF HAVING TO DEPEND ON **PEOPLE** FOR EVERYTHING!
IF I WERE A WOLF AND I SAW SOMETHING I WANTED, I COULD JUST **TAKE** IT..
AARGH!!
!
SCHULZ

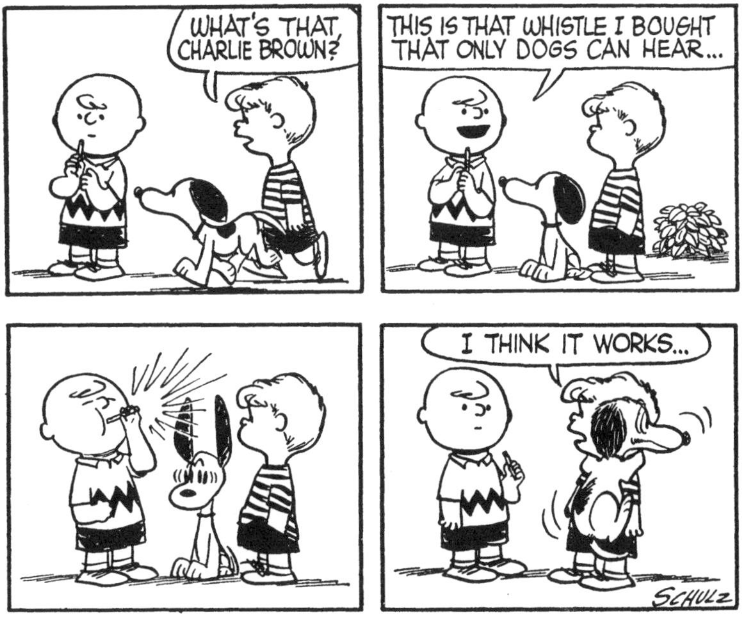
WHAT'S THAT, CHARLIE BROWN?
THIS IS THAT WHISTLE I BOUGHT THAT ONLY DOGS CAN HEAR...
I THINK IT WORKS...
SCHULZ

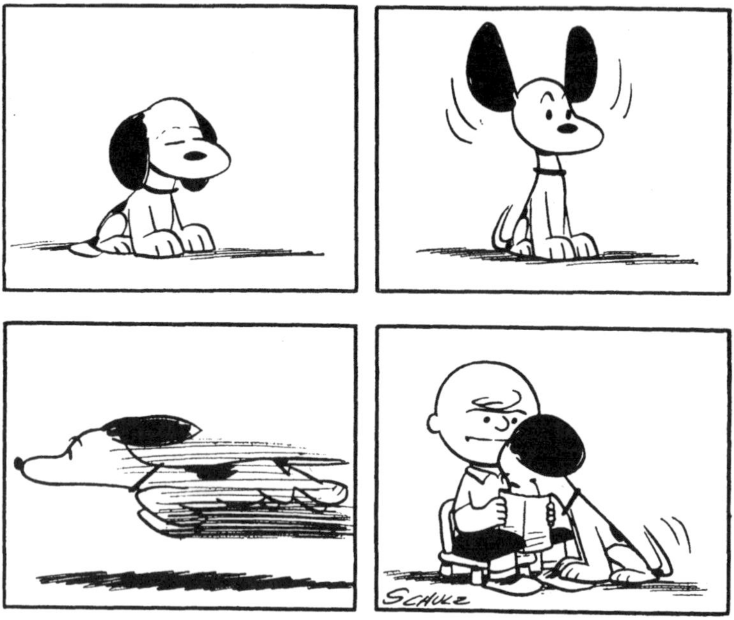

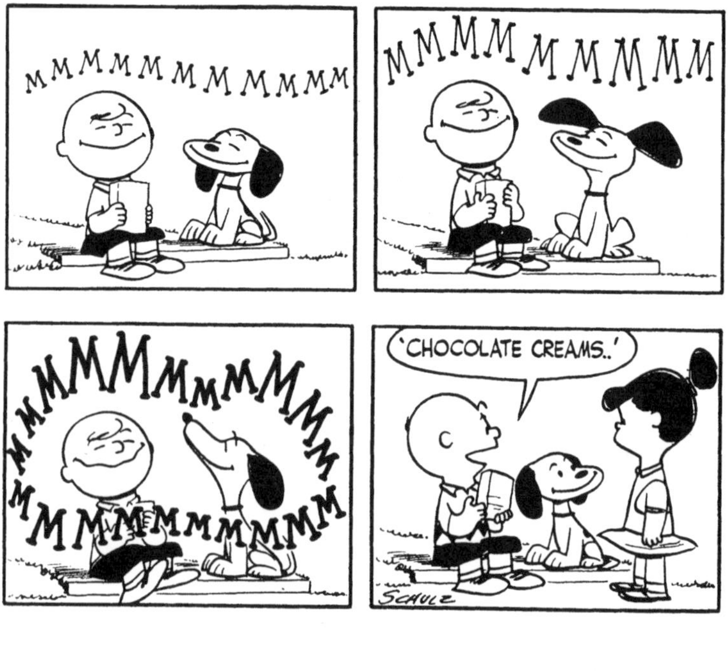
'CHOCOLATE CREAMS..'

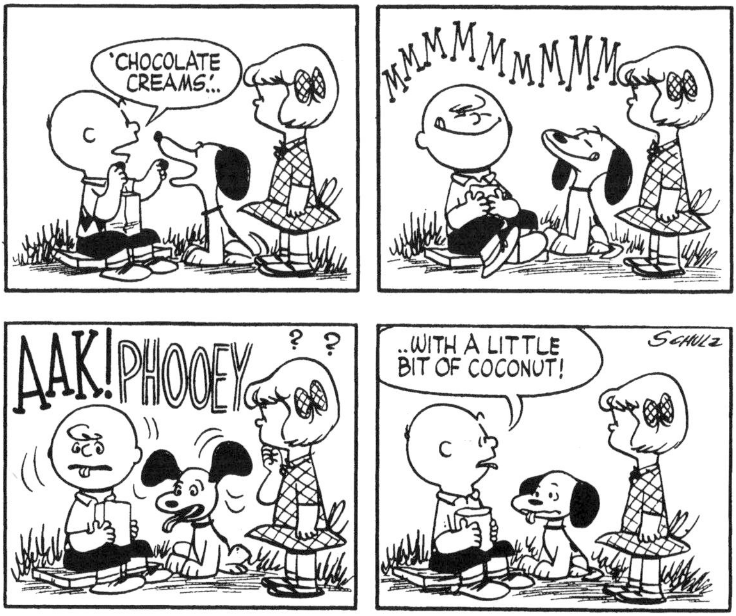
'CHOCOLATE CREAMS'...
MMMMMMMMMMM
AAK! PHOOEY
? ?
..WITH A LITTLE BIT OF COCONUT!
SCHULZ

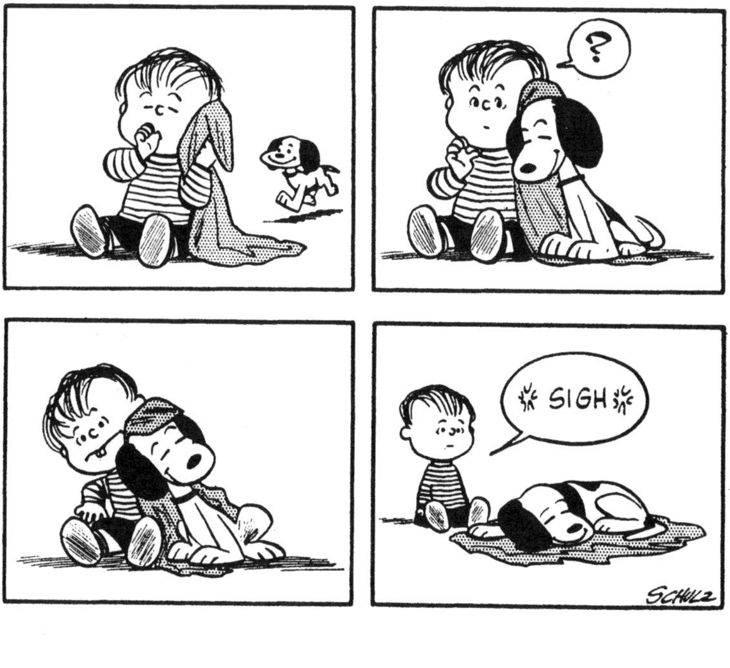
?
SIGH
SCHULZ

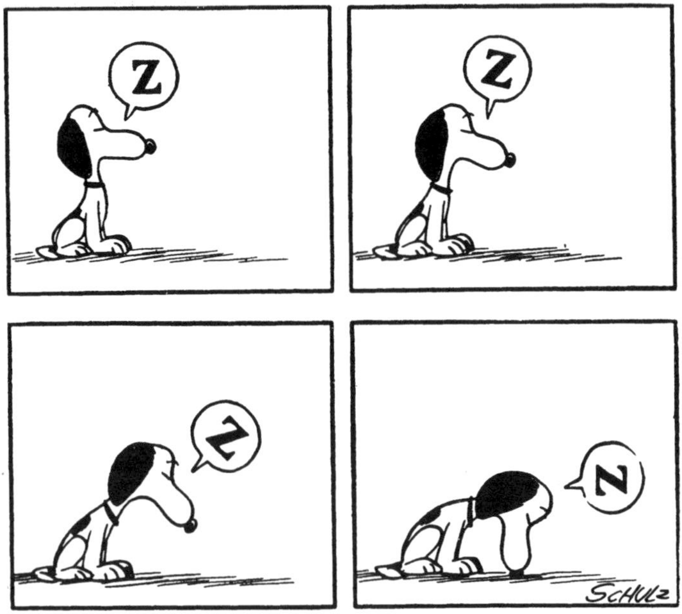
Z
Z
Z
Z
SCHULZ

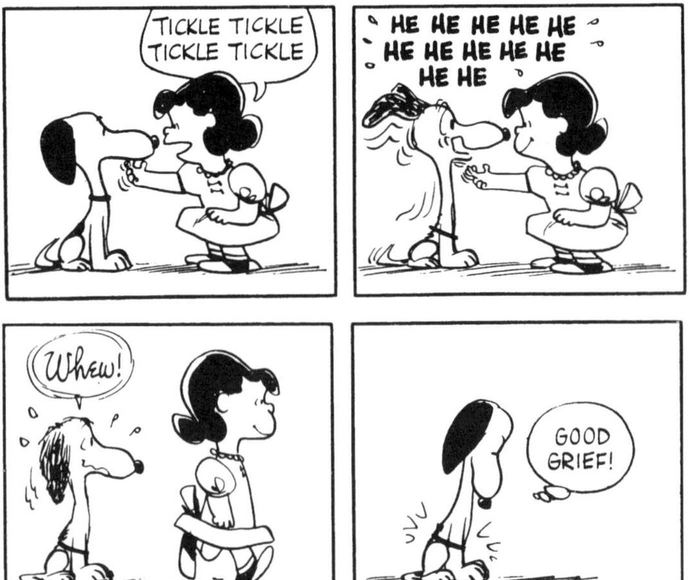
TICKLE TICKLE TICKLE TICKLE
HE HE HE HE HE HE HE HE HE HE HE HE
Whew!
GOOD GRIEF!
SCHULZ

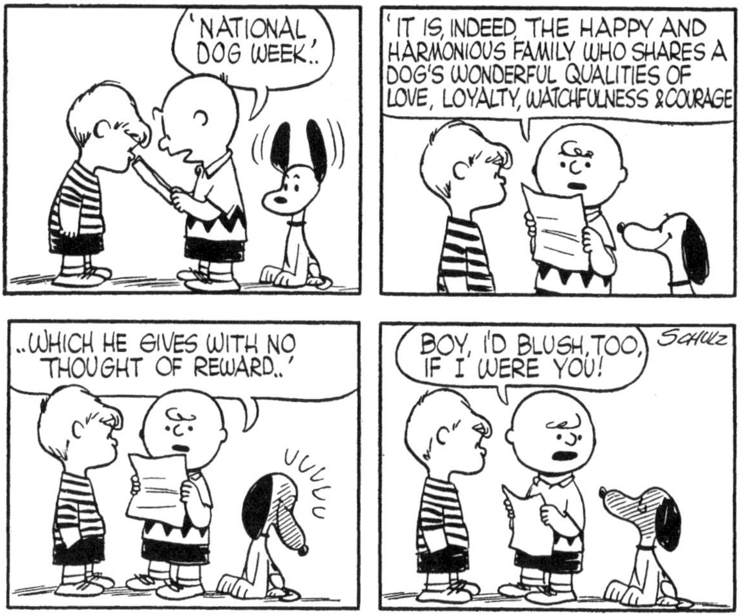
'NATIONAL DOG WEEK'..
'IT IS, INDEED, THE HAPPY AND HARMONIOUS FAMILY WHO SHARES A DOG'S WONDERFUL QUALITIES OF LOVE, LOYALTY, WATCHFULNESS & COURAGE
..WHICH HE GIVES WITH NO THOUGHT OF REWARD..'
BOY, I'D BLUSH, TOO, IF I WERE YOU!
SCHULZ

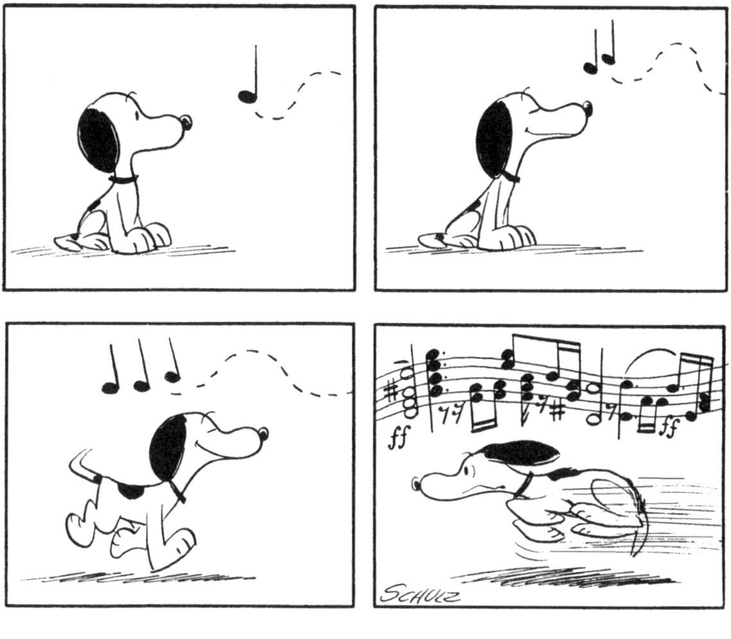
ff
ff
SCHULZ

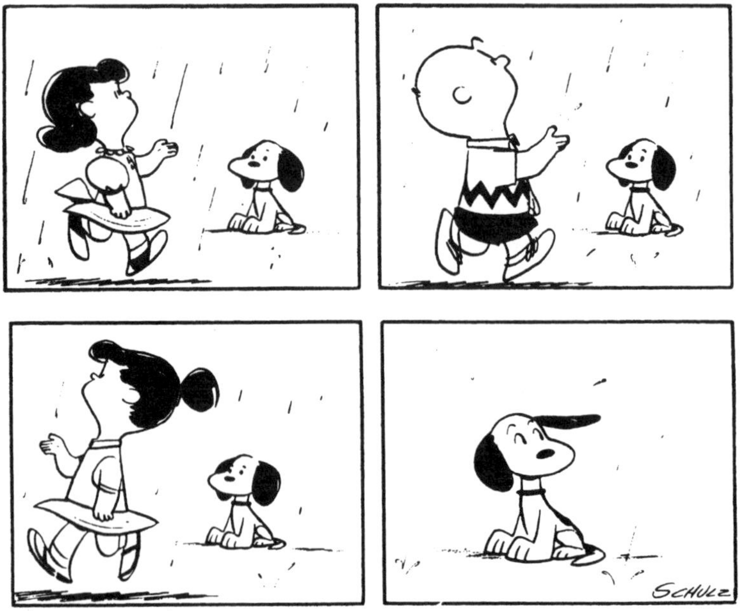
SCHULZ

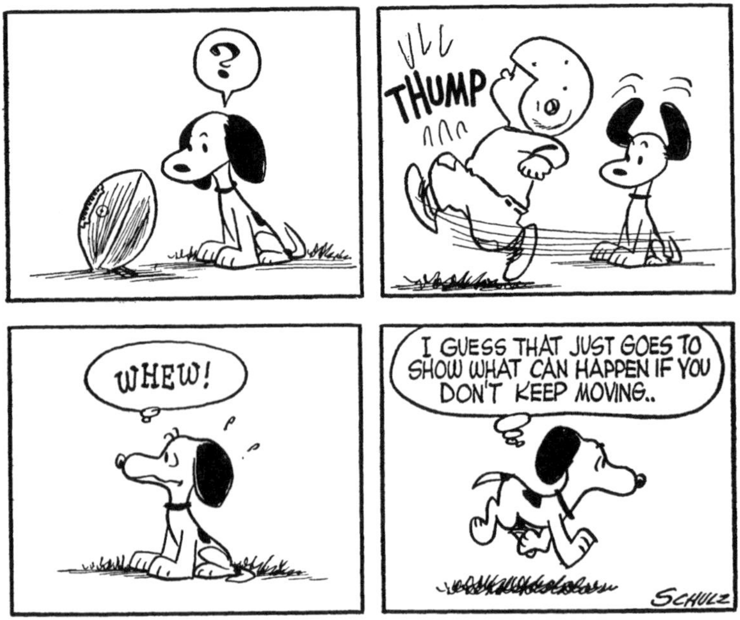
?
THUMP
WHEW!
I GUESS THAT JUST GOES TO SHOW WHAT CAN HAPPEN IF YOU DON'T KEEP MOVING..
SCHULZ

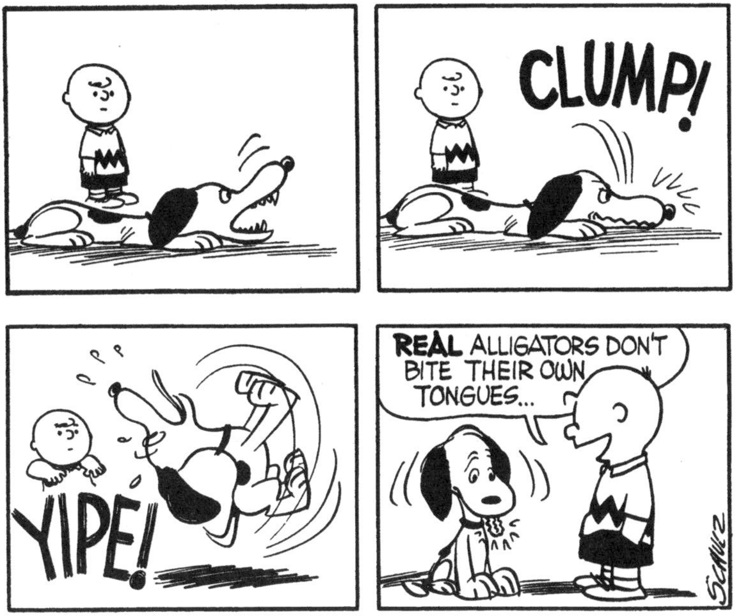
CLUMP!
YIPE!
REAL ALLIGATORS DON'T BITE THEIR OWN TONGUES...
SCHULZ

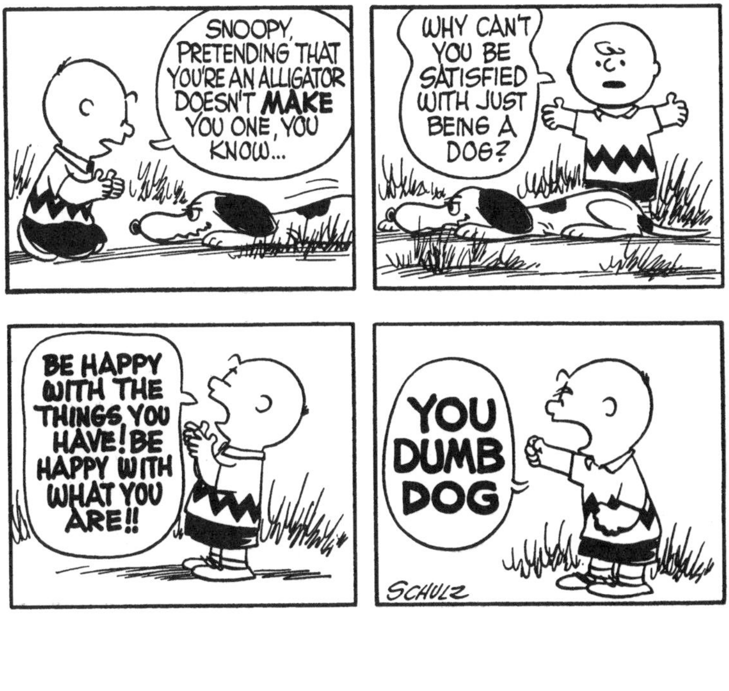
SNOOPY, PRETENDING THAT YOU'RE AN ALLIGATOR DOESN'T MAKE YOU ONE, YOU KNOW...
WHY CAN'T YOU BE SATISFIED WITH JUST BEING A DOG?
BE HAPPY WITH THE THINGS YOU HAVE! BE HAPPY WITH WHAT YOU ARE!!
YOU DUMB DOG
SCHULZ

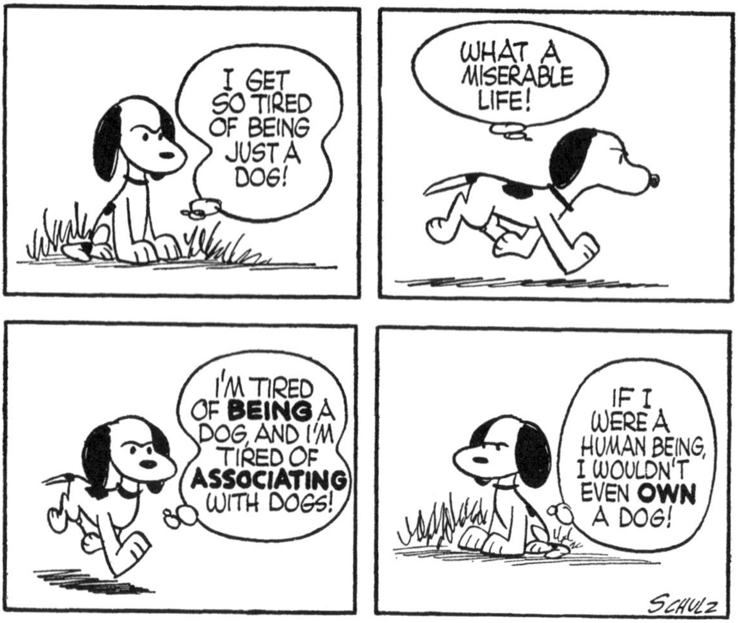
I GET SO TIRED OF BEING JUST A DOG!
WHAT A MISERABLE LIFE!
I'M TIRED OF **BEING** A DOG, AND I'M TIRED OF **ASSOCIATING** WITH DOGS!
IF I WERE A HUMAN BEING, I WOULDN'T EVEN **OWN** A DOG!
SCHULZ

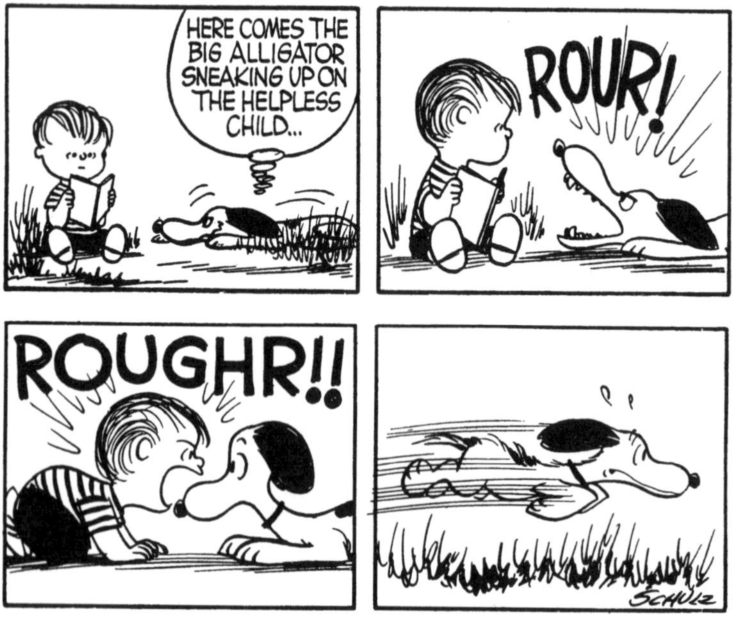
HERE COMES THE BIG ALLIGATOR SNEAKING UP ON THE HELPLESS CHILD...
ROUR!
ROUGHR!!
SCHULZ

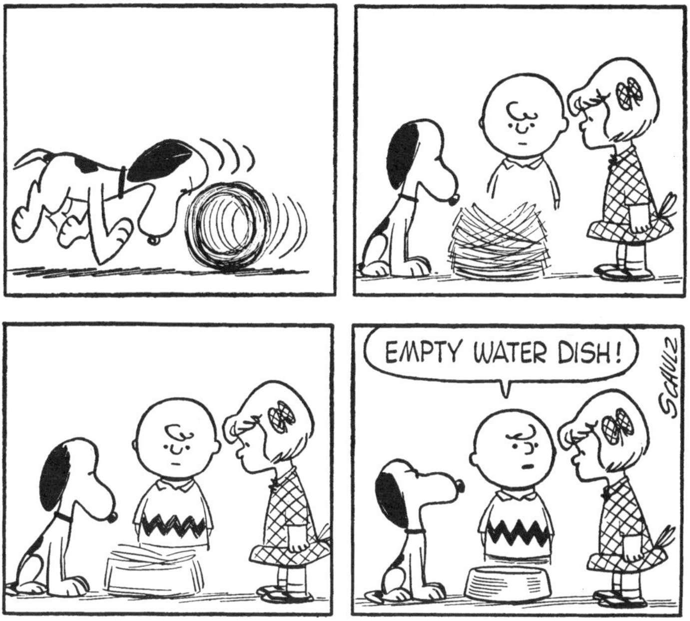
EMPTY WATER DISH!
SCHULZ

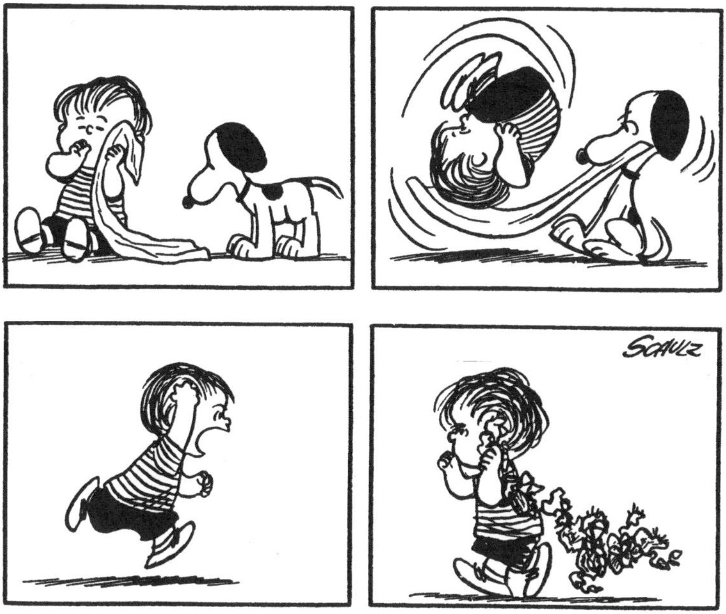
SCHULZ

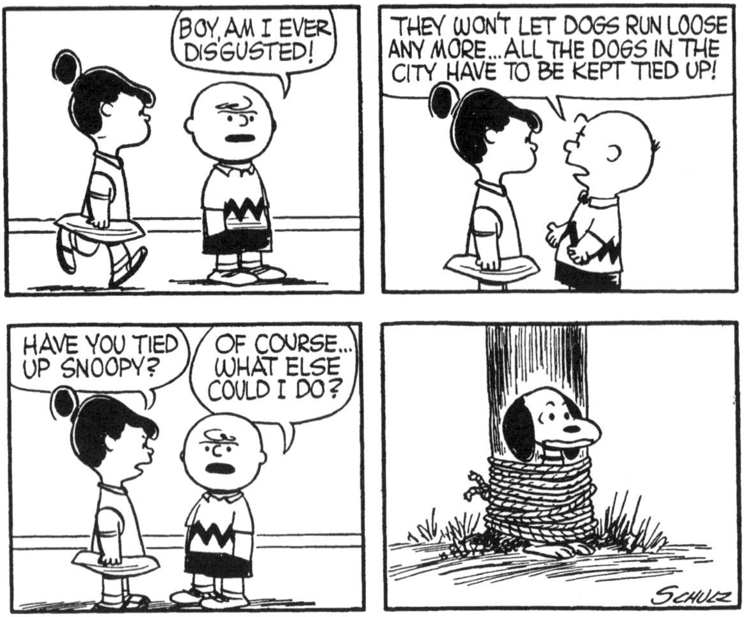
BOY, AM I EVER DISGUSTED!
THEY WON'T LET DOGS RUN LOOSE ANY MORE...ALL THE DOGS IN THE CITY HAVE TO BE KEPT TIED UP!
HAVE YOU TIED UP SNOOPY?
OF COURSE... WHAT ELSE COULD I DO?
SCHULZ

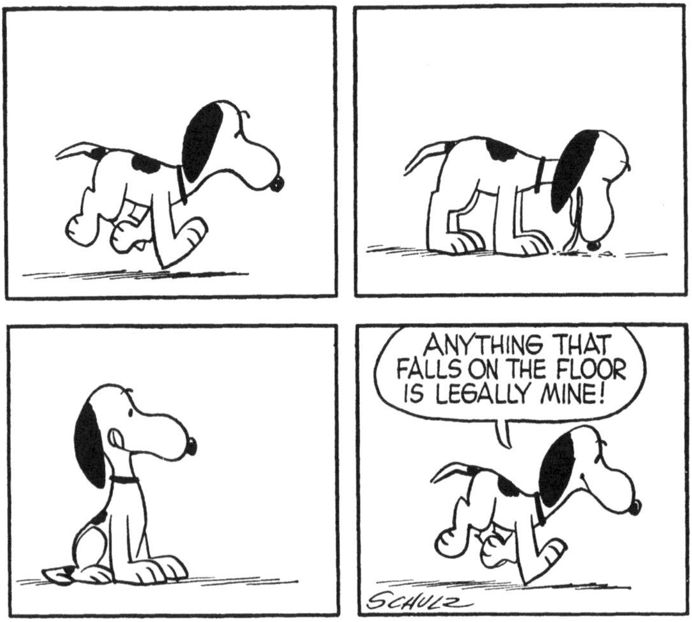
ANYTHING THAT FALLS ON THE FLOOR IS LEGALLY MINE!
SCHULZ

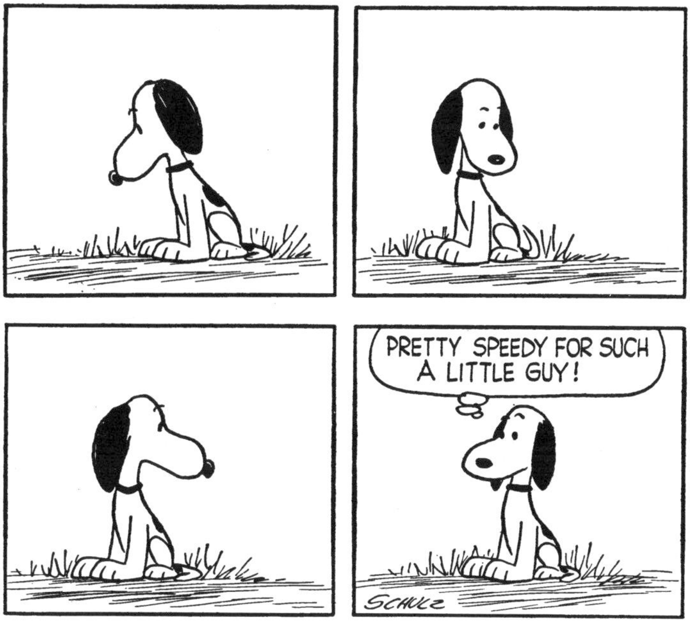
PRETTY SPEEDY FOR SUCH A LITTLE GUY!
SCHULZ

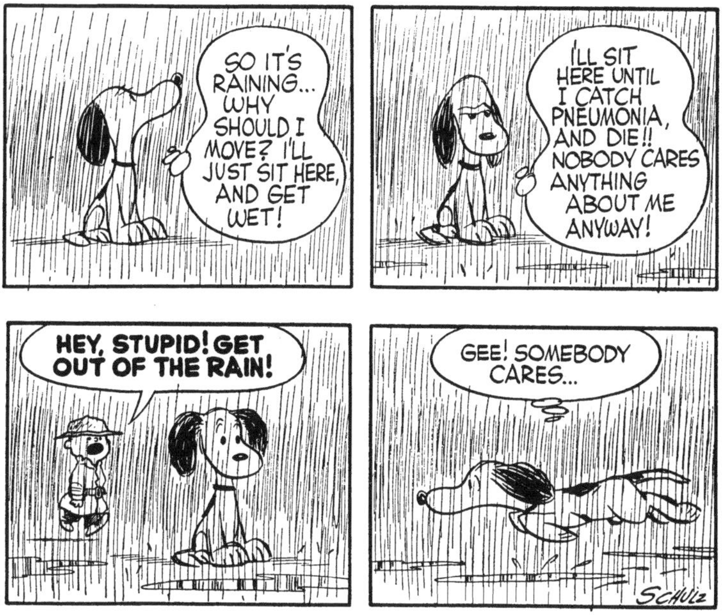
SO IT'S RAINING... WHY SHOULD I MOVE? I'LL JUST SIT HERE, AND GET WET!
I'LL SIT HERE UNTIL I CATCH PNEUMONIA, AND DIE!! NOBODY CARES ANYTHING ABOUT ME ANYWAY!
HEY, STUPID! GET OUT OF THE RAIN!
GEE! SOMEBODY CARES...
SCHULZ

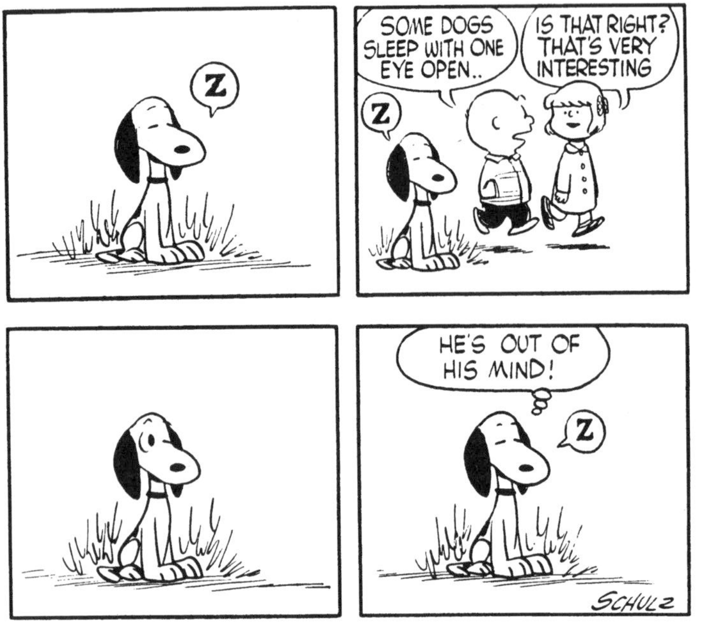
Z
SOME DOGS SLEEP WITH ONE EYE OPEN..
IS THAT RIGHT? THAT'S VERY INTERESTING
Z
HE'S OUT OF HIS MIND!
Z
SCHULZ

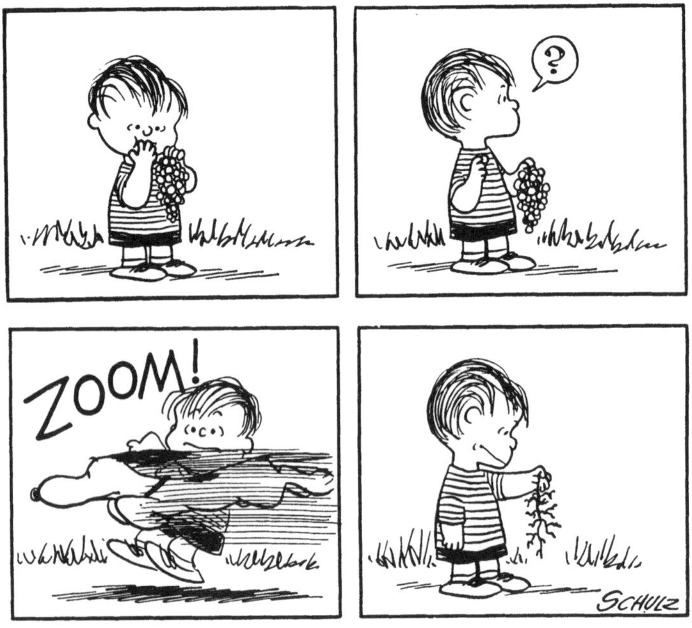
?
ZOOM!
SCHULZ

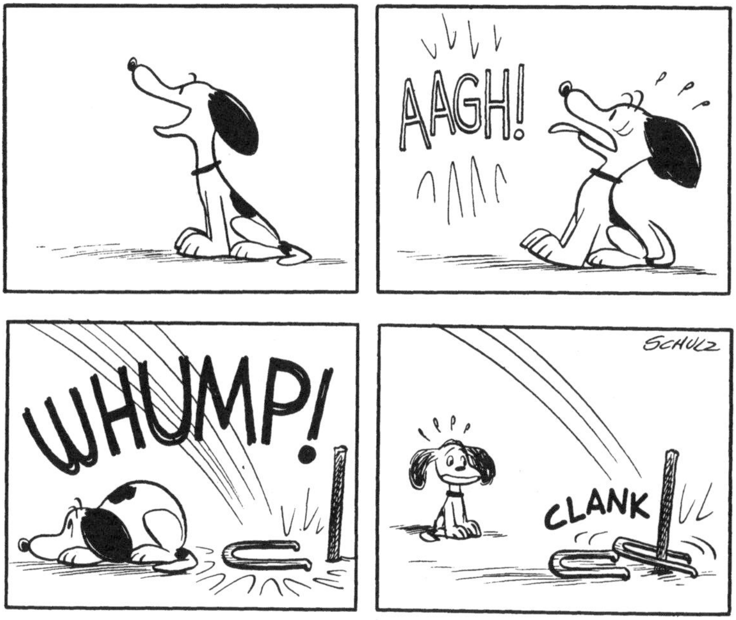
AAGH!
WHUMP!
CLANK
SCHULZ

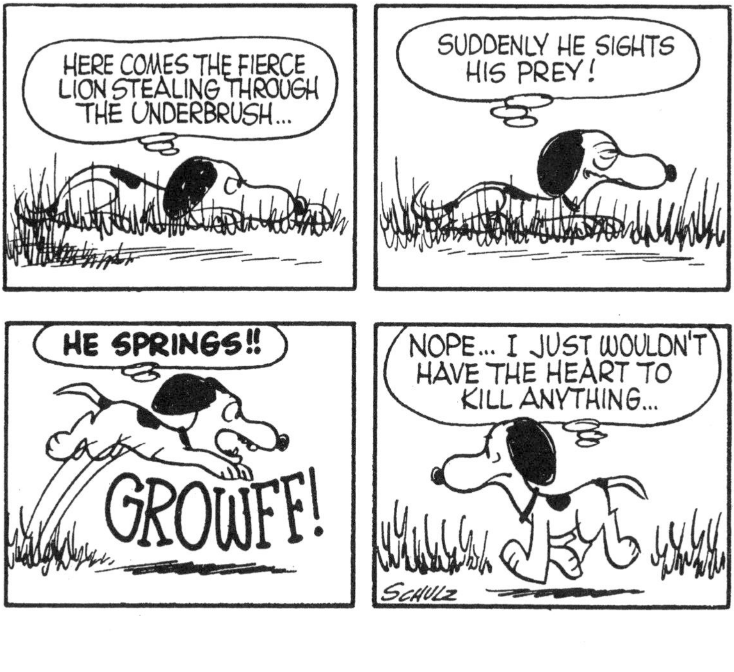
HERE COMES THE FIERCE LION STEALING THROUGH THE UNDERBRUSH...
SUDDENLY HE SIGHTS HIS PREY!
HE SPRINGS!!
GROWFF!
NOPE... I JUST WOULDN'T HAVE THE HEART TO KILL ANYTHING...
SCHULZ

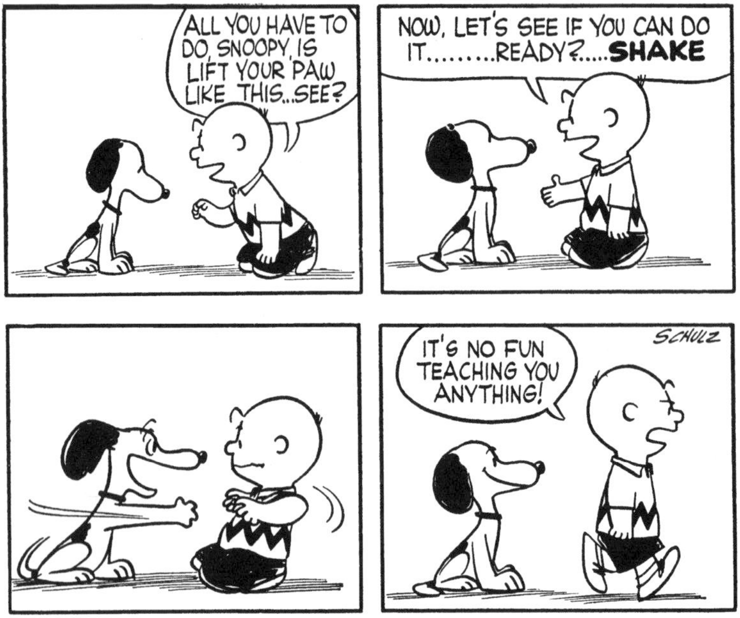
ALL YOU HAVE TO DO, SNOOPY, IS LIFT YOUR PAW LIKE THIS...SEE?
NOW, LET'S SEE IF YOU CAN DO IT.........READY?.....SHAKE
SCHULZ
IT'S NO FUN TEACHING YOU ANYTHING!

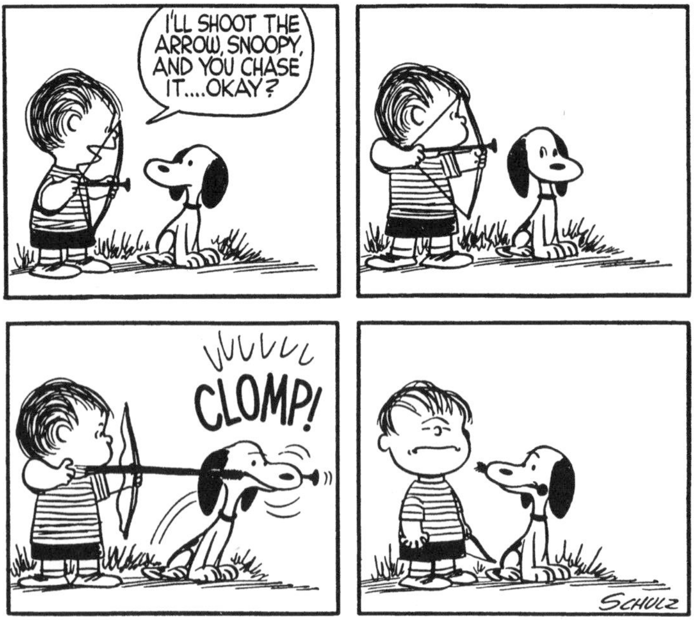
I'LL SHOOT THE ARROW, SNOOPY, AND YOU CHASE IT....OKAY?
VVUVVV
CLOMP!
SCHULZ

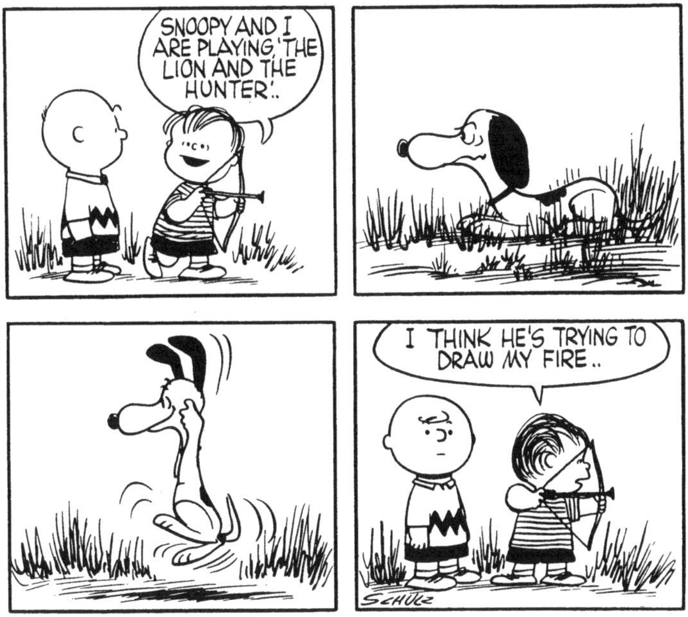
SNOOPY AND I ARE PLAYING 'THE LION AND THE HUNTER'..
I THINK HE'S TRYING TO DRAW MY FIRE..
SCHULZ

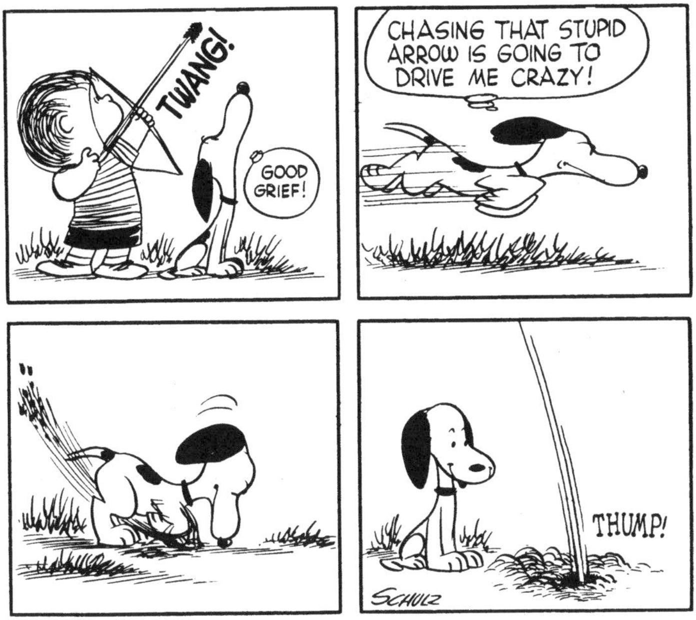
TWANG!
GOOD GRIEF!
CHASING THAT STUPID ARROW IS GOING TO DRIVE ME CRAZY!
THUMP!
SCHULZ

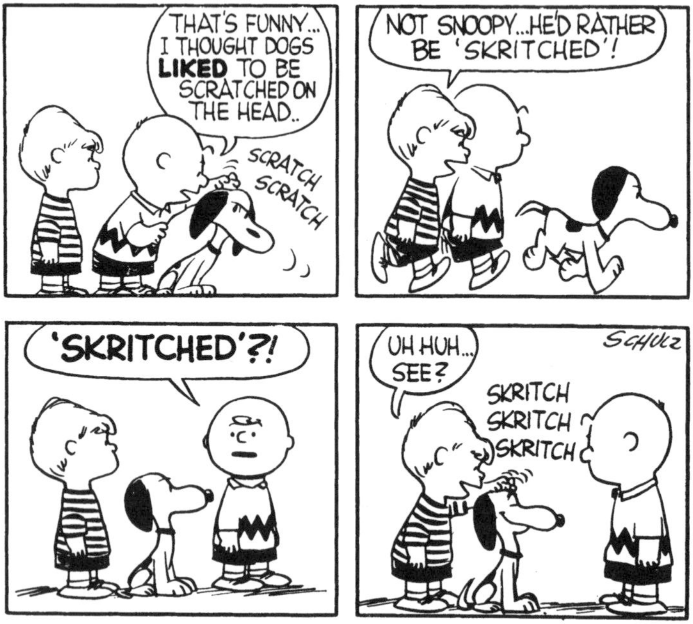
THAT'S FUNNY... I THOUGHT DOGS **LIKED** TO BE SCRATCHED ON THE HEAD..
SCRATCH SCRATCH
NOT SNOOPY...HE'D RATHER BE 'SKRITCHED'!
'SKRITCHED'?!
SCHULZ
UH HUH... SEE?
SKRITCH SKRITCH SKRITCH

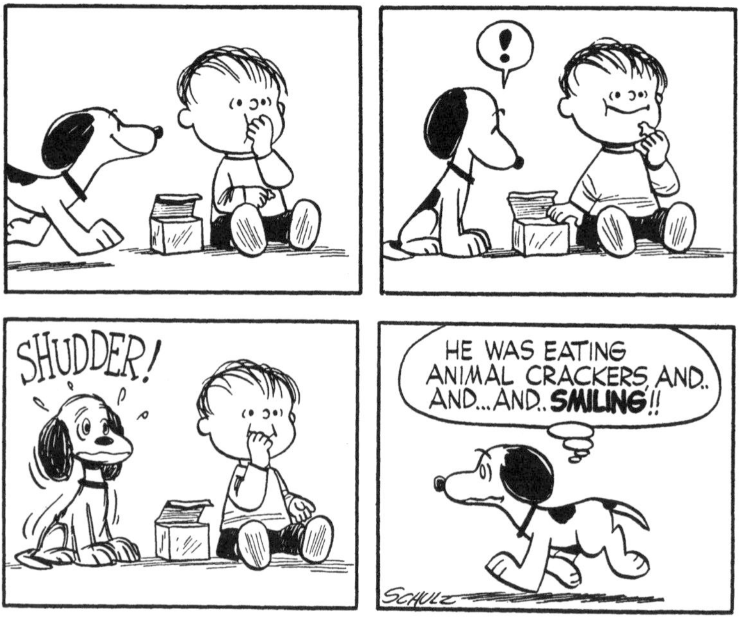
!
SHUDDER!
HE WAS EATING ANIMAL CRACKERS AND.. AND...AND..**SMILING**!!
SCHULZ

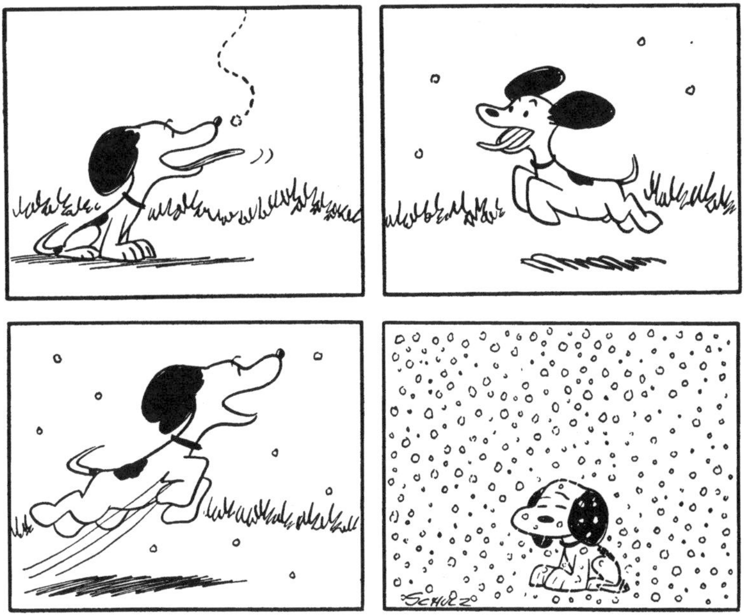
SCHULZ

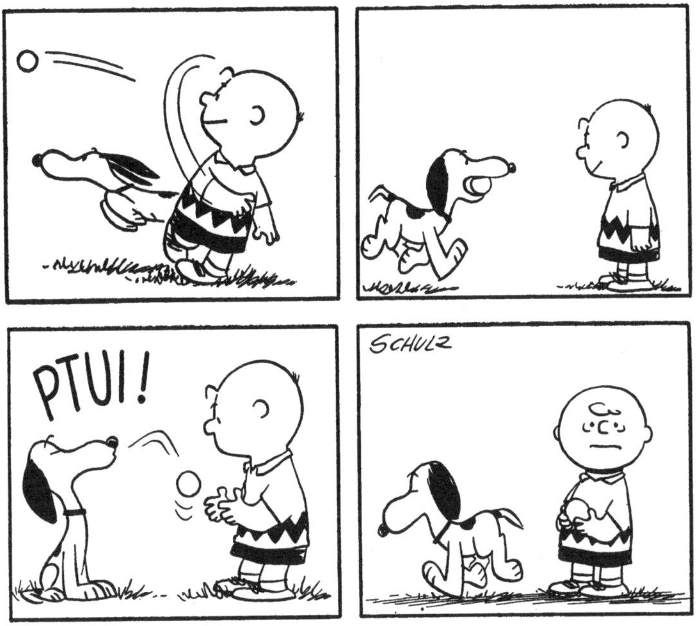
PTUI!
SCHULZ

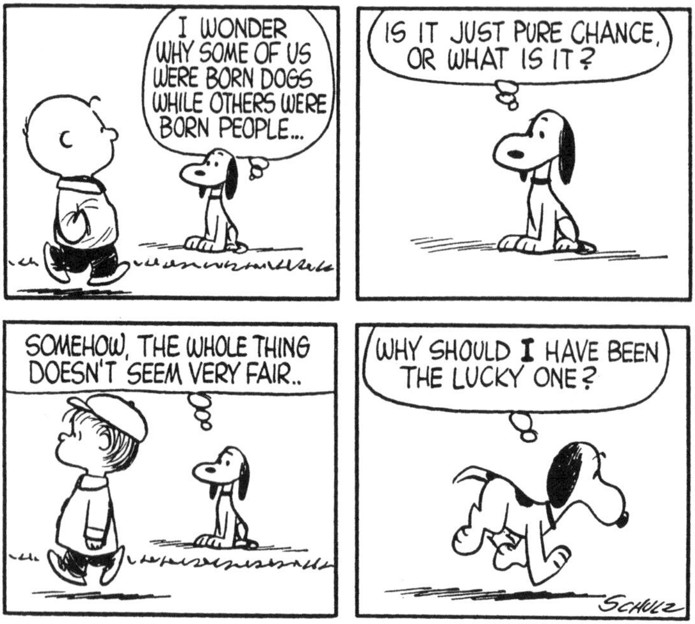
I WONDER WHY SOME OF US WERE BORN DOGS WHILE OTHERS WERE BORN PEOPLE...
IS IT JUST PURE CHANCE, OR WHAT IS IT?
SOMEHOW, THE WHOLE THING DOESN'T SEEM VERY FAIR..
WHY SHOULD I HAVE BEEN THE LUCKY ONE?
SCHULZ

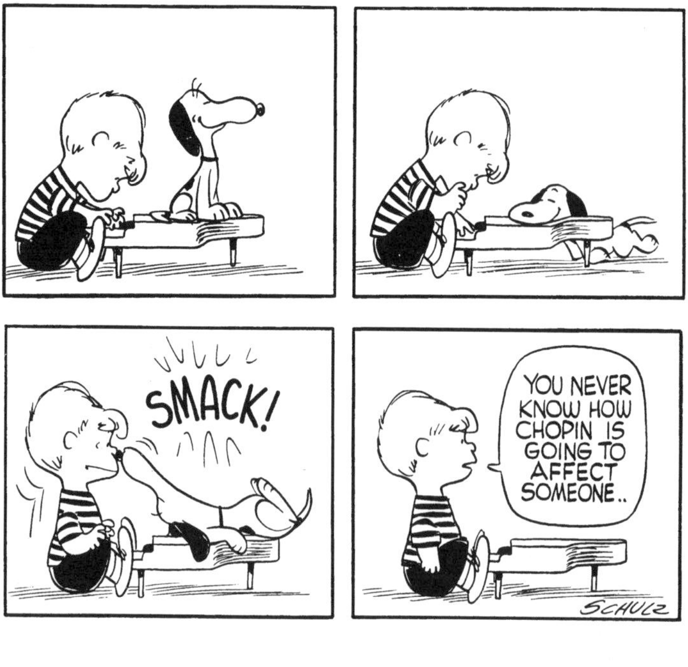
SMACK!
YOU NEVER KNOW HOW CHOPIN IS GOING TO AFFECT SOMEONE..
SCHULZ

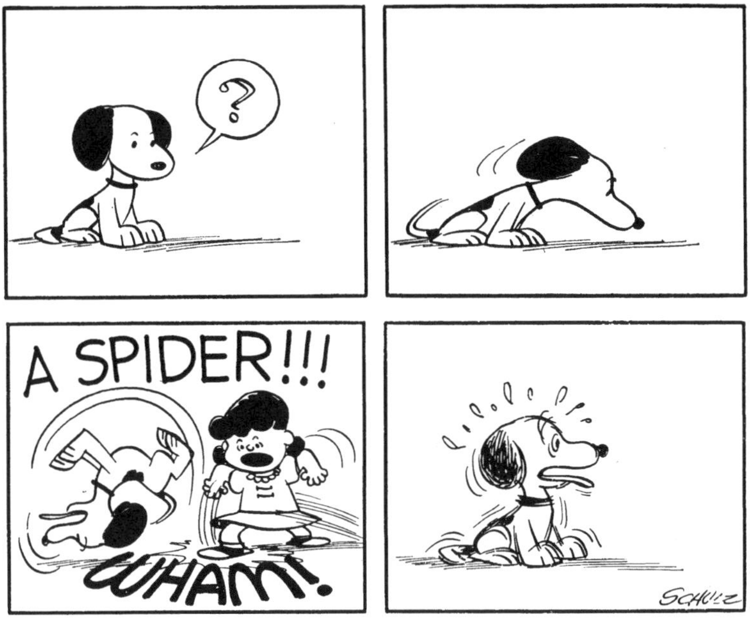
?
A SPIDER!!!
WHAM!

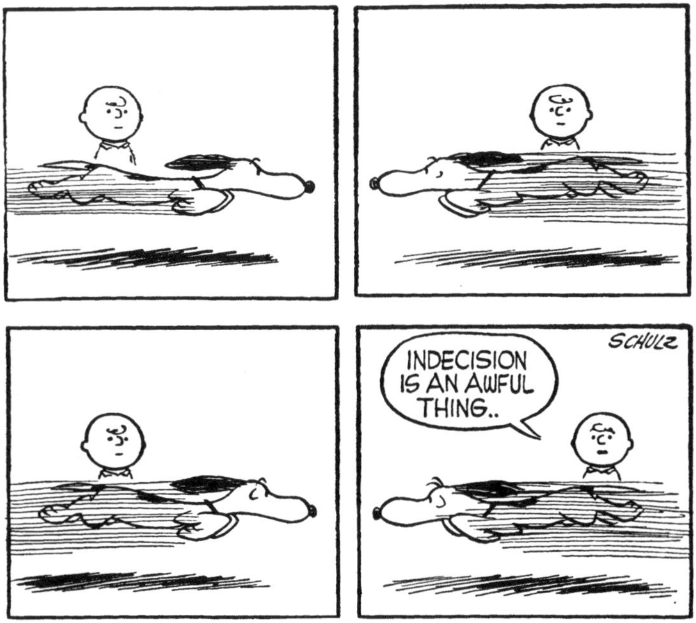
SCHULZ
INDECISION IS AN AWFUL THING..

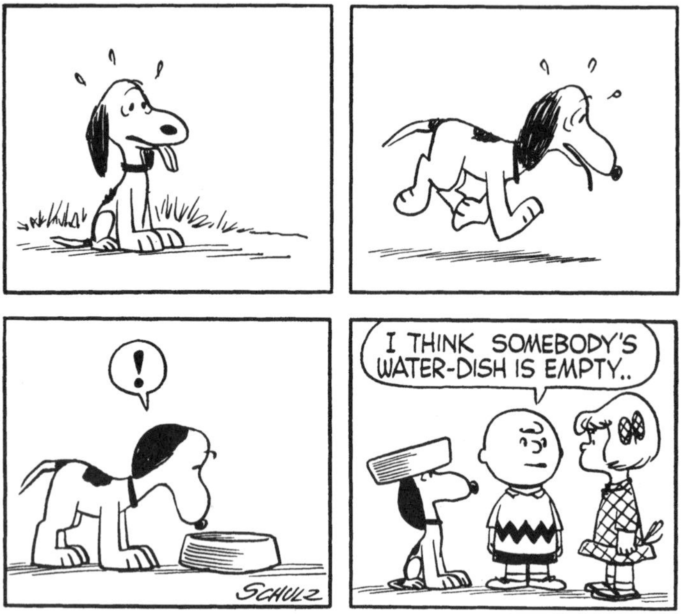
!
I THINK SOMEBODY'S WATER-DISH IS EMPTY..
SCHULZ

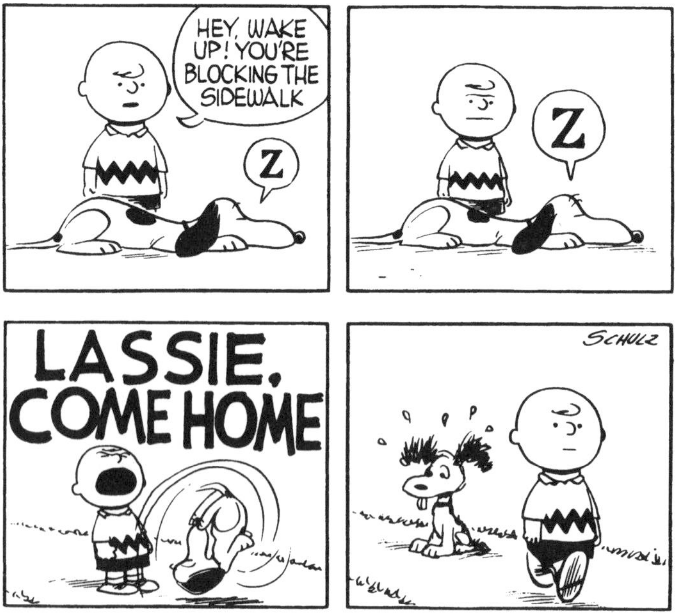
HEY, WAKE UP! YOU'RE BLOCKING THE SIDEWALK
Z
Z
LASSIE, COME HOME
SCHULZ

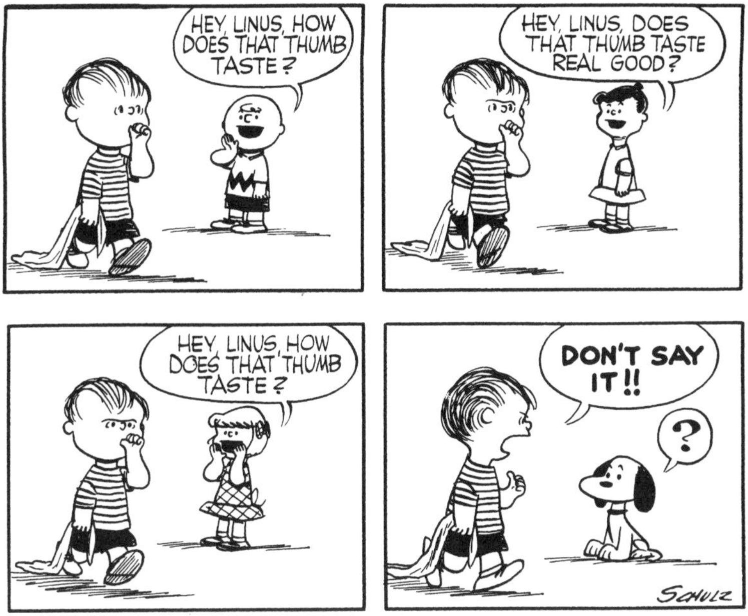
HEY, LINUS, HOW DOES THAT THUMB TASTE?
HEY, LINUS, DOES THAT THUMB TASTE REAL GOOD?
HEY, LINUS, HOW DOES THAT THUMB TASTE?
DON'T SAY IT!!
?
SCHULZ

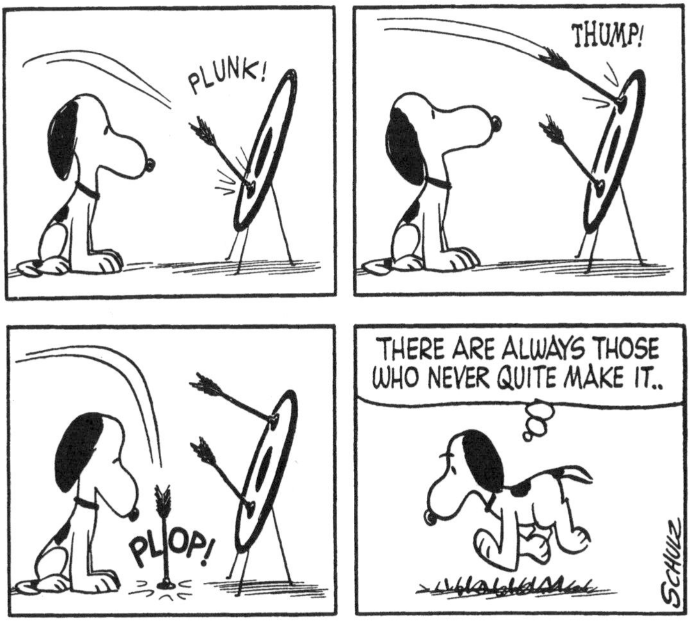
PLUNK!
THUMP!
PLOP!
THERE ARE ALWAYS THOSE WHO NEVER QUITE MAKE IT..
SCHULZ

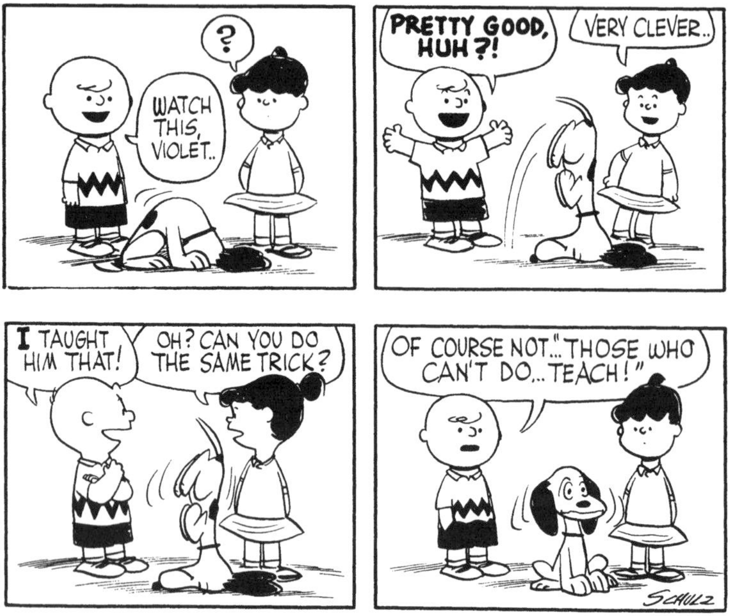
?
WATCH THIS, VIOLET..
PRETTY GOOD, HUH ?!
VERY CLEVER..
I TAUGHT HIM THAT!
OH? CAN YOU DO THE SAME TRICK?
OF COURSE NOT.."THOSE WHO CAN'T DO... TEACH!"
SCHULZ

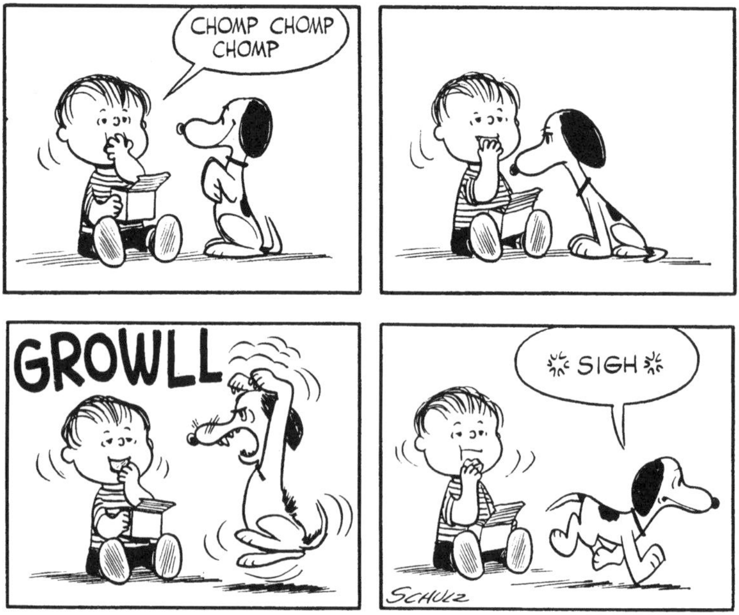
CHOMP CHOMP CHOMP
GROWLL
SIGH
SCHULZ

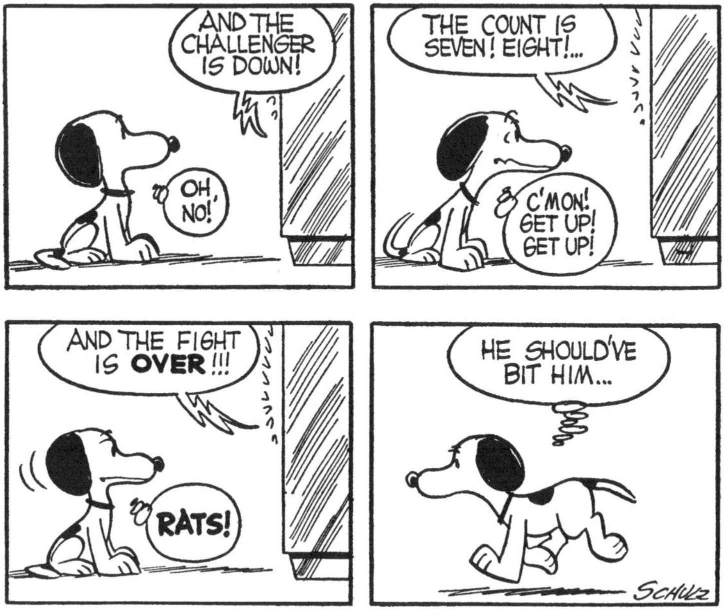
AND THE CHALLENGER IS DOWN!
OH, NO!
THE COUNT IS SEVEN! EIGHT!...
C'MON! GET UP! GET UP!
AND THE FIGHT IS **OVER**!!!
RATS!
HE SHOULD'VE BIT HIM...
SCHULZ

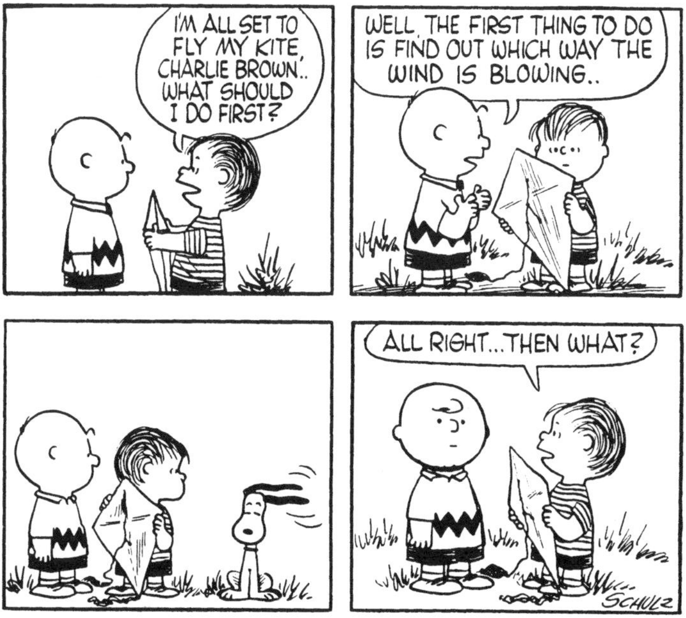
I'M ALL SET TO FLY MY KITE, CHARLIE BROWN.. WHAT SHOULD I DO FIRST?
WELL, THE FIRST THING TO DO IS FIND OUT WHICH WAY THE WIND IS BLOWING..
ALL RIGHT...THEN WHAT?
SCHULZ

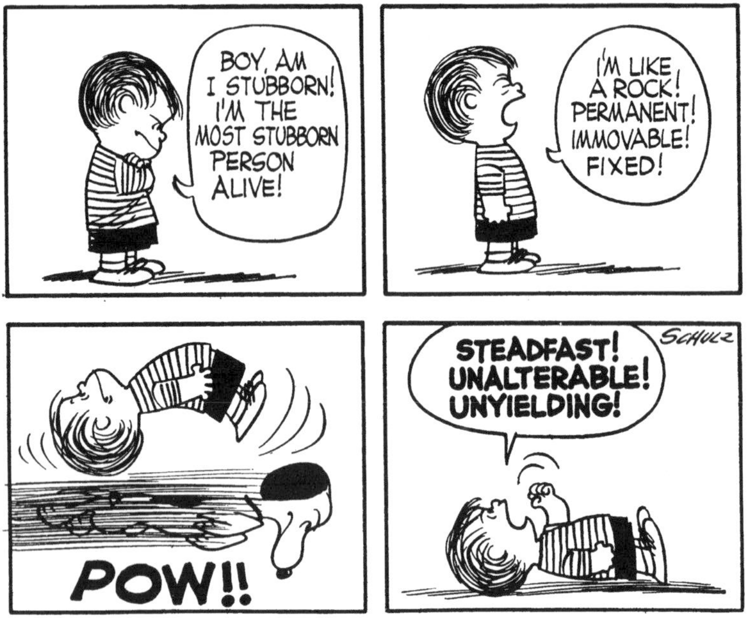
BOY, AM I STUBBORN! I'M THE MOST STUBBORN PERSON ALIVE!
I'M LIKE A ROCK! PERMANENT! IMMOVABLE! FIXED!
POW!!
STEADFAST! UNALTERABLE! UNYIELDING!
SCHULZ

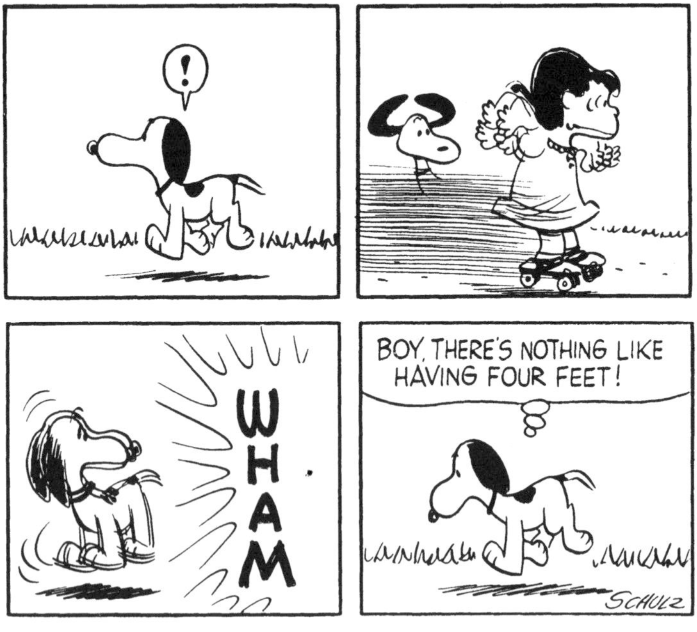
!
WHAM
BOY, THERE'S NOTHING LIKE HAVING FOUR FEET!
SCHULZ

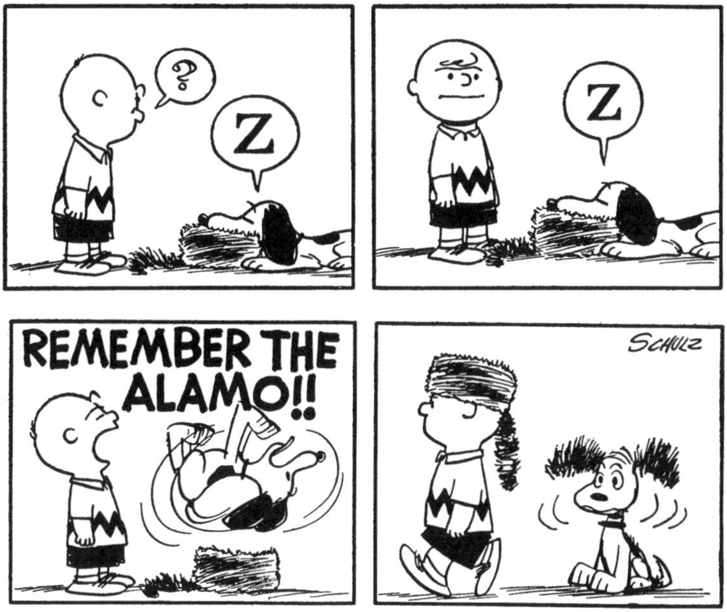
?
Z
Z
REMEMBER THE ALAMO!!
SCHULZ

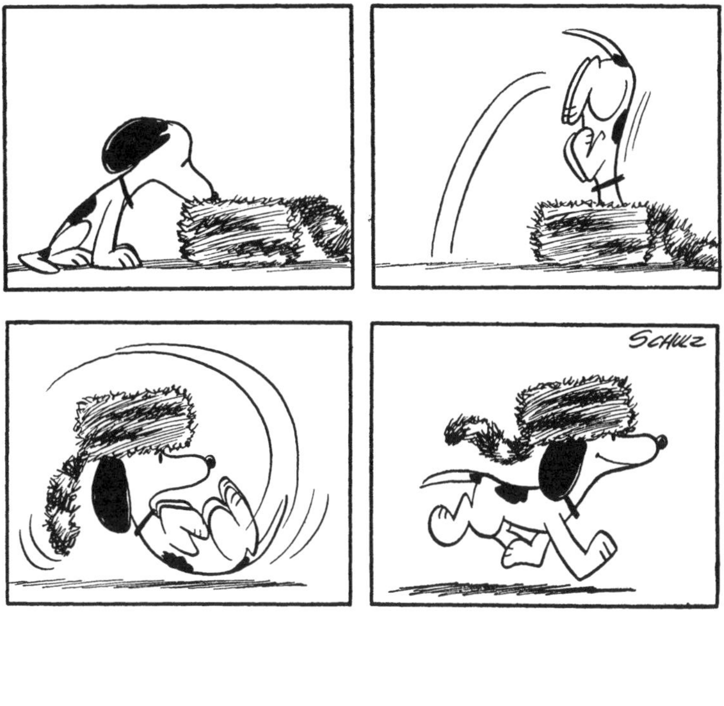
SCHULZ

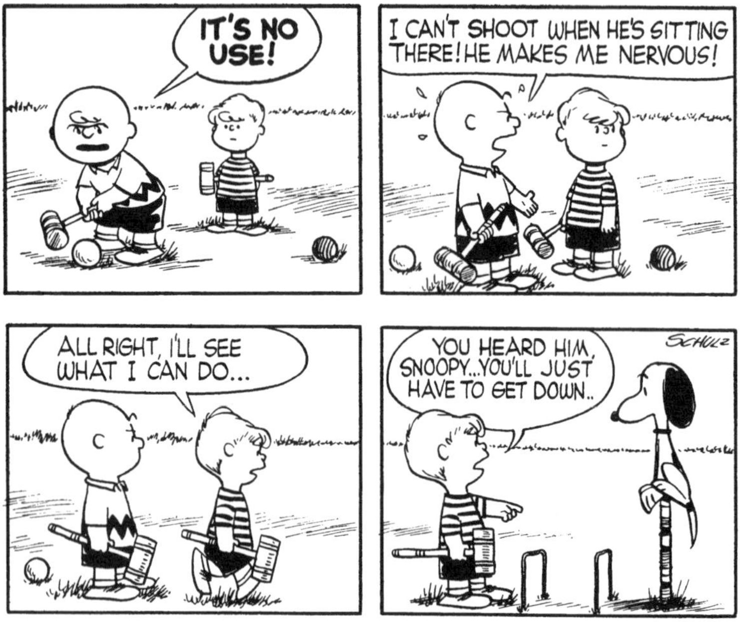
IT'S NO USE!
I CAN'T SHOOT WHEN HE'S SITTING THERE! HE MAKES ME NERVOUS!
ALL RIGHT, I'LL SEE WHAT I CAN DO...
YOU HEARD HIM, SNOOPY...YOU'LL JUST HAVE TO GET DOWN..
SCHULZ

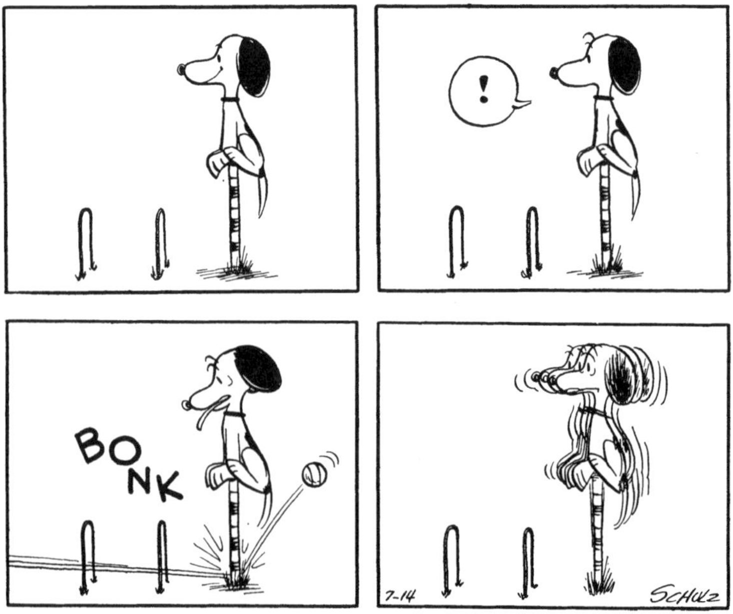
!
BONK
7-14
SCHULZ

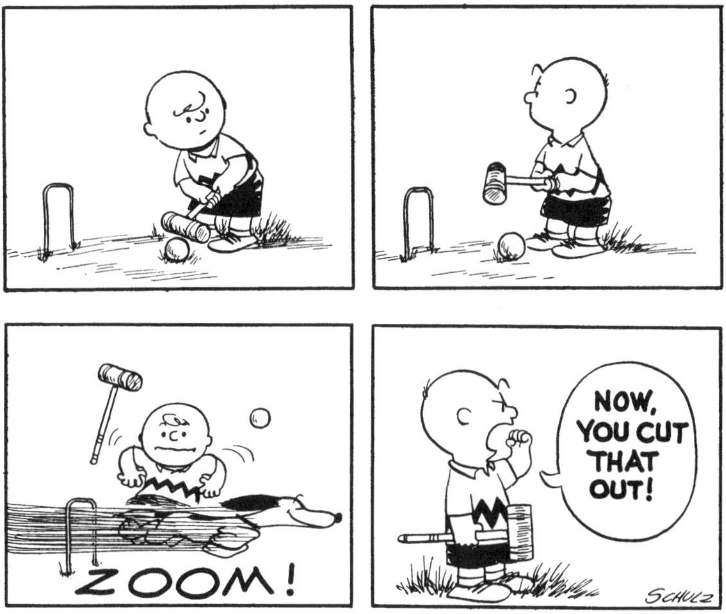
ZOOM!
NOW, YOU CUT THAT OUT!
SCHULZ

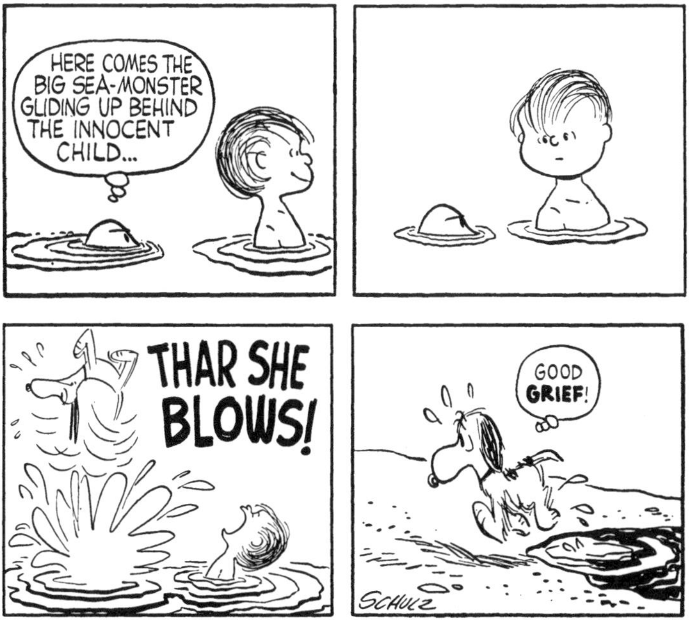
HERE COMES THE BIG SEA-MONSTER GLIDING UP BEHIND THE INNOCENT CHILD...
THAR SHE BLOWS!
GOOD GRIEF!
SCHULZ

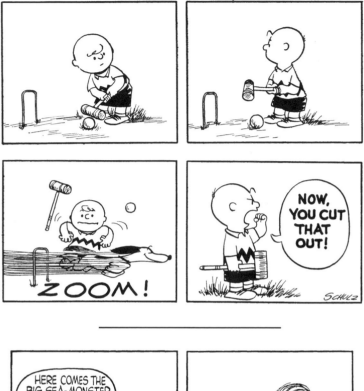

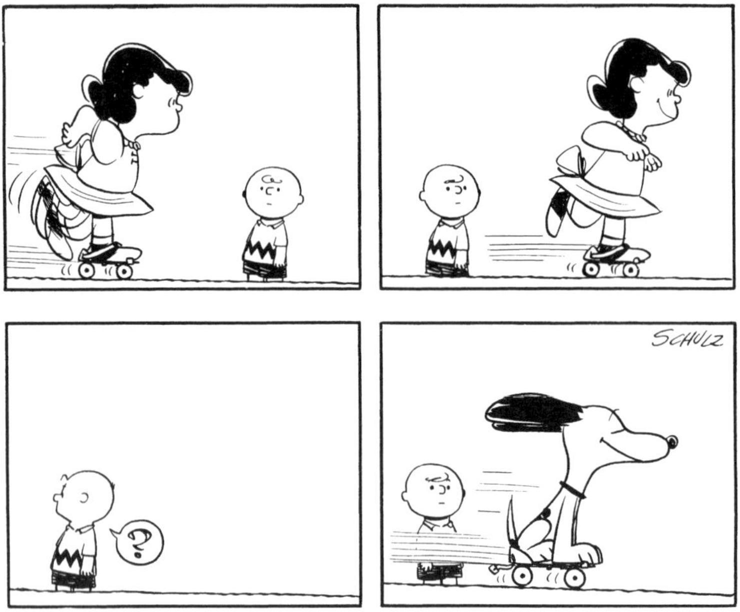
?
SCHULZ

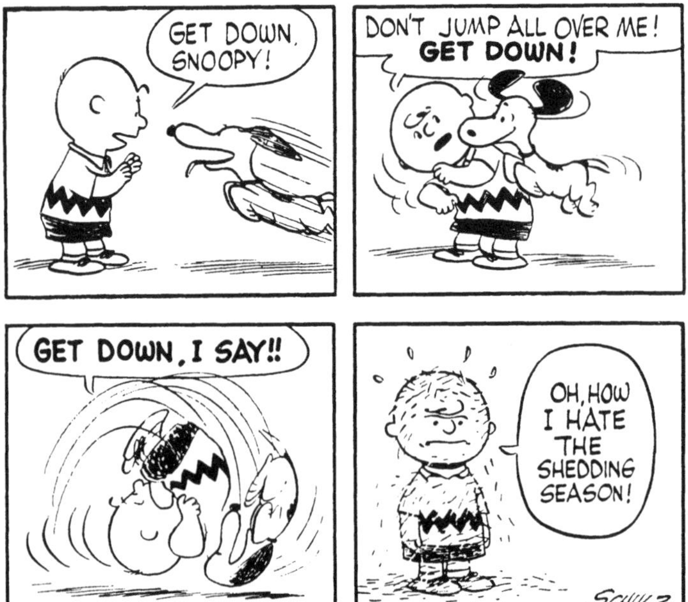
GET DOWN, SNOOPY!
DON'T JUMP ALL OVER ME! GET DOWN!
GET DOWN, I SAY!!
OH, HOW I HATE THE SHEDDING SEASON!
SCHULZ

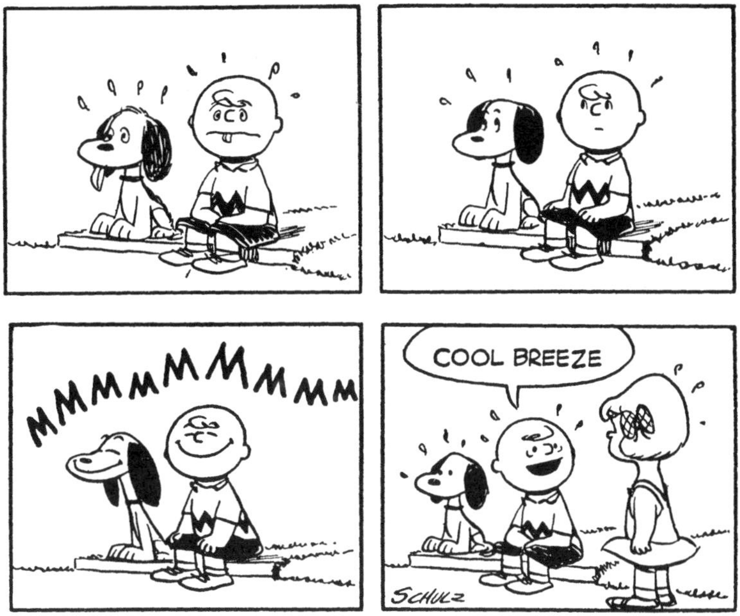
MMMMMMMMM
COOL BREEZE
SCHULZ

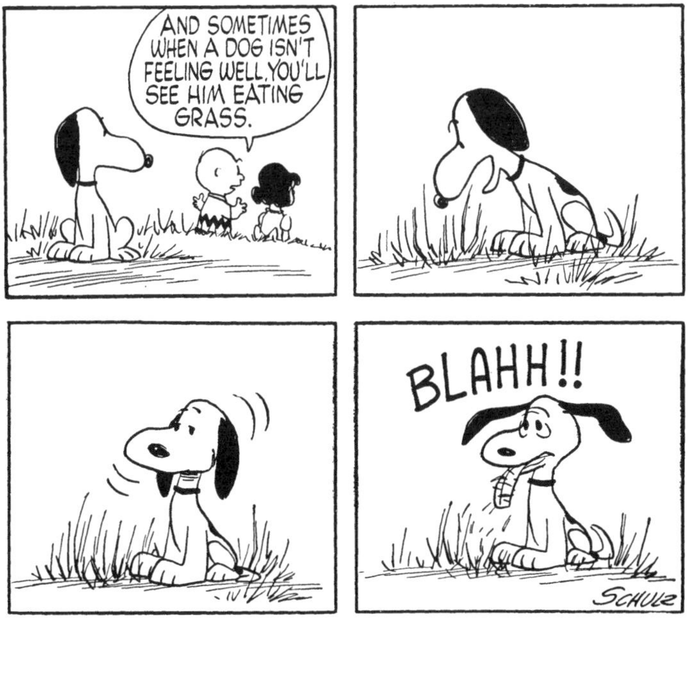
AND SOMETIMES WHEN A DOG ISN'T FEELING WELL, YOU'LL SEE HIM EATING GRASS.
BLAHH!!
SCHULZ

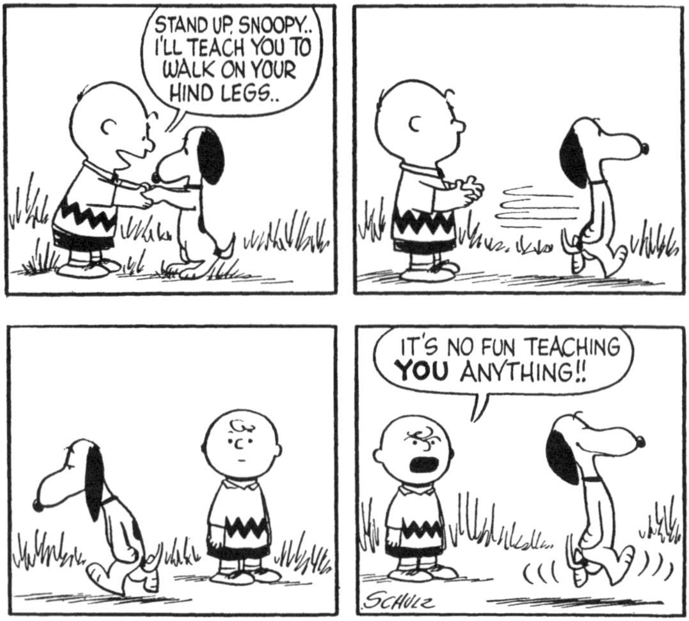
STAND UP, SNOOPY.. I'LL TEACH YOU TO WALK ON YOUR HIND LEGS..
IT'S NO FUN TEACHING **YOU** ANYTHING!!
SCHULZ

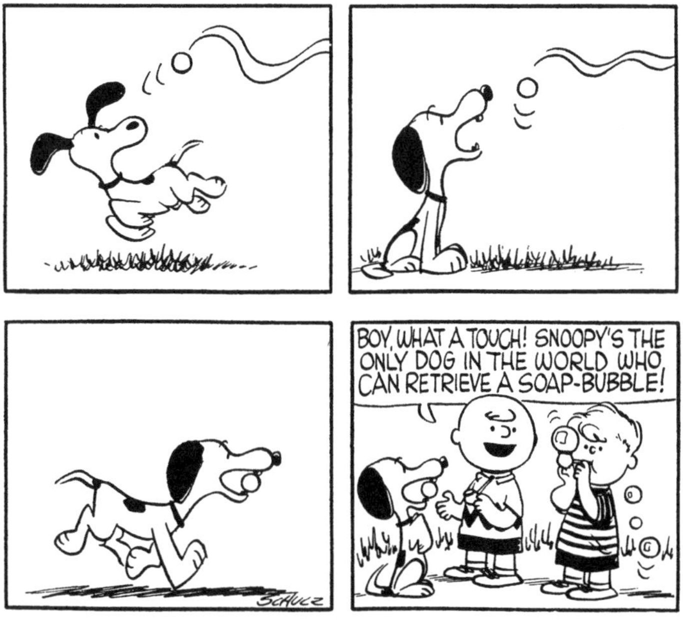
SCHULZ
BOY, WHAT A TOUCH! SNOOPY'S THE ONLY DOG IN THE WORLD WHO CAN RETRIEVE A SOAP-BUBBLE!

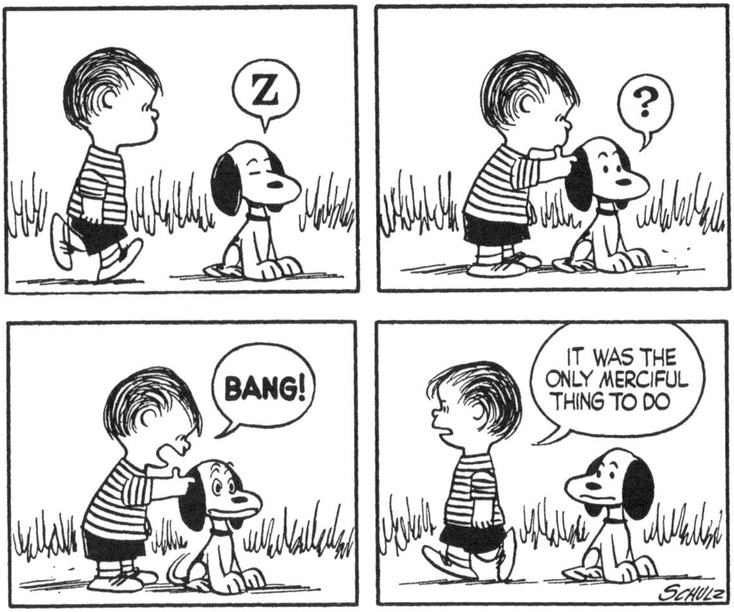
Z
?
BANG!
IT WAS THE ONLY MERCIFUL THING TO DO
SCHULZ

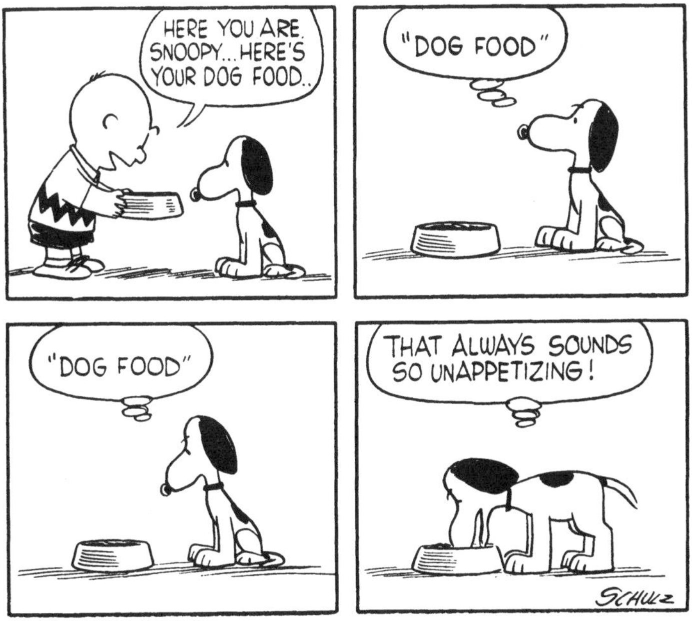
HERE YOU ARE, SNOOPY... HERE'S YOUR DOG FOOD..
"DOG FOOD"
"DOG FOOD"
THAT ALWAYS SOUNDS SO UNAPPETIZING!
SCHULZ

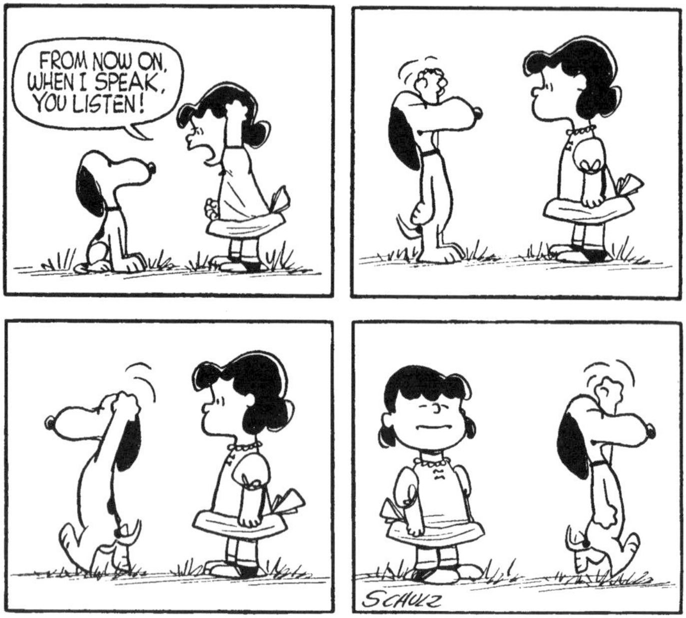
FROM NOW ON, WHEN I SPEAK, YOU LISTEN!
SCHULZ

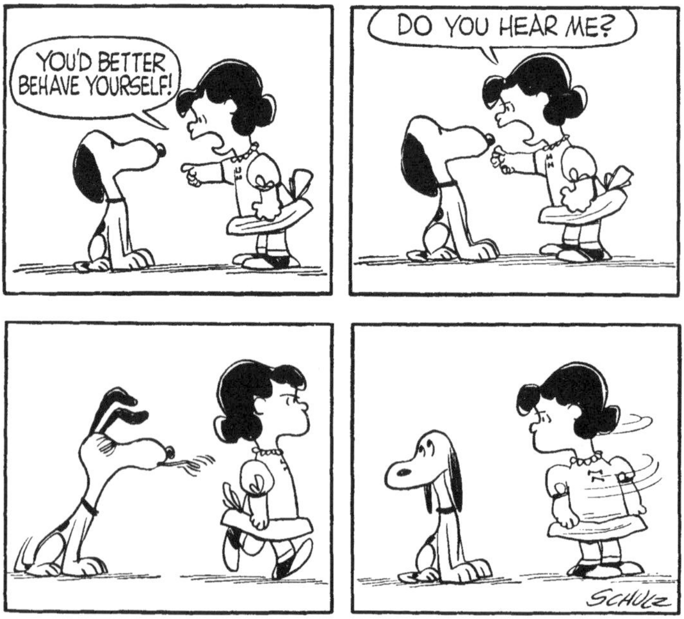
YOU'D BETTER BEHAVE YOURSELF!
DO YOU HEAR ME?
SCHULZ

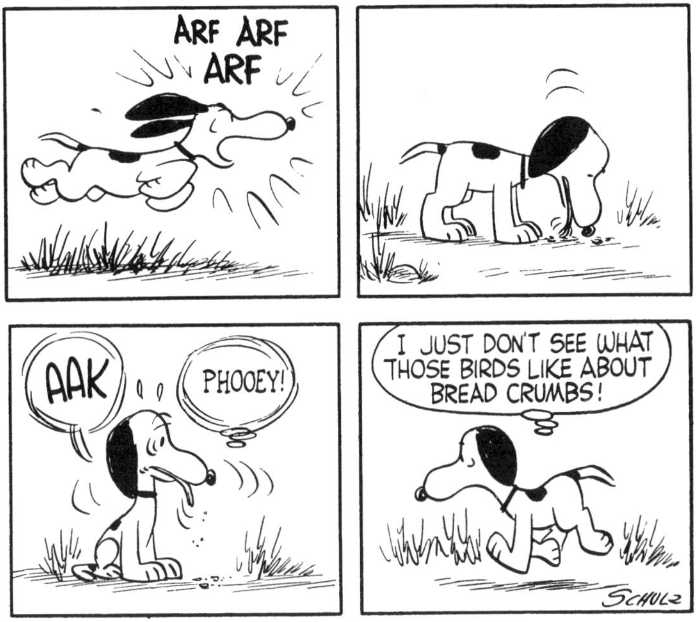
ARF ARF ARF
AAK
PHOOEY!
I JUST DON'T SEE WHAT THOSE BIRDS LIKE ABOUT BREAD CRUMBS!
SCHULZ

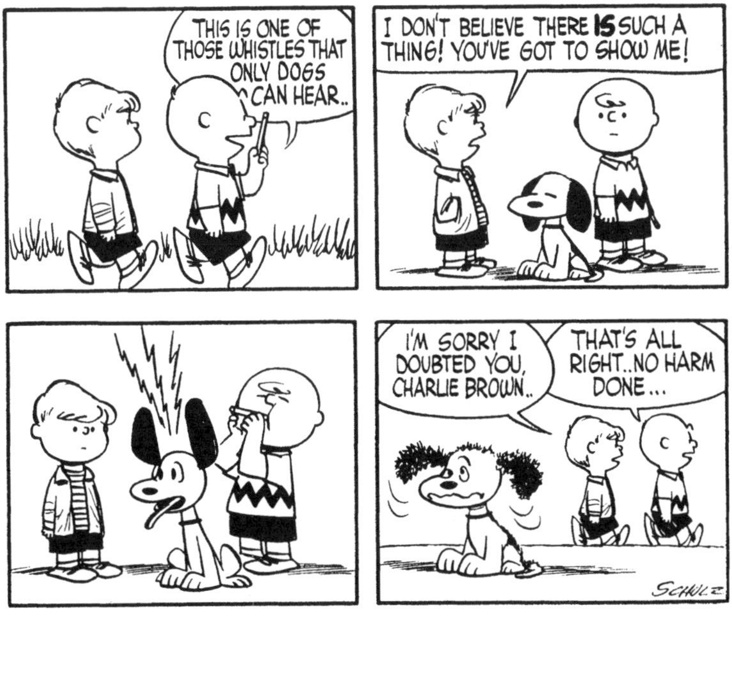
THIS IS ONE OF THOSE WHISTLES THAT ONLY DOGS CAN HEAR..
I DON'T BELIEVE THERE IS SUCH A THING! YOU'VE GOT TO SHOW ME!
I'M SORRY I DOUBTED YOU, CHARLIE BROWN..
THAT'S ALL RIGHT..NO HARM DONE...
SCHULZ

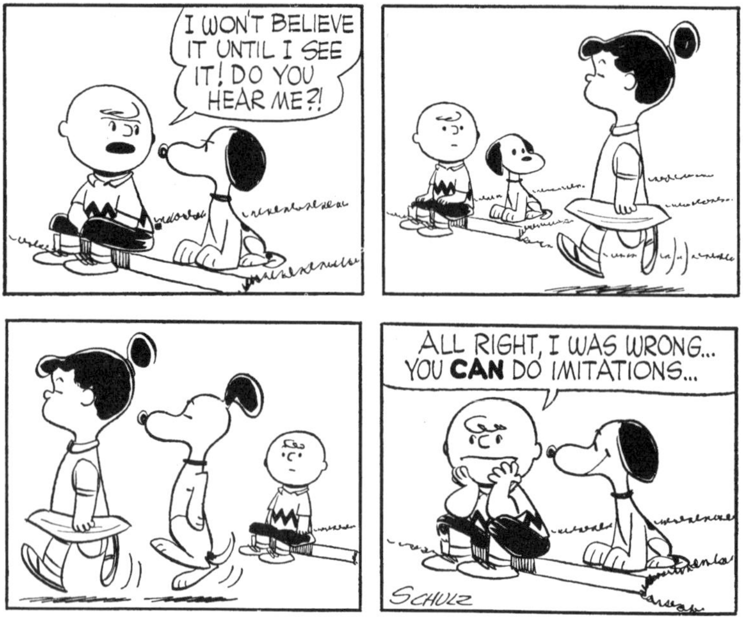
I WON'T BELIEVE IT UNTIL I SEE IT! DO YOU HEAR ME?!
ALL RIGHT, I WAS WRONG... YOU **CAN** DO IMITATIONS...
SCHULZ

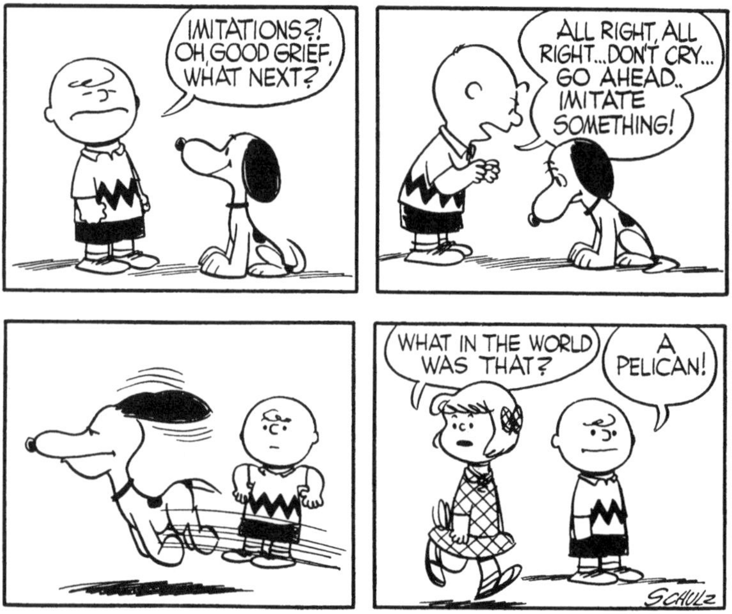
IMITATIONS?! OH, GOOD GRIEF, WHAT NEXT?
ALL RIGHT, ALL RIGHT...DON'T CRY... GO AHEAD.. IMITATE SOMETHING!
WHAT IN THE WORLD WAS THAT?
A PELICAN!
SCHULZ

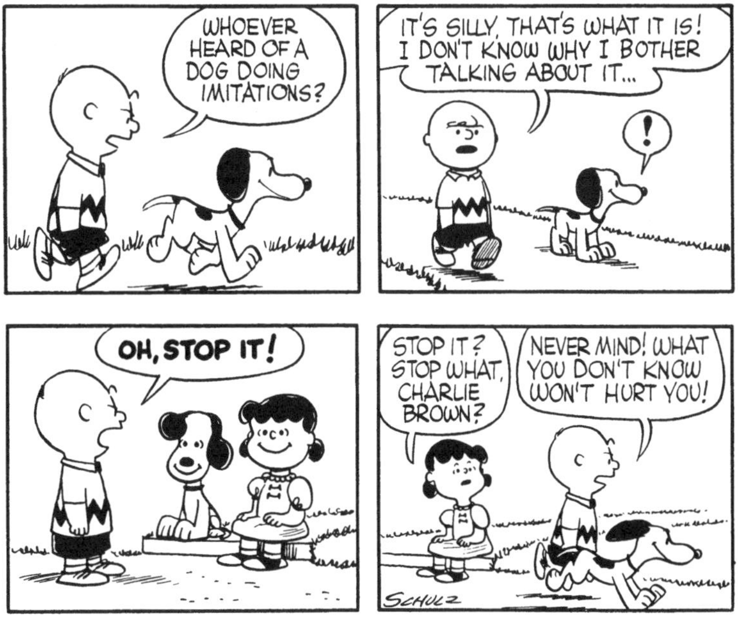
WHOEVER HEARD OF A DOG DOING IMITATIONS?
IT'S SILLY, THAT'S WHAT IT IS! I DON'T KNOW WHY I BOTHER TALKING ABOUT IT...
!
OH, STOP IT!
STOP IT? STOP WHAT, CHARLIE BROWN?
NEVER MIND! WHAT YOU DON'T KNOW WON'T HURT YOU!
SCHULZ

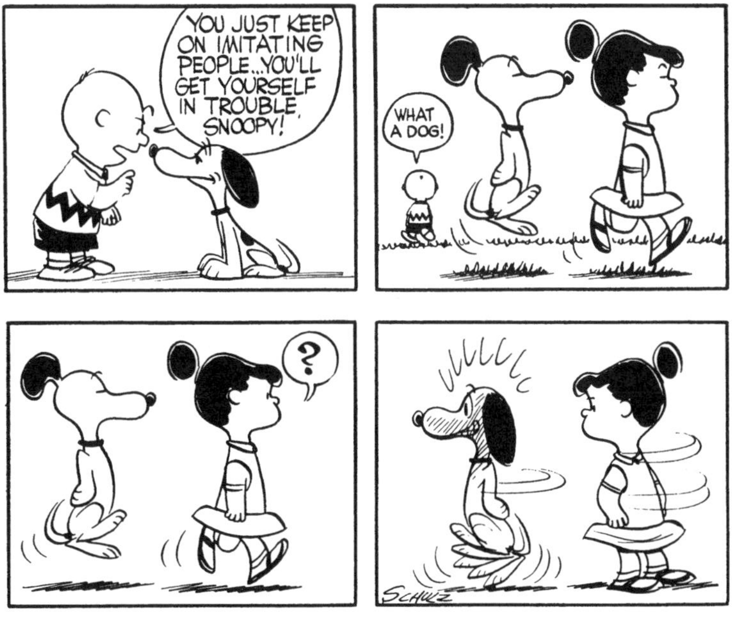
YOU JUST KEEP ON IMITATING PEOPLE...YOU'LL GET YOURSELF IN TROUBLE, SNOOPY!
WHAT A DOG!
?
SCHULZ

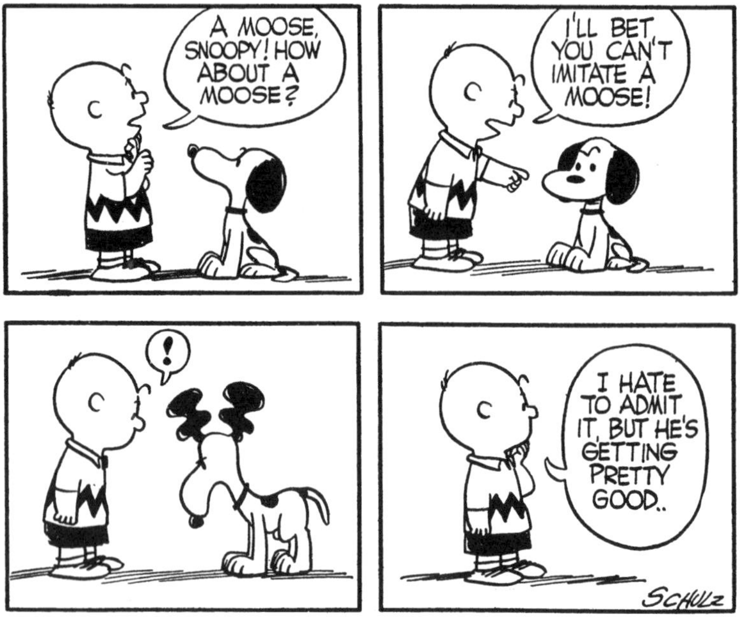
A MOOSE, SNOOPY! HOW ABOUT A MOOSE?
I'LL BET YOU CAN'T IMITATE A MOOSE!
!
I HATE TO ADMIT IT, BUT HE'S GETTING PRETTY GOOD..
SCHULZ

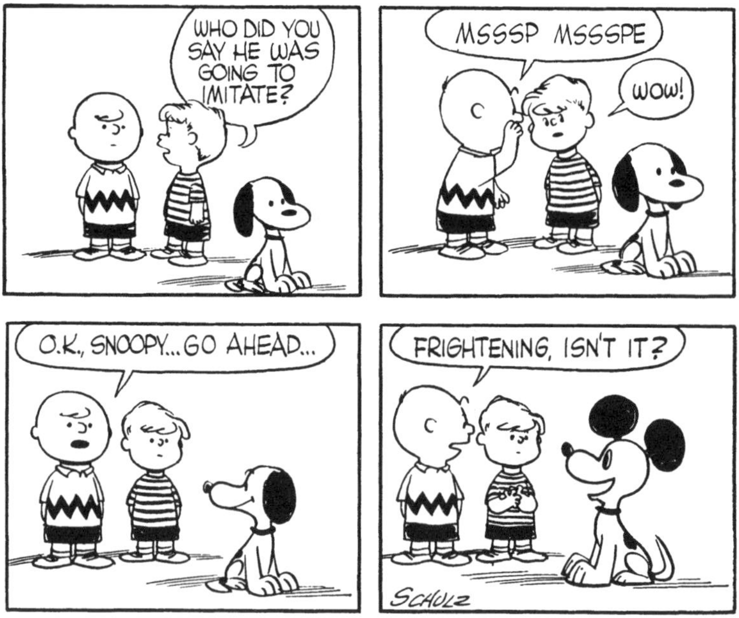
WHO DID YOU SAY HE WAS GOING TO IMITATE?
MSSSP MSSSPE
WOW!
O.K., SNOOPY...GO AHEAD...
FRIGHTENING, ISN'T IT?
SCHULZ

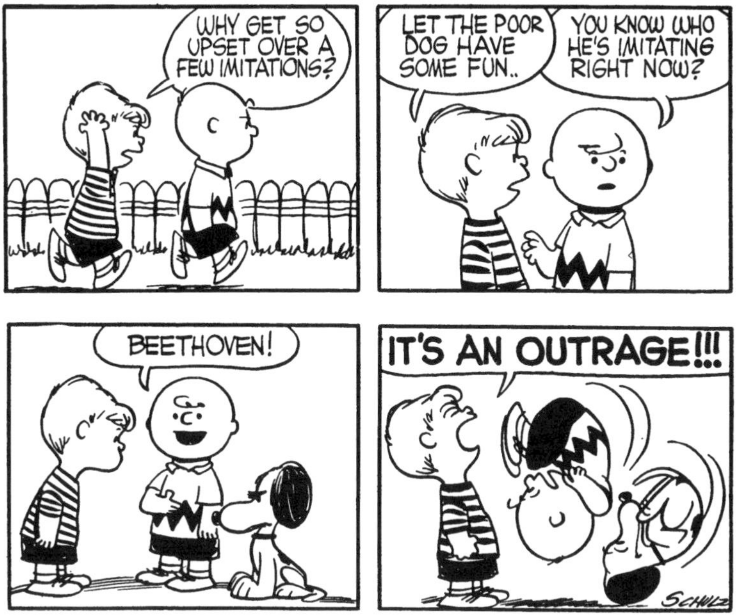
WHY GET SO UPSET OVER A FEW IMITATIONS?
LET THE POOR DOG HAVE SOME FUN..
YOU KNOW WHO HE'S IMITATING RIGHT NOW?
BEETHOVEN!
IT'S AN OUTRAGE!!!
SCHULZ

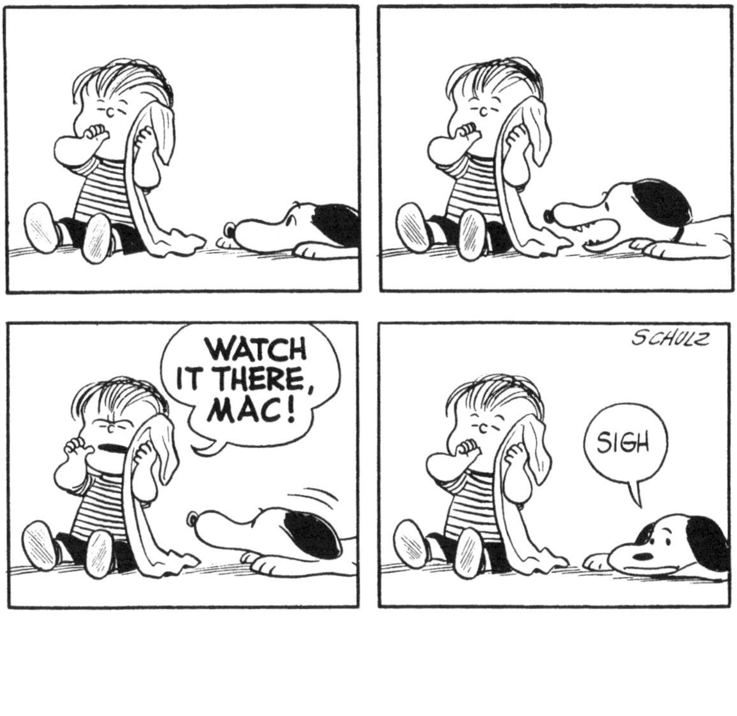
SCHULZ
WATCH IT THERE, MAC!
SIGH

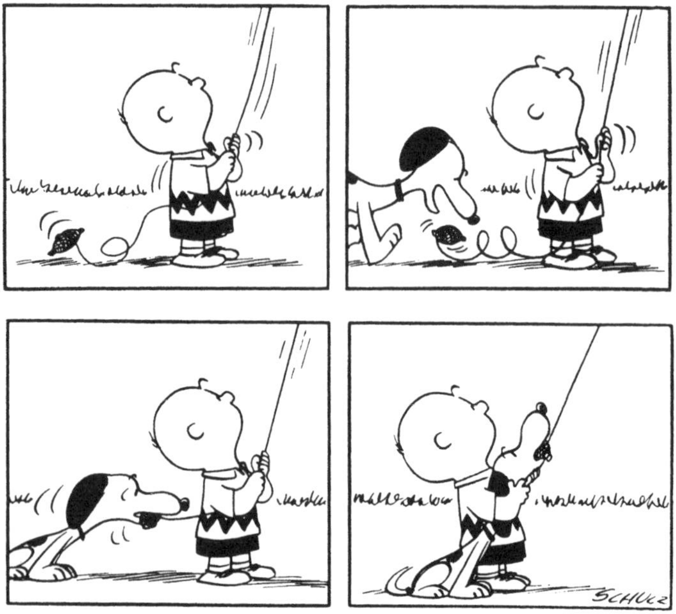
SCHULZ

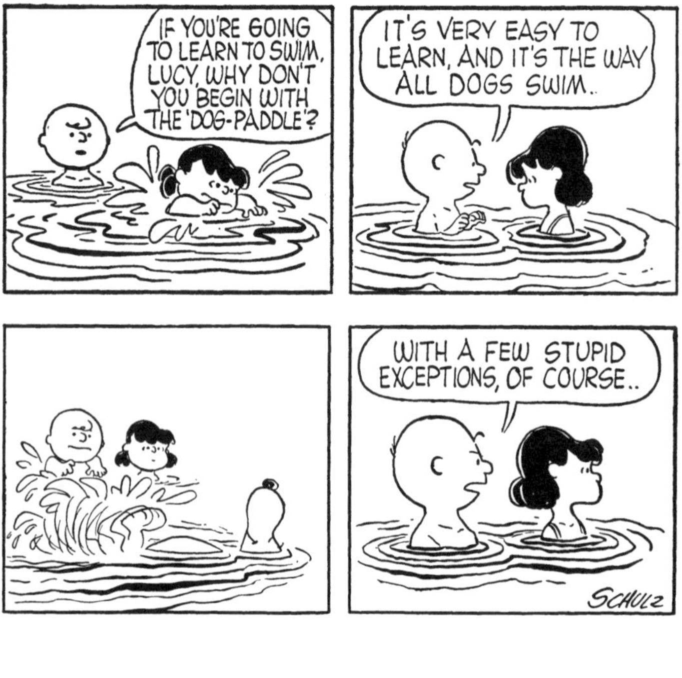
IF YOU'RE GOING TO LEARN TO SWIM, LUCY, WHY DON'T YOU BEGIN WITH THE 'DOG-PADDLE'?
IT'S VERY EASY TO LEARN, AND IT'S THE WAY ALL DOGS SWIM..
WITH A FEW STUPID EXCEPTIONS, OF COURSE..
SCHULZ

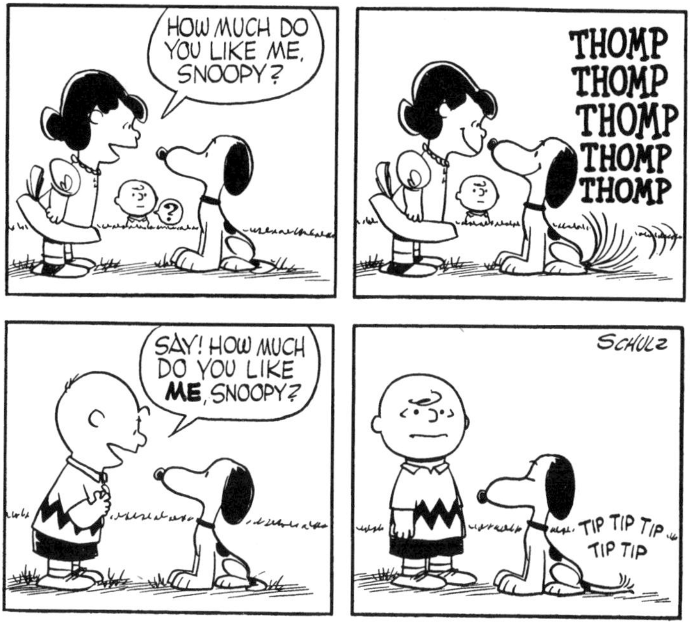
HOW MUCH DO YOU LIKE ME, SNOOPY?
?
THOMP THOMP THOMP THOMP THOMP
SAY! HOW MUCH DO YOU LIKE **ME**, SNOOPY?
SCHULZ
TIP TIP TIP TIP TIP

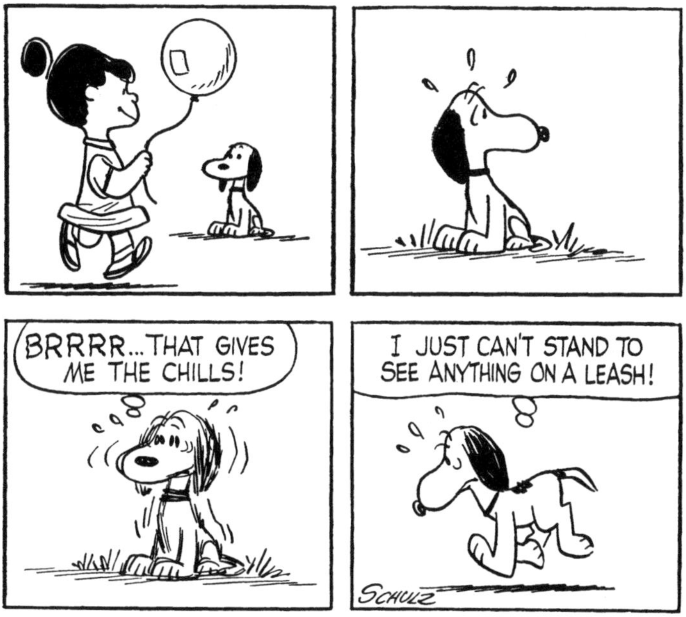
BRRRR...THAT GIVES ME THE CHILLS!
I JUST CAN'T STAND TO SEE ANYTHING ON A LEASH!
SCHULZ

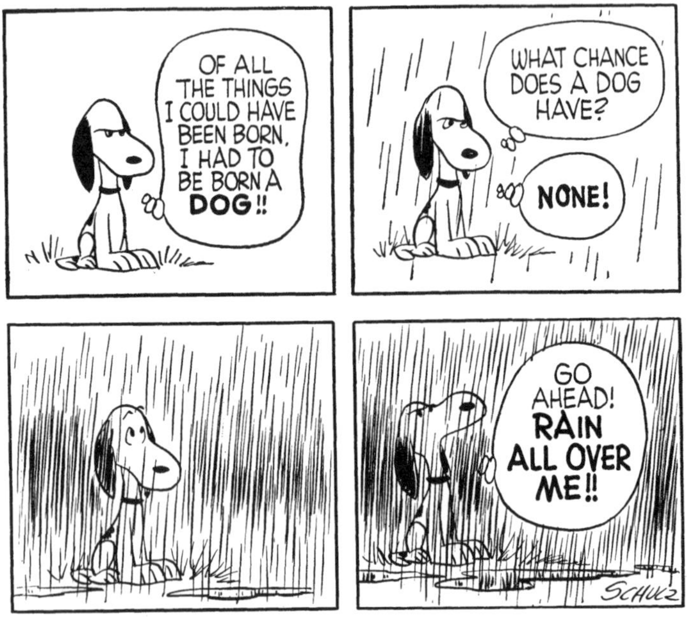
OF ALL THE THINGS I COULD HAVE BEEN BORN, I HAD TO BE BORN A **DOG**!!
WHAT CHANCE DOES A DOG HAVE?
NONE!
GO AHEAD! **RAIN ALL OVER ME!!**
SCHULZ

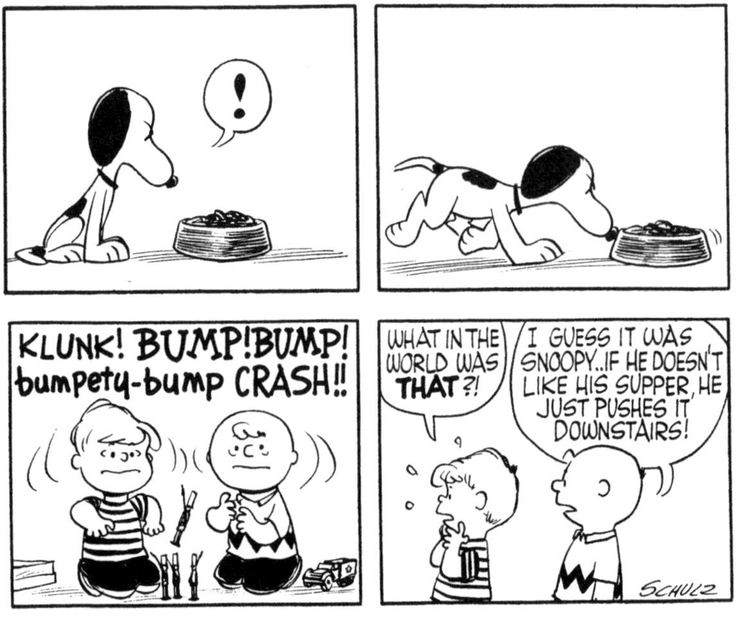
!
KLUNK! BUMP! BUMP! bumpety-bump CRASH!!
WHAT IN THE WORLD WAS **THAT**?!
I GUESS IT WAS SNOOPY..IF HE DOESN'T LIKE HIS SUPPER, HE JUST PUSHES IT DOWNSTAIRS!
SCHULZ

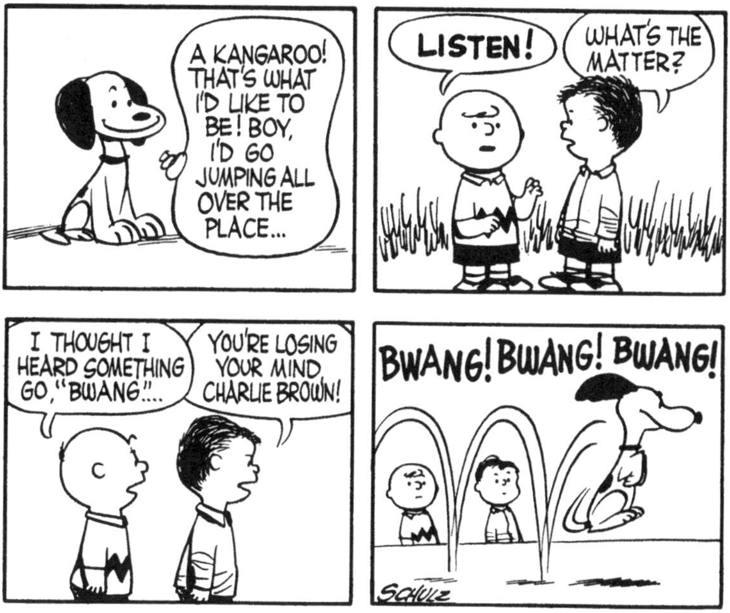
A KANGAROO! THAT'S WHAT I'D LIKE TO BE! BOY, I'D GO JUMPING ALL OVER THE PLACE...
LISTEN!
WHAT'S THE MATTER?
I THOUGHT I HEARD SOMETHING GO, "BWANG!"...
YOU'RE LOSING YOUR MIND CHARLIE BROWN!
BWANG! BWANG! BWANG!
SCHULZ

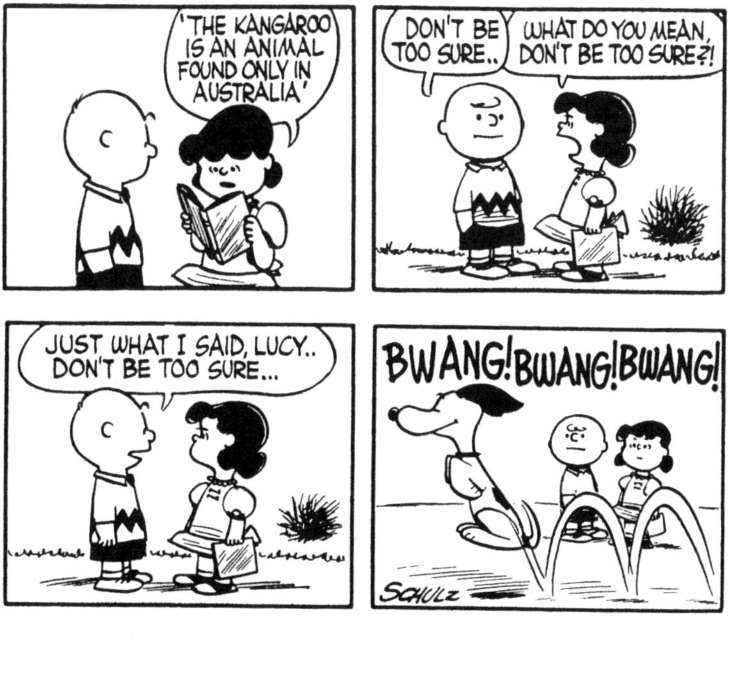
'THE KANGAROO IS AN ANIMAL FOUND ONLY IN AUSTRALIA'
DON'T BE TOO SURE..
WHAT DO YOU MEAN, DON'T BE TOO SURE?!
JUST WHAT I SAID, LUCY.. DON'T BE TOO SURE...
BWANG! BWANG! BWANG!
SCHULZ

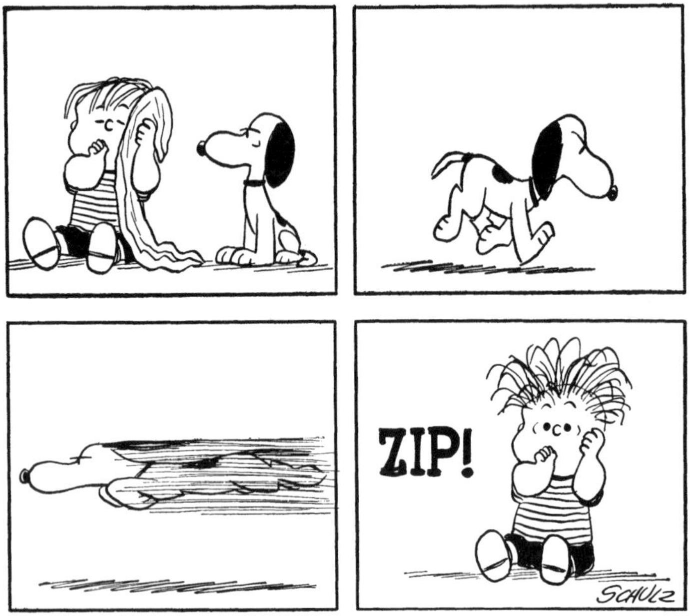
ZIP!
SCHULZ

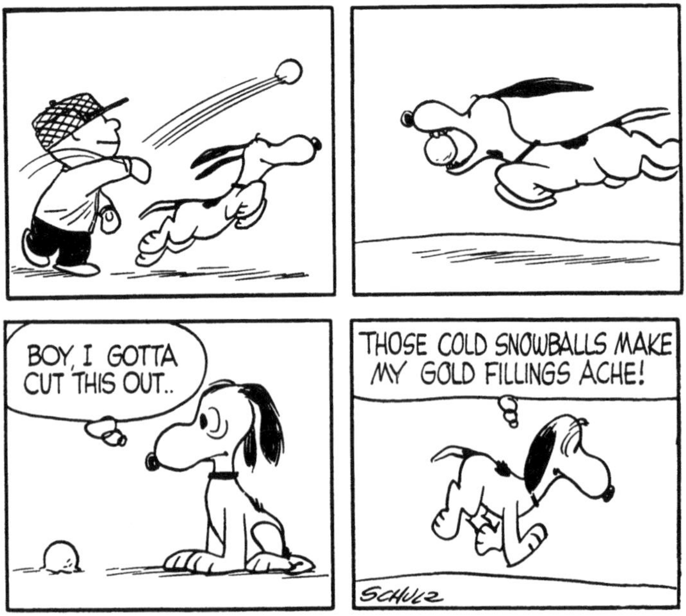
BOY, I GOTTA CUT THIS OUT..
THOSE COLD SNOWBALLS MAKE MY GOLD FILLINGS ACHE!
SCHULZ

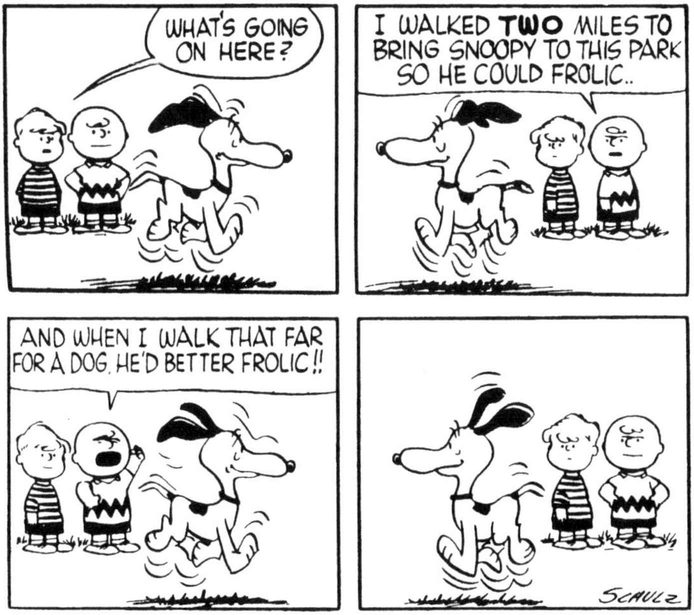
WHAT'S GOING ON HERE?
I WALKED TWO MILES TO BRING SNOOPY TO THIS PARK SO HE COULD FROLIC..
AND WHEN I WALK THAT FAR FOR A DOG, HE'D BETTER FROLIC!!
SCHULZ

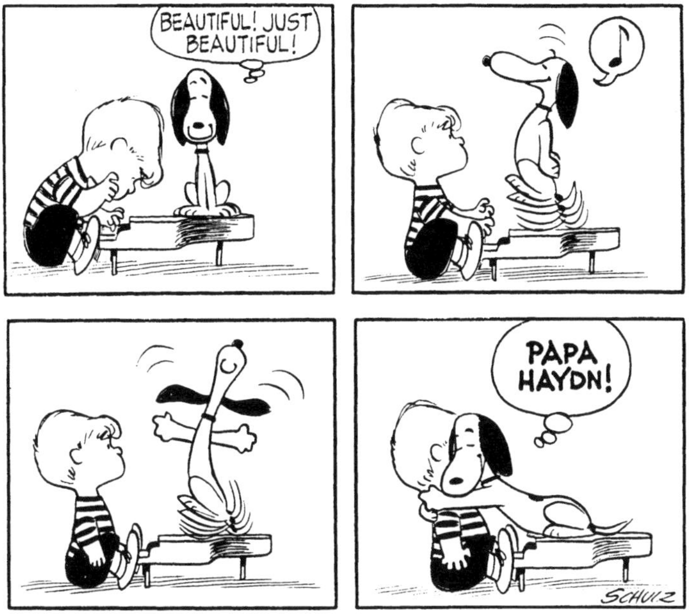
BEAUTIFUL! JUST BEAUTIFUL!
PAPA HAYDN!
SCHULZ

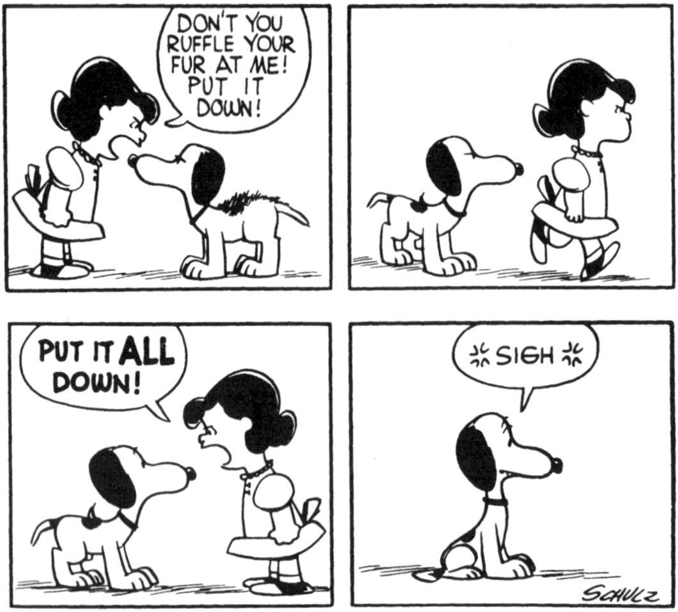
DON'T YOU RUFFLE YOUR FUR AT ME! PUT IT DOWN!
PUT IT **ALL** DOWN!
SIGH
SCHULZ

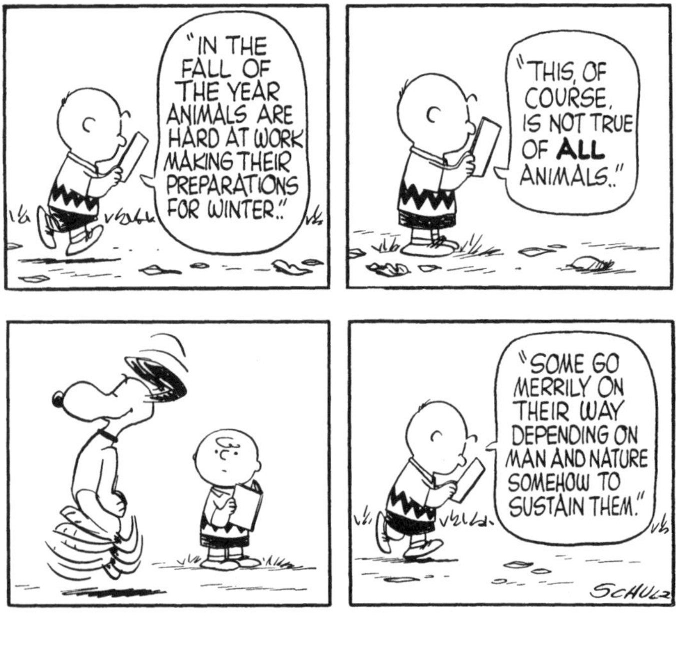
"IN THE FALL OF THE YEAR ANIMALS ARE HARD AT WORK MAKING THEIR PREPARATIONS FOR WINTER."
"THIS, OF COURSE, IS NOT TRUE OF **ALL** ANIMALS."
"SOME GO MERRILY ON THEIR WAY DEPENDING ON MAN AND NATURE SOMEHOW TO SUSTAIN THEM."
SCHULZ

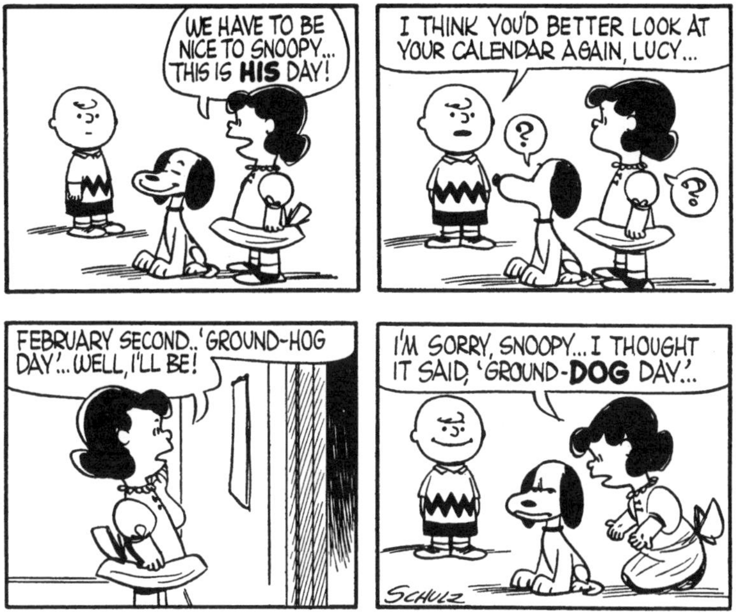
WE HAVE TO BE NICE TO SNOOPY... THIS IS **HIS** DAY!
I THINK YOU'D BETTER LOOK AT YOUR CALENDAR AGAIN, LUCY...
?
?
FEBRUARY SECOND..'GROUND-HOG DAY'...WELL, I'LL BE!
I'M SORRY, SNOOPY... I THOUGHT IT SAID, 'GROUND-**DOG** DAY.'...
SCHULZ

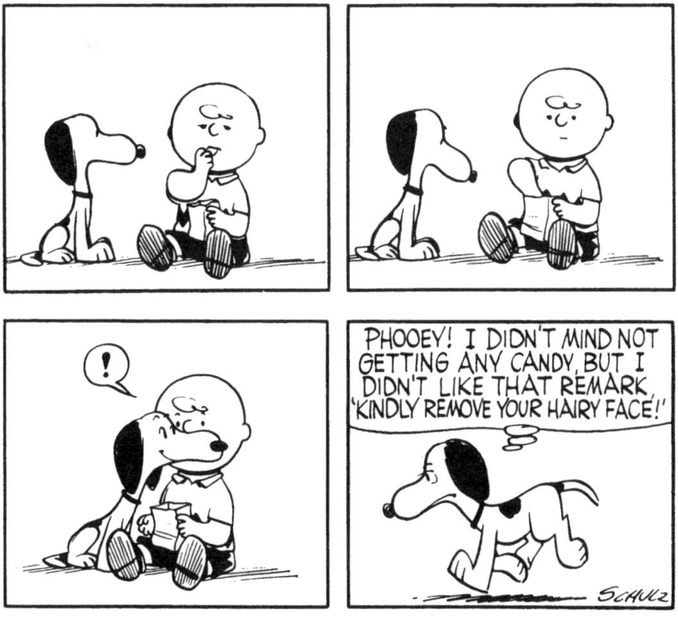
!
PHOOEY! I DIDN'T MIND NOT GETTING ANY CANDY, BUT I DIDN'T LIKE THAT REMARK, 'KINDLY REMOVE YOUR HAIRY FACE!'
SCHULZ

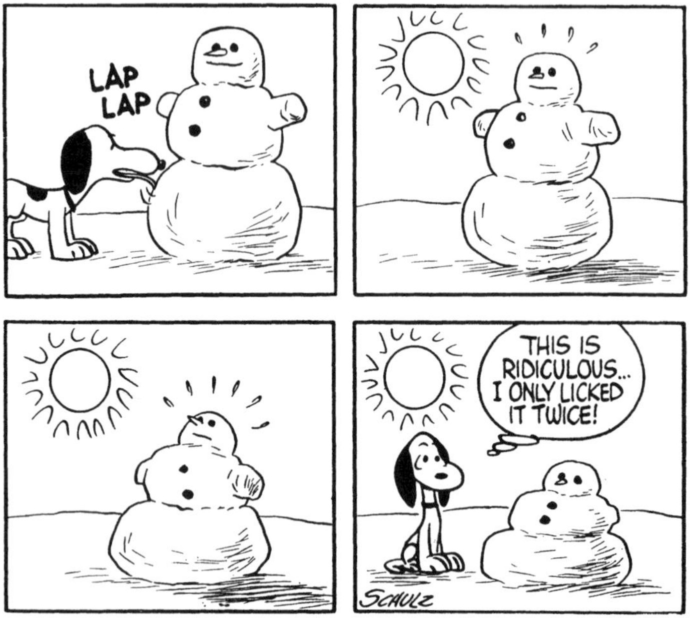
LAP
LAP
THIS IS RIDICULOUS... I ONLY LICKED IT TWICE!
SCHULZ

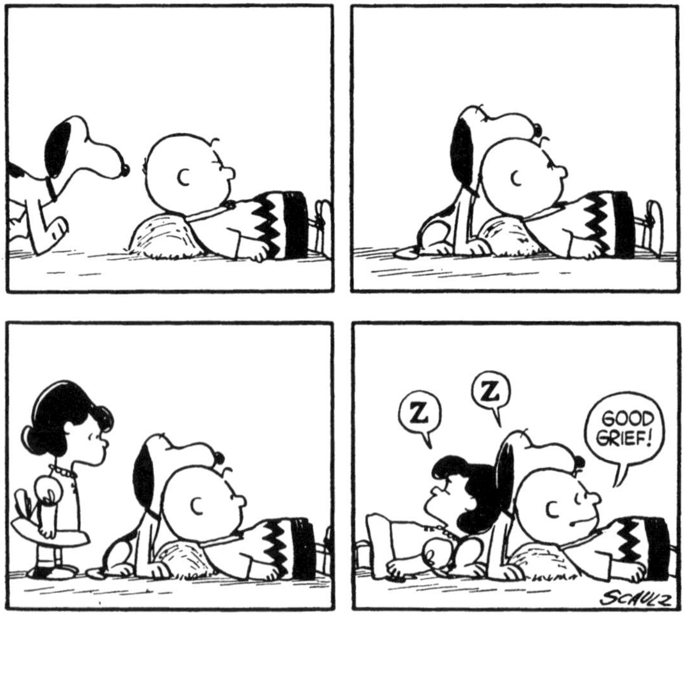
Z
Z
GOOD GRIEF!
SCHULZ

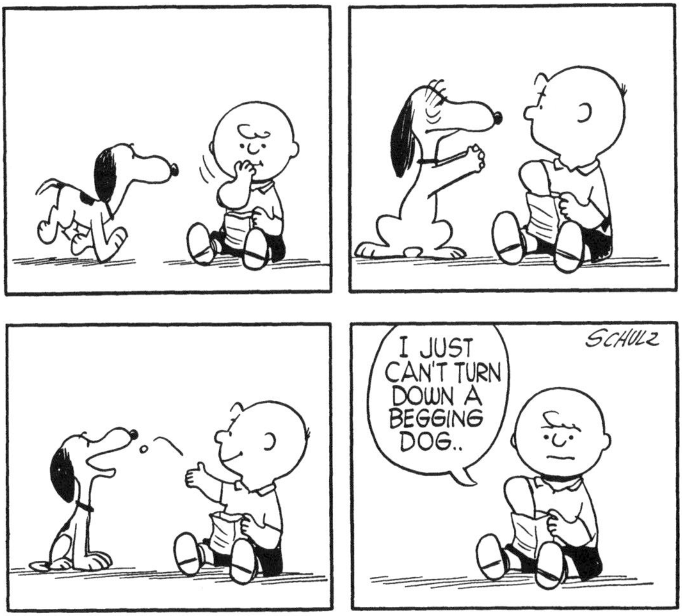
SCHULZ
I JUST CAN'T TURN DOWN A BEGGING DOG..

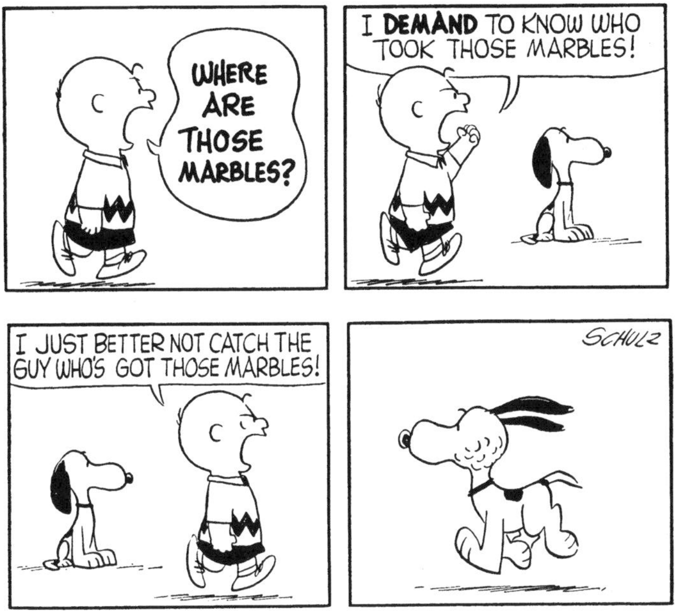
WHERE ARE THOSE MARBLES?
I **DEMAND** TO KNOW WHO TOOK THOSE MARBLES!
I JUST BETTER NOT CATCH THE GUY WHO'S GOT THOSE MARBLES!
SCHULZ

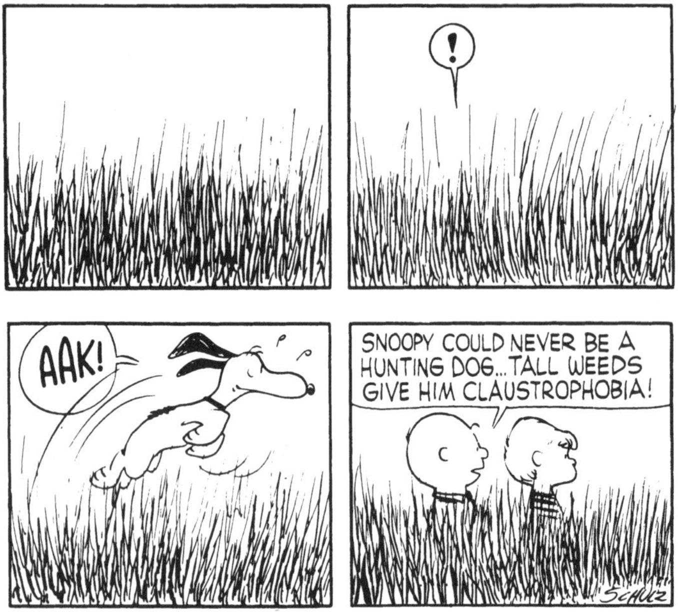
!
AAK!
SNOOPY COULD NEVER BE A HUNTING DOG...TALL WEEDS GIVE HIM CLAUSTROPHOBIA!
SCHULZ

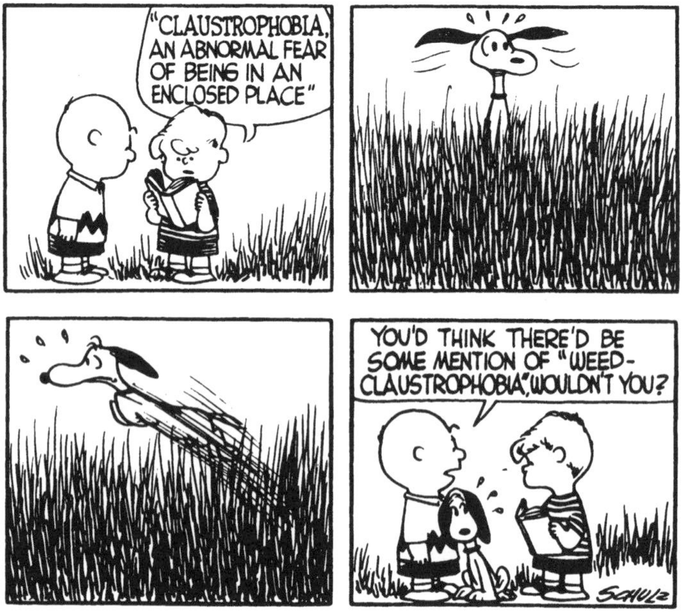
"CLAUSTROPHOBIA, AN ABNORMAL FEAR OF BEING IN AN ENCLOSED PLACE"
YOU'D THINK THERE'D BE SOME MENTION OF "WEED-CLAUSTROPHOBIA," WOULDN'T YOU?
SCHULZ

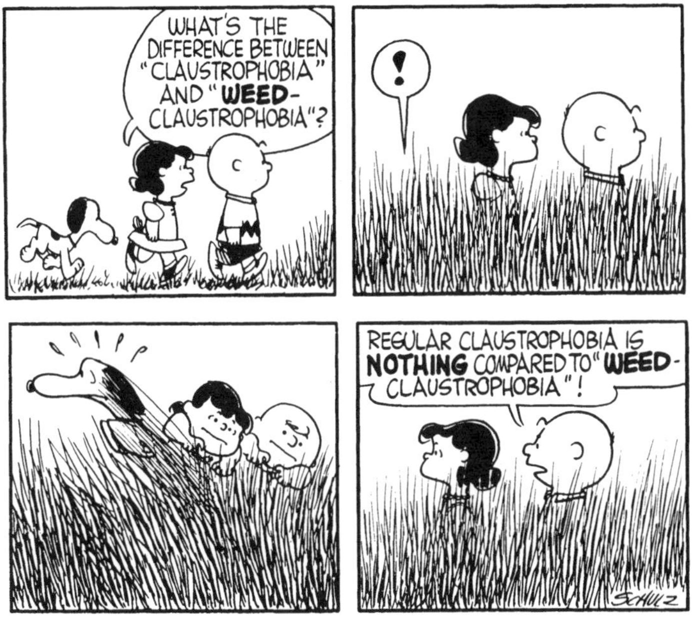
WHAT'S THE DIFFERENCE BETWEEN "CLAUSTROPHOBIA" AND "WEED-CLAUSTROPHOBIA"?
!
REGULAR CLAUSTROPHOBIA IS NOTHING COMPARED TO "WEED-CLAUSTROPHOBIA"!
SCHULZ

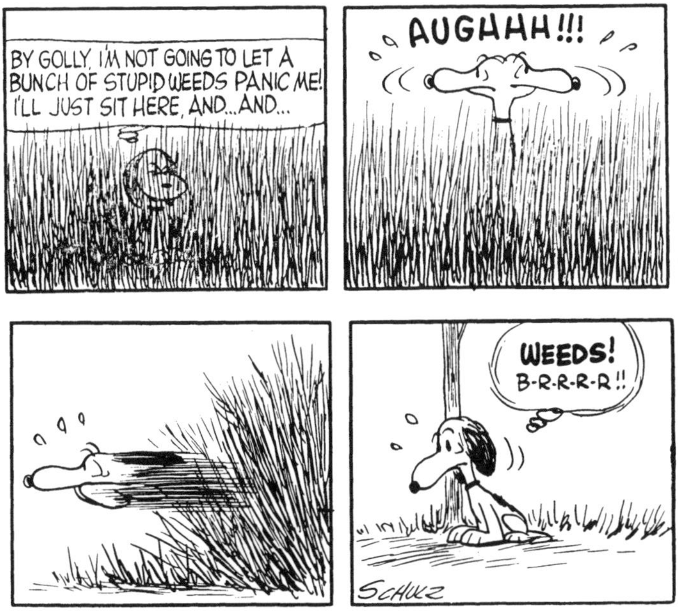
BY GOLLY, I'M NOT GOING TO LET A BUNCH OF STUPID WEEDS PANIC ME! I'LL JUST SIT HERE, AND...AND...
AUGHHH!!!
WEEDS! B-R-R-R-R!!
SCHULZ

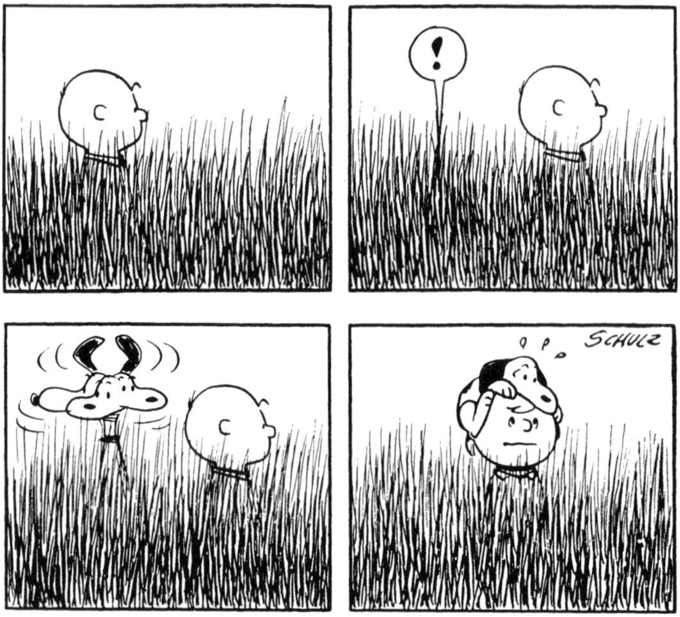
!
SCHULZ

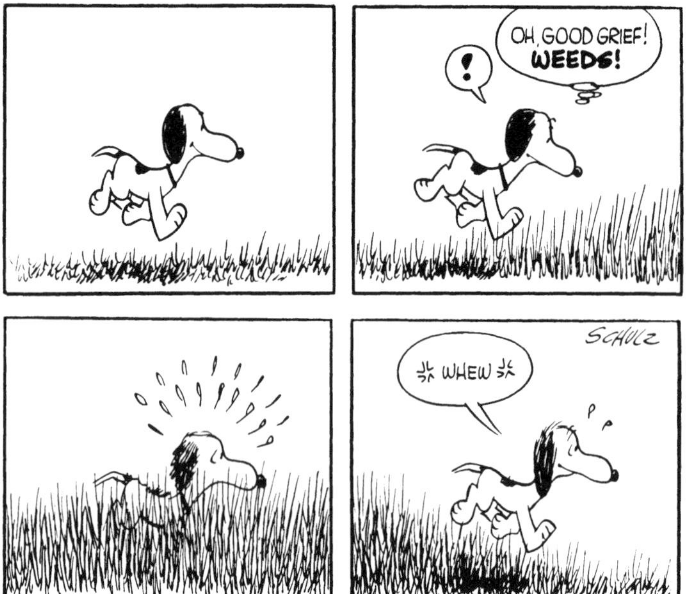
!
OH, GOOD GRIEF! WEEDS!
WHEW
SCHULZ

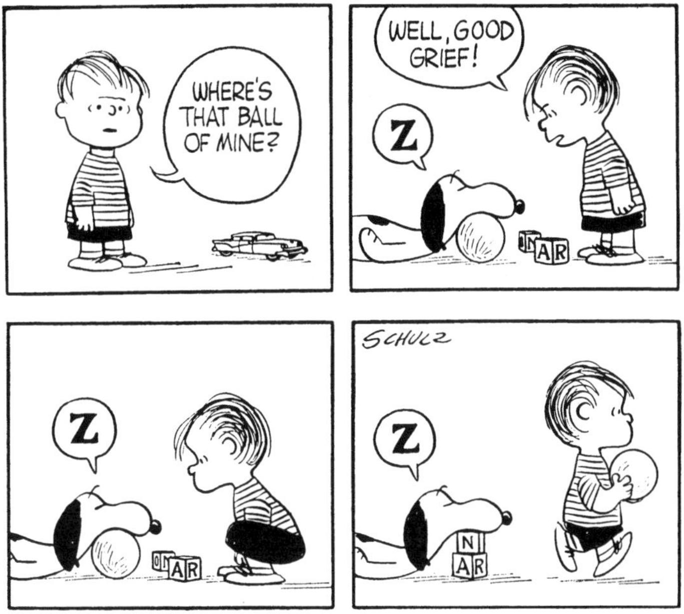
WHERE'S THAT BALL OF MINE?
WELL, GOOD GRIEF!
Z
Z
Z
SCHULZ

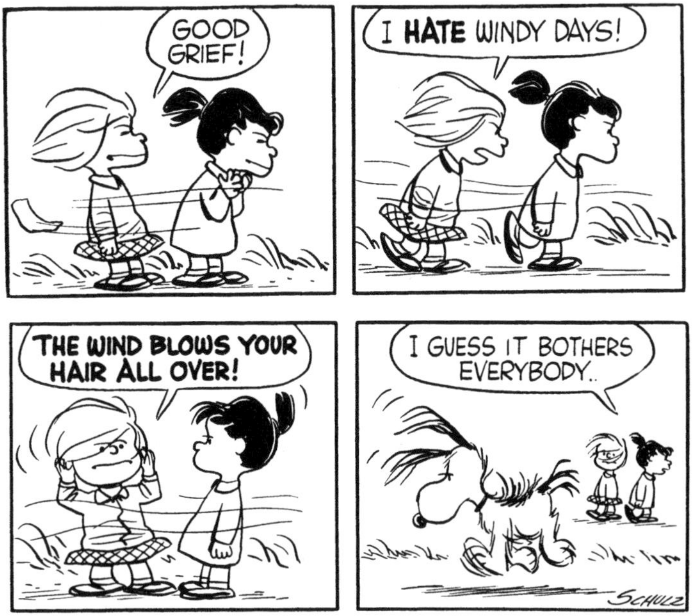
GOOD GRIEF!
I HATE WINDY DAYS!
THE WIND BLOWS YOUR HAIR ALL OVER!
I GUESS IT BOTHERS EVERYBODY..
SCHULZ

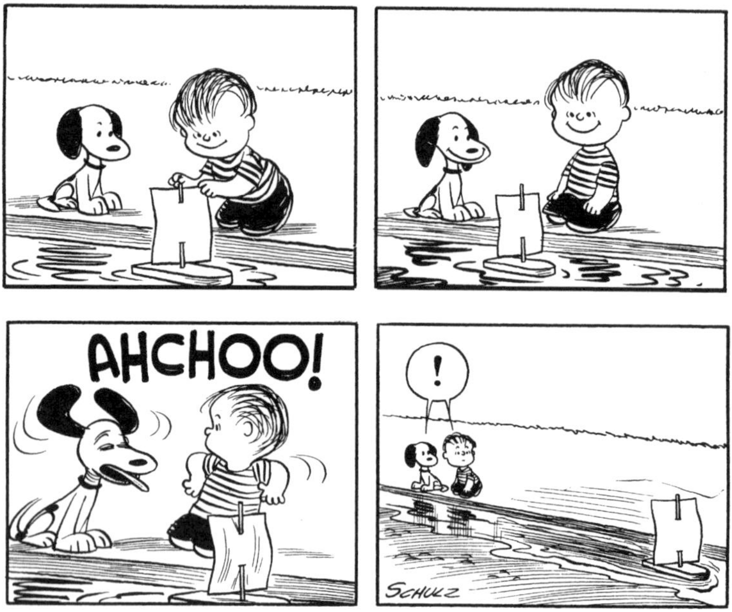
AHCHOO!
!
SCHULZ

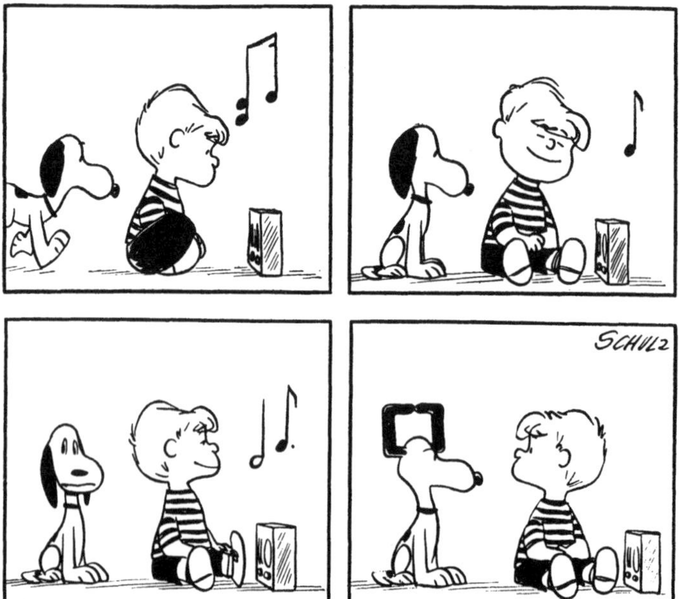
SCHULZ

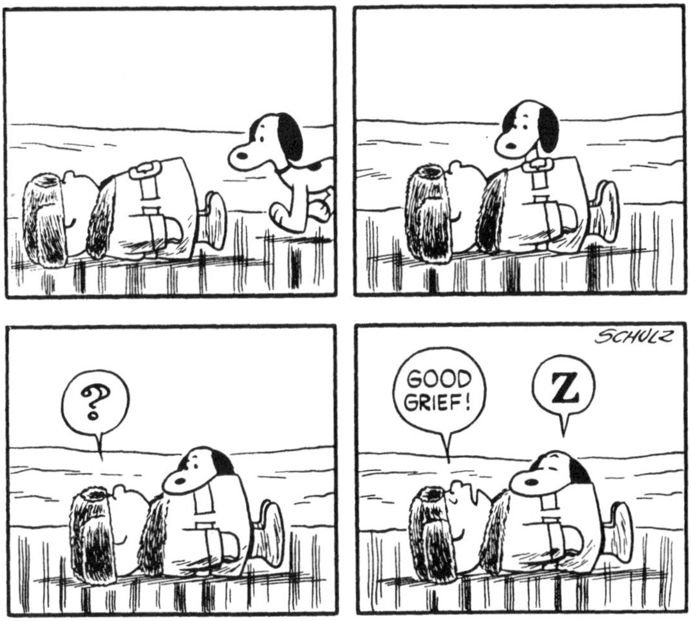
SCHULZ
?
GOOD GRIEF!
Z

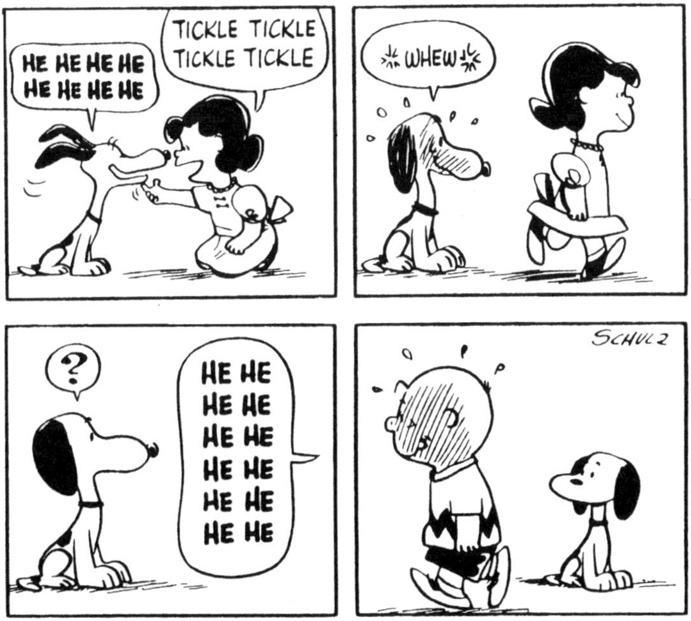
HE HE HE HE HE HE HE HE
TICKLE TICKLE TICKLE TICKLE
WHEW
SCHULZ
?
HE HE HE HE HE HE HE HE HE HE HE HE

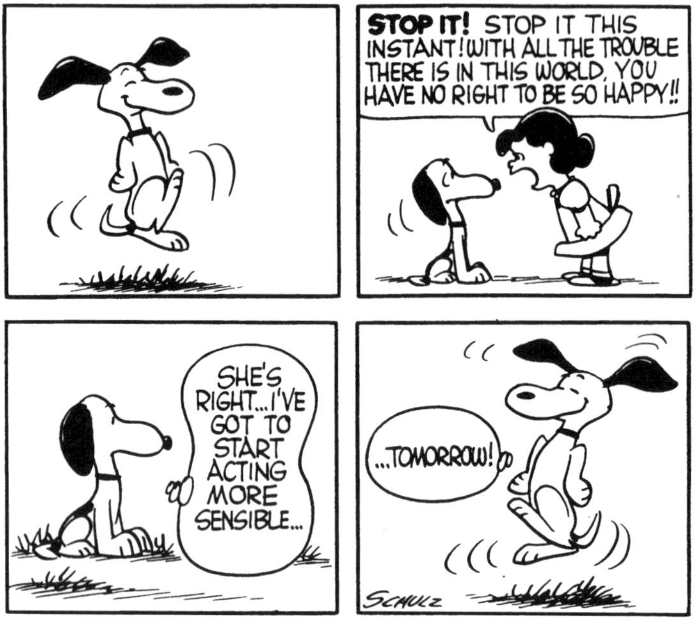
STOP IT! STOP IT THIS INSTANT! WITH ALL THE TROUBLE THERE IS IN THIS WORLD, YOU HAVE NO RIGHT TO BE SO HAPPY!!
SHE'S RIGHT...I'VE GOT TO START ACTING MORE SENSIBLE...
...TOMORROW!
SCHULZ

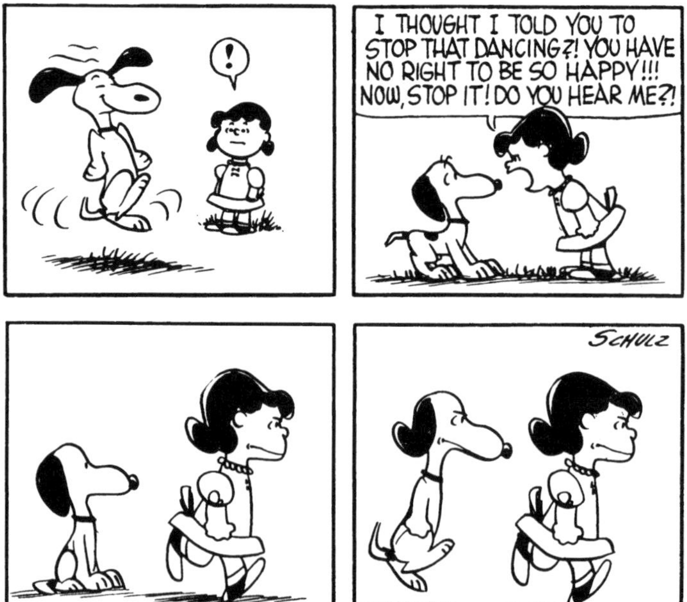
!
I THOUGHT I TOLD YOU TO STOP THAT DANCING?! YOU HAVE NO RIGHT TO BE SO HAPPY!!! NOW, STOP IT! DO YOU HEAR ME?!
SCHULZ

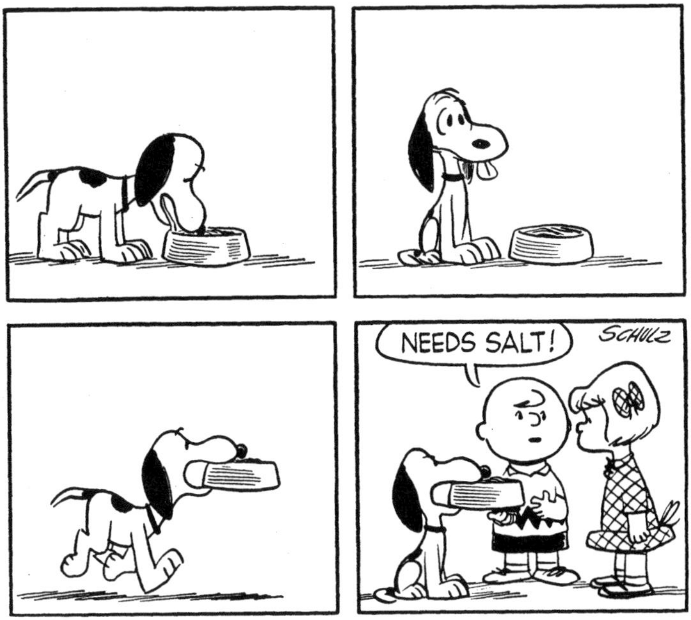
NEEDS SALT!
SCHULZ

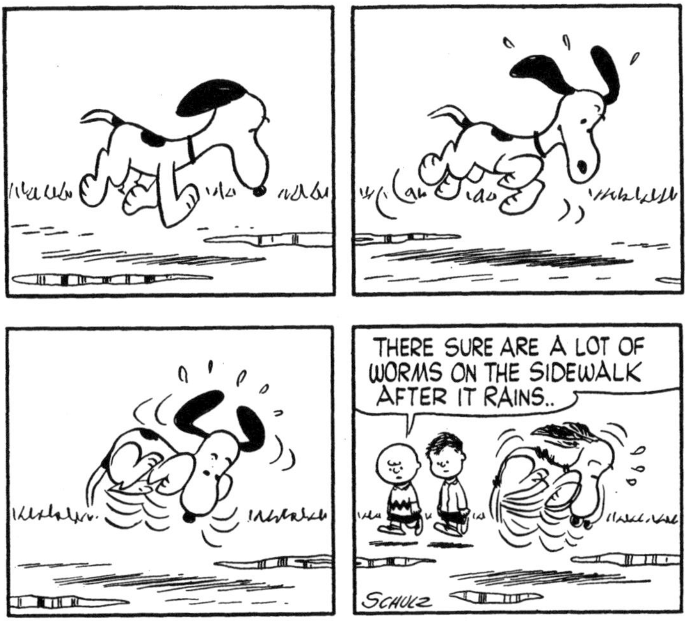
THERE SURE ARE A LOT OF WORMS ON THE SIDEWALK AFTER IT RAINS..
SCHULZ

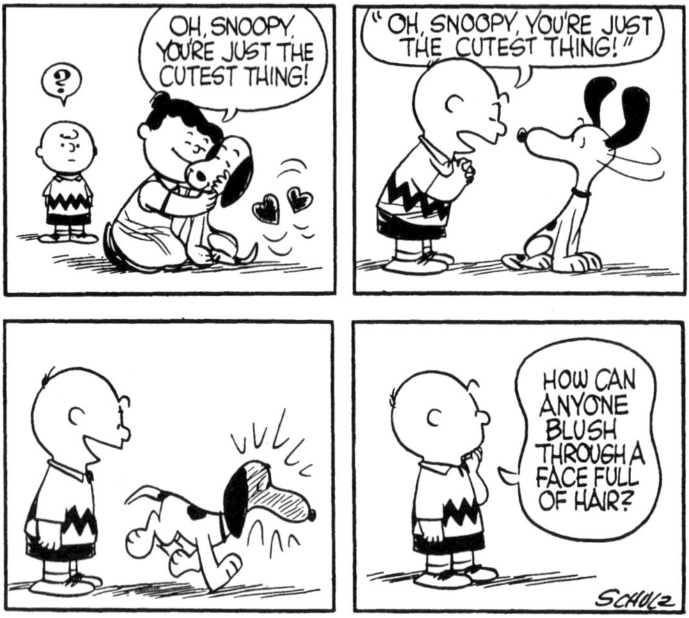

OH, SNOOPY, YOU'RE JUST THE CUTEST THING!
"OH, SNOOPY, YOU'RE JUST THE CUTEST THING!"
HOW CAN ANYONE BLUSH THROUGH A FACE FULL OF HAIR?
SCHULZ

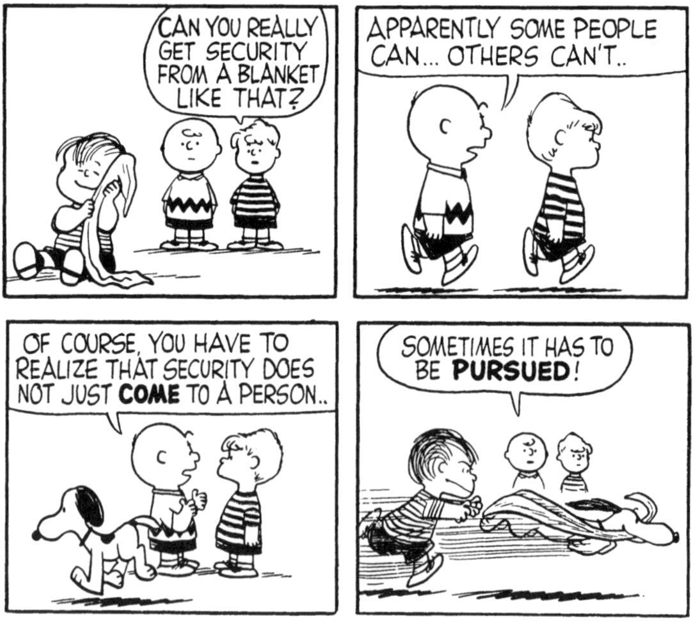

CAN YOU REALLY GET SECURITY FROM A BLANKET LIKE THAT?
APPARENTLY SOME PEOPLE CAN... OTHERS CAN'T..
OF COURSE, YOU HAVE TO REALIZE THAT SECURITY DOES NOT JUST **COME** TO A PERSON..
SOMETIMES IT HAS TO BE **PURSUED**!

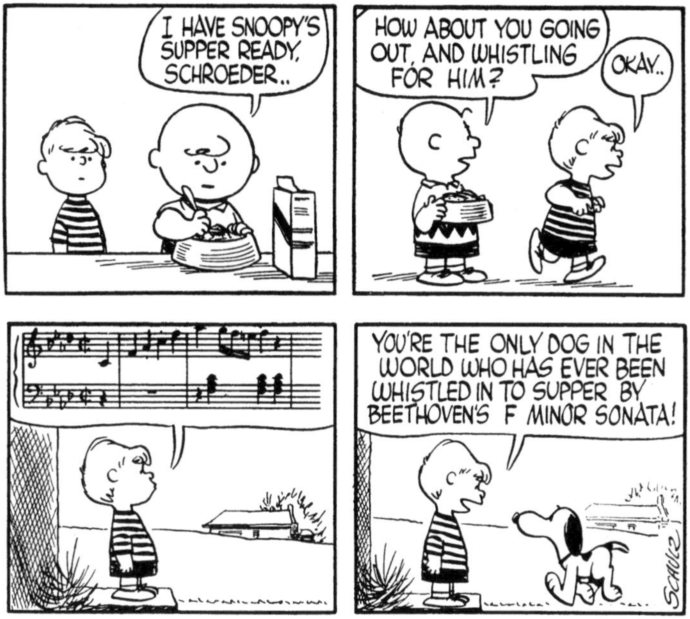
I HAVE SNOOPY'S SUPPER READY, SCHROEDER..
HOW ABOUT YOU GOING OUT, AND WHISTLING FOR HIM?
OKAY..
YOU'RE THE ONLY DOG IN THE WORLD WHO HAS EVER BEEN WHISTLED IN TO SUPPER BY BEETHOVEN'S F MINOR SONATA!
SCHULZ

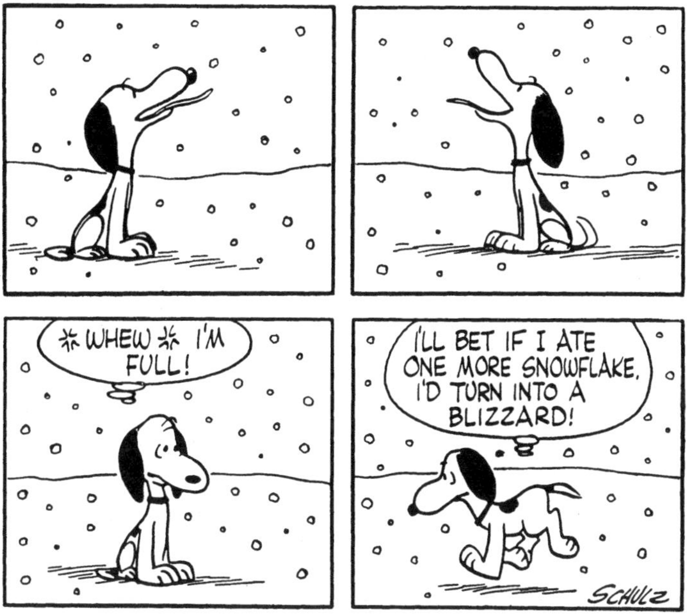
WHEW I'M FULL!
I'LL BET IF I ATE ONE MORE SNOWFLAKE, I'D TURN INTO A BLIZZARD!
SCHULZ

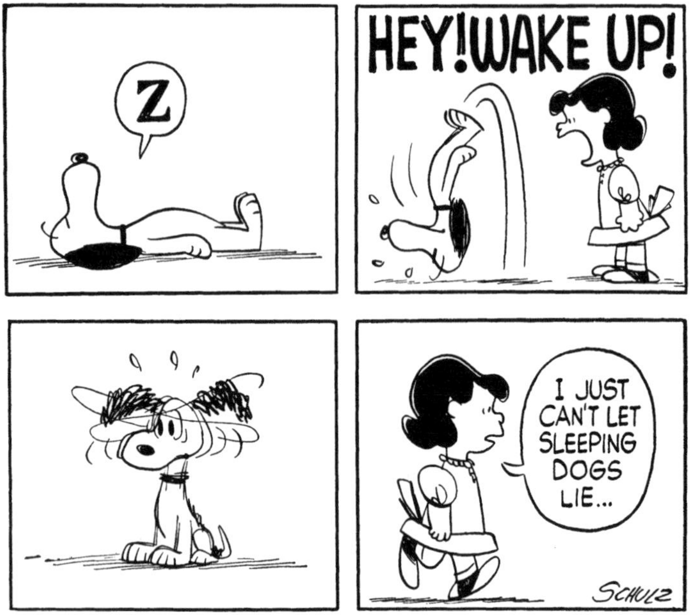
Z
HEY! WAKE UP!
I JUST CAN'T LET SLEEPING DOGS LIE...
SCHULZ

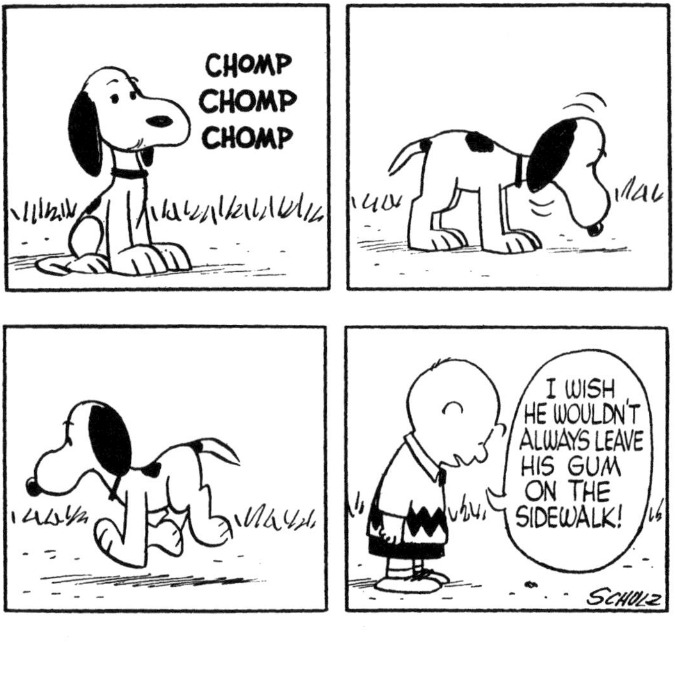
CHOMP CHOMP CHOMP
I WISH HE WOULDN'T ALWAYS LEAVE HIS GUM ON THE SIDEWALK!
SCHULZ

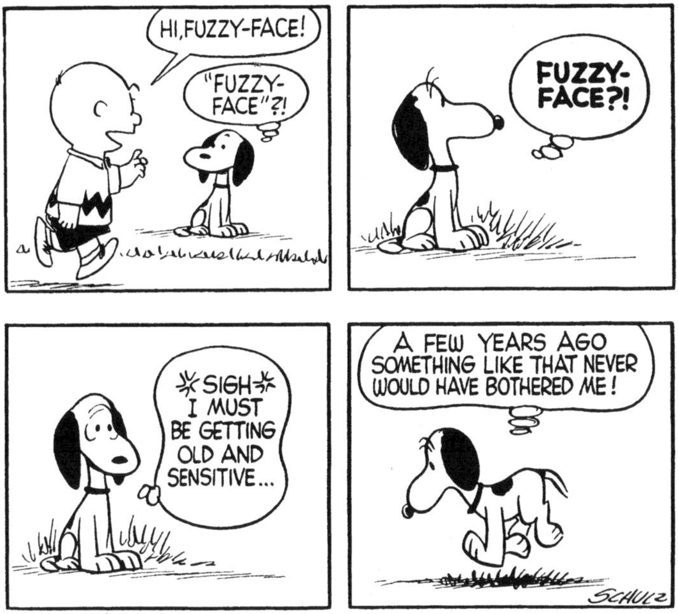
HI, FUZZY-FACE!
"FUZZY-FACE"?!
FUZZY-FACE?!
SIGH I MUST BE GETTING OLD AND SENSITIVE...
A FEW YEARS AGO SOMETHING LIKE THAT NEVER WOULD HAVE BOTHERED ME!
SCHULZ

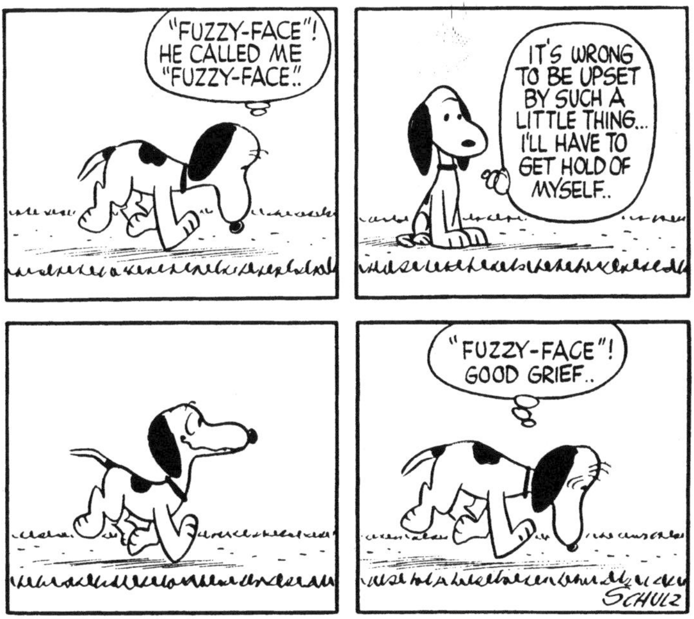
"FUZZY-FACE"! HE CALLED ME "FUZZY-FACE"..
IT'S WRONG TO BE UPSET BY SUCH A LITTLE THING... I'LL HAVE TO GET HOLD OF MYSELF..
"FUZZY-FACE"! GOOD GRIEF..
SCHULZ

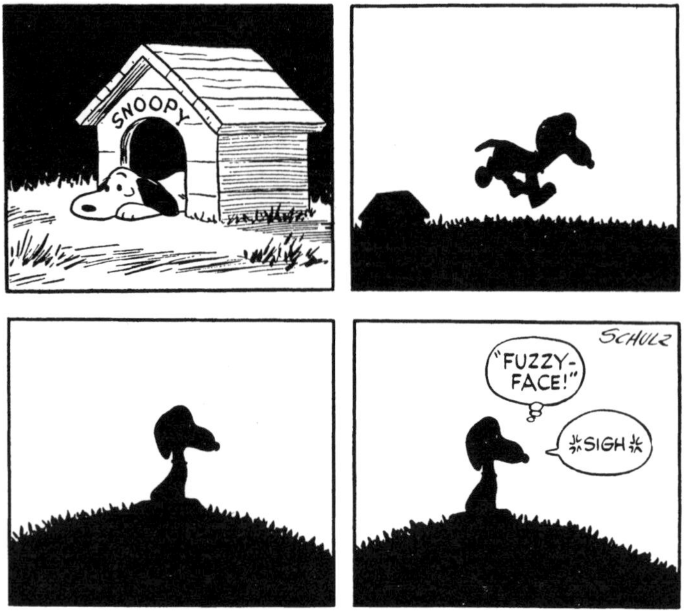
SNOOPY
"FUZZY-FACE!"
SIGH
SCHULZ

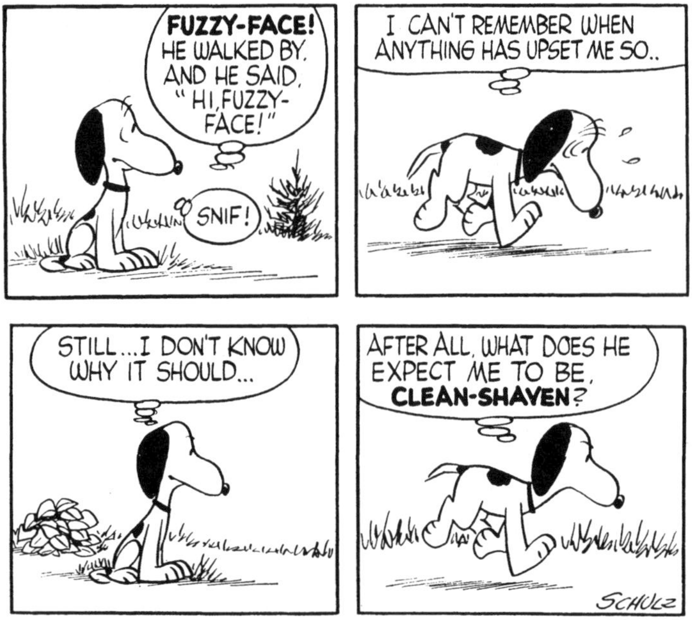
FUZZY-FACE! HE WALKED BY, AND HE SAID, "HI, FUZZY-FACE!"
SNIF!
I CAN'T REMEMBER WHEN ANYTHING HAS UPSET ME SO..
STILL...I DON'T KNOW WHY IT SHOULD...
AFTER ALL, WHAT DOES HE EXPECT ME TO BE, **CLEAN-SHAVEN**?
SCHULZ

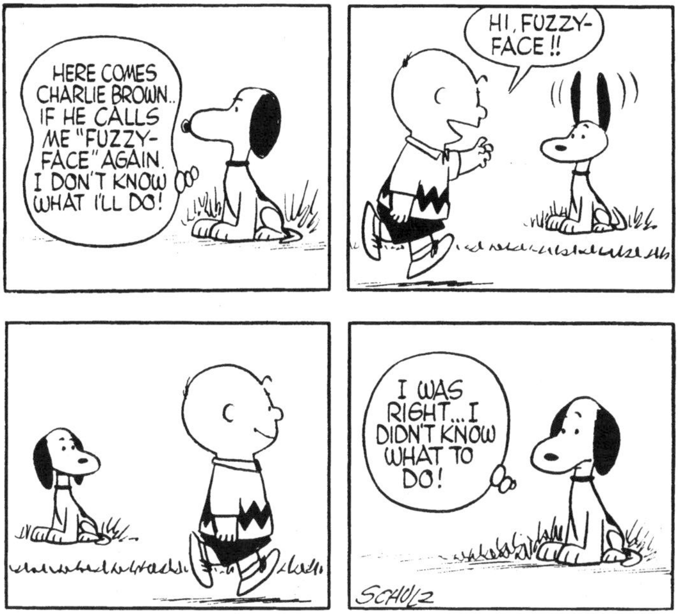
HERE COMES CHARLIE BROWN.. IF HE CALLS ME "FUZZY-FACE" AGAIN, I DON'T KNOW WHAT I'LL DO!
HI, FUZZY-FACE !!
I WAS RIGHT...I DIDN'T KNOW WHAT TO DO!
SCHULZ

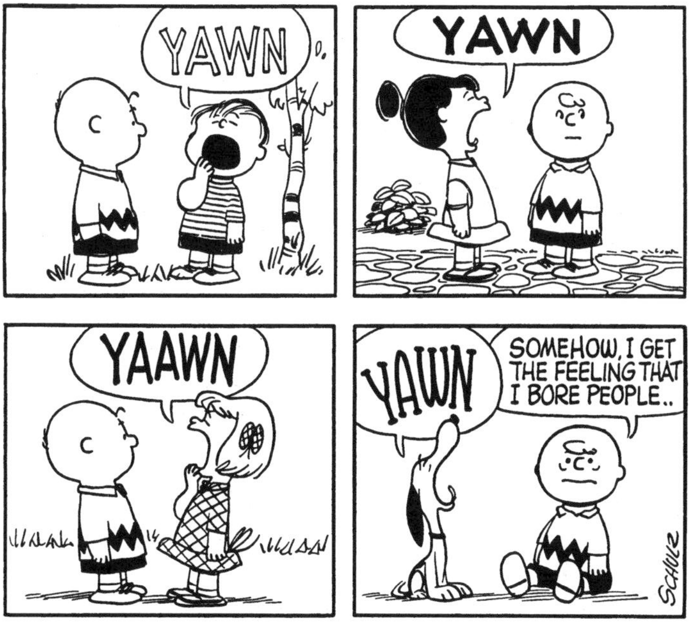
YAWN
YAWN
YAAWN
YAWN
SOMEHOW, I GET THE FEELING THAT I BORE PEOPLE..
SCHULZ

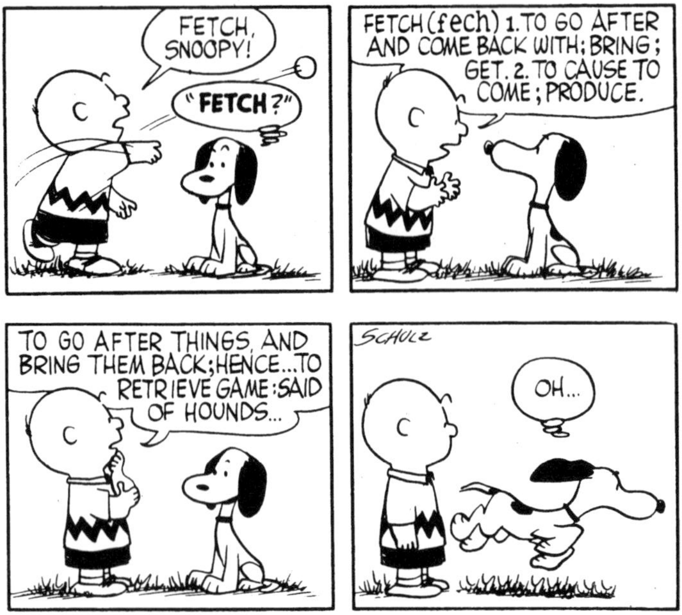
FETCH, SNOOPY!
"FETCH?"
FETCH (fech) 1. TO GO AFTER AND COME BACK WITH; BRING; GET. 2. TO CAUSE TO COME; PRODUCE.
TO GO AFTER THINGS, AND BRING THEM BACK; HENCE...TO RETRIEVE GAME: SAID OF HOUNDS...
SCHULZ
OH...

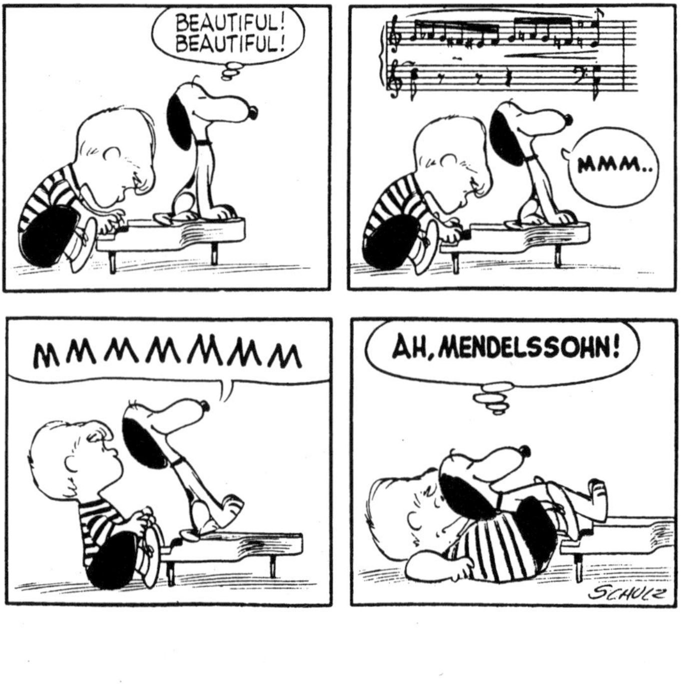
BEAUTIFUL! BEAUTIFUL!
MMM..
MMMMMMMM
AH, MENDELSSOHN!
SCHULZ

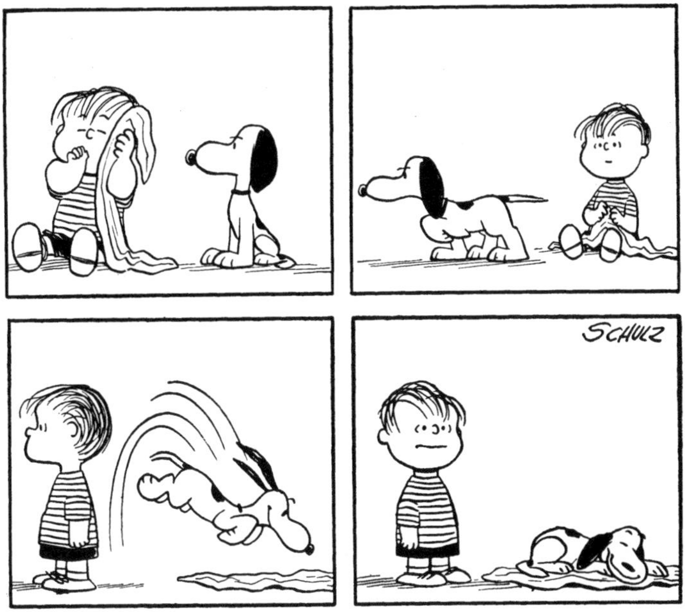
SCHULZ

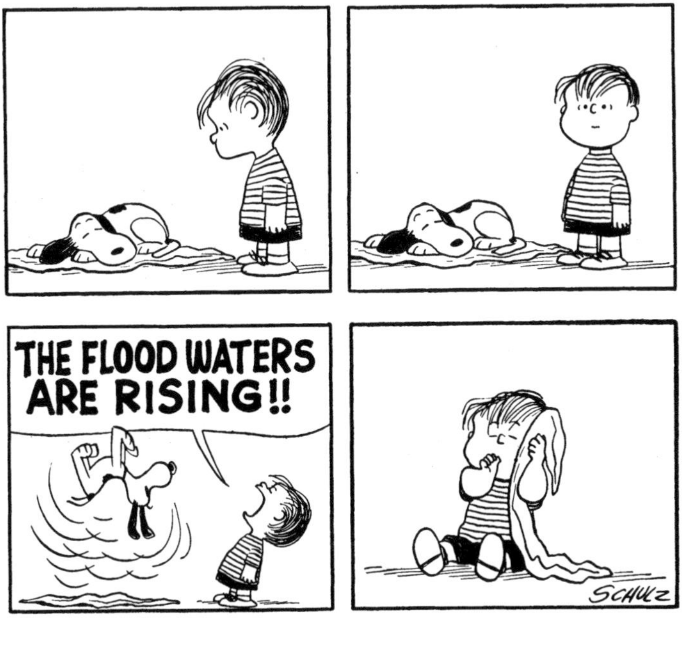
THE FLOOD WATERS ARE RISING!!
SCHULZ

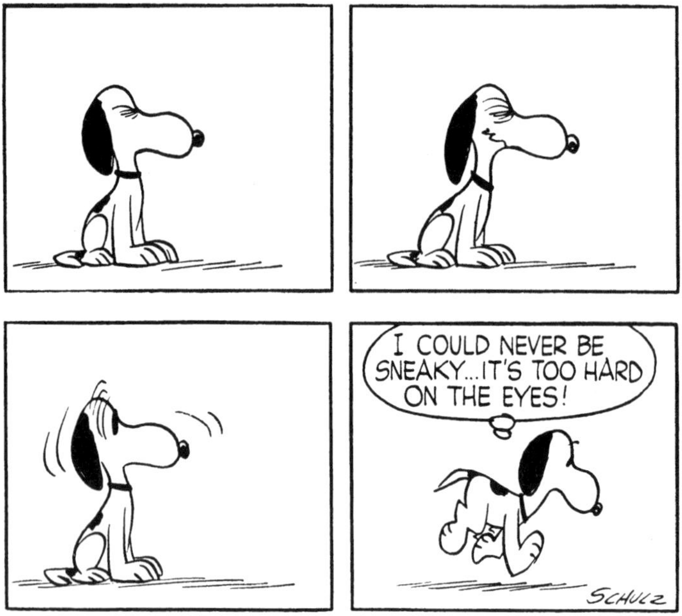
I COULD NEVER BE SNEAKY...IT'S TOO HARD ON THE EYES!
SCHULZ

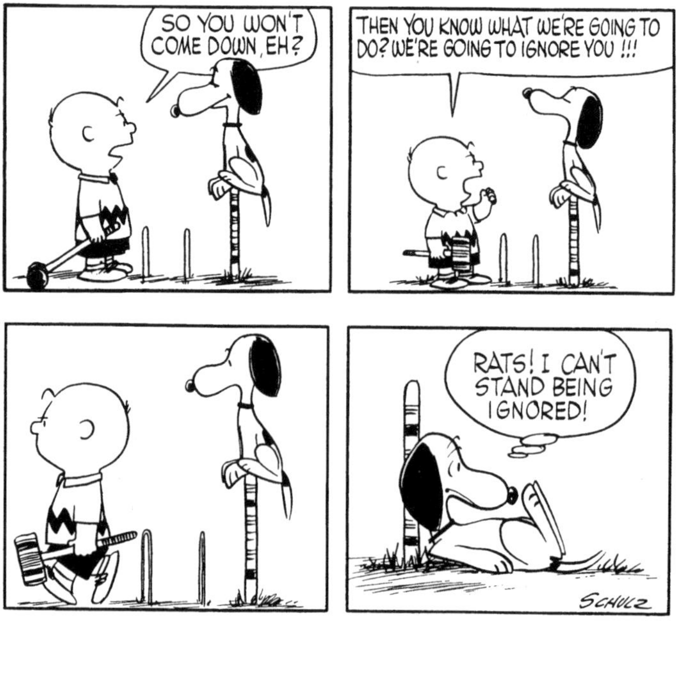
SO YOU WON'T COME DOWN, EH?
THEN YOU KNOW WHAT WE'RE GOING TO DO? WE'RE GOING TO IGNORE YOU !!!
RATS! I CAN'T STAND BEING IGNORED!
SCHULZ

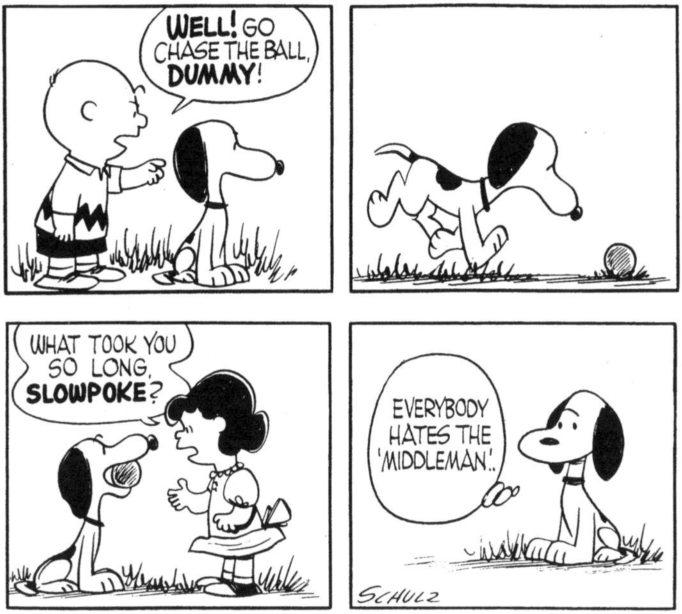
WELL! GO CHASE THE BALL, DUMMY!
WHAT TOOK YOU SO LONG, SLOWPOKE?
EVERYBODY HATES THE 'MIDDLEMAN'..
SCHULZ

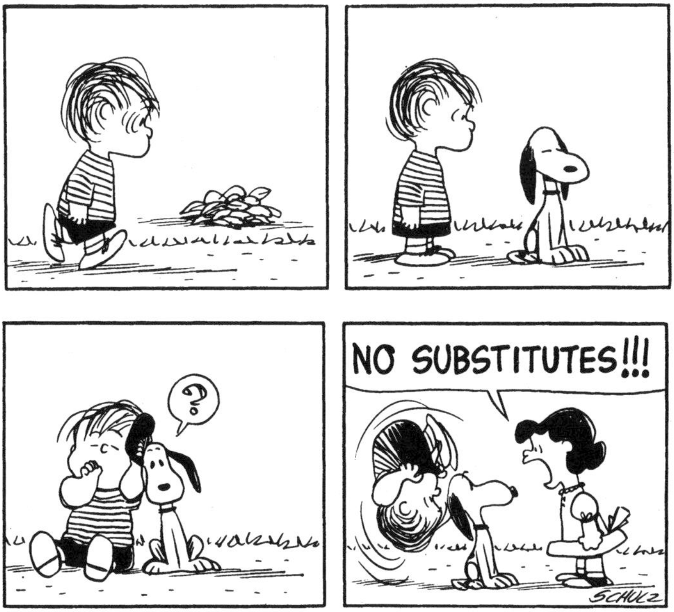
?
NO SUBSTITUTES!!!
SCHULZ

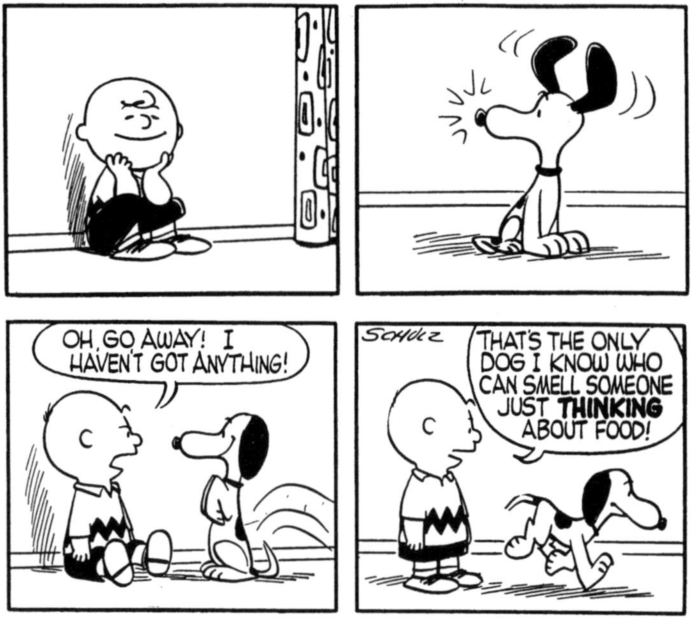
OH, GO AWAY! I HAVEN'T GOT ANYTHING!
SCHULZ
THAT'S THE ONLY DOG I KNOW WHO CAN SMELL SOMEONE JUST **THINKING** ABOUT FOOD!

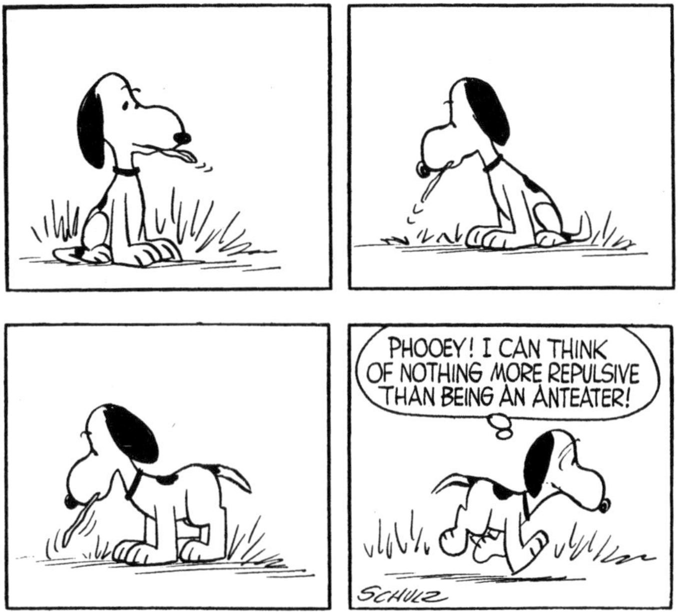
PHOOEY! I CAN THINK OF NOTHING MORE REPULSIVE THAN BEING AN ANTEATER!
SCHULZ

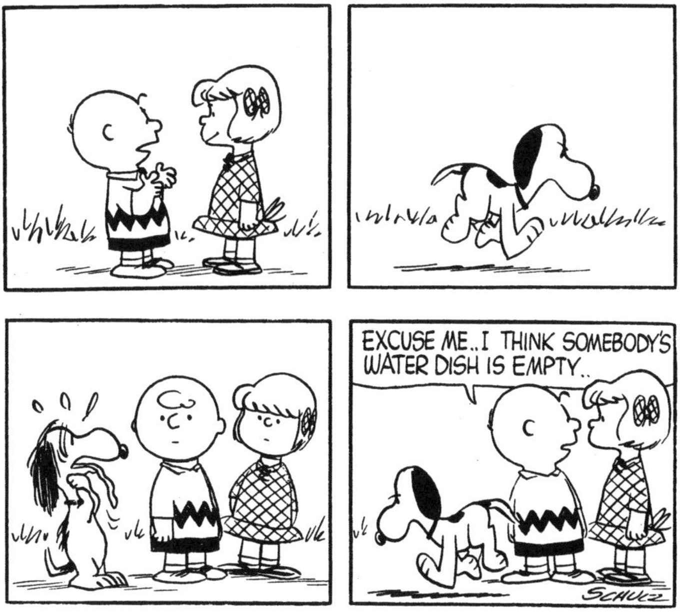
EXCUSE ME..I THINK SOMEBODY'S WATER DISH IS EMPTY..
SCHULZ

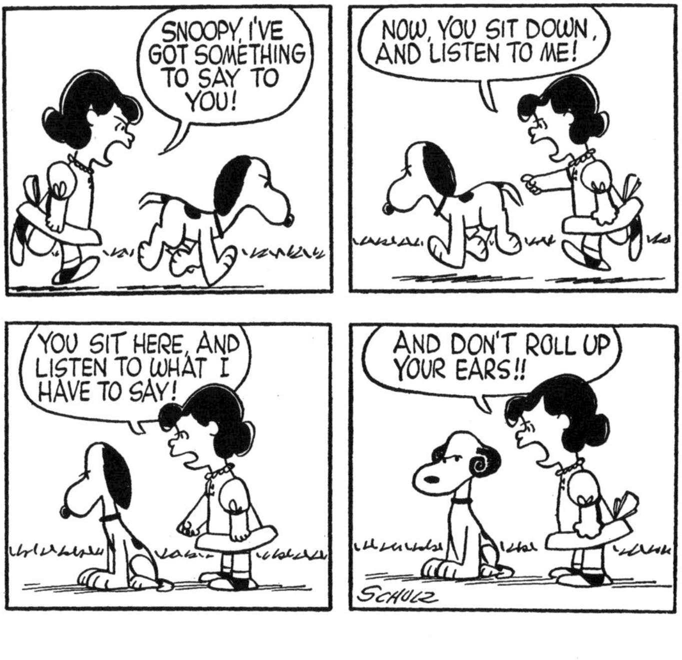
SNOOPY, I'VE GOT SOMETHING TO SAY TO YOU!
NOW, YOU SIT DOWN, AND LISTEN TO ME!
YOU SIT HERE, AND LISTEN TO WHAT I HAVE TO SAY!
AND DON'T ROLL UP YOUR EARS!!
SCHULZ

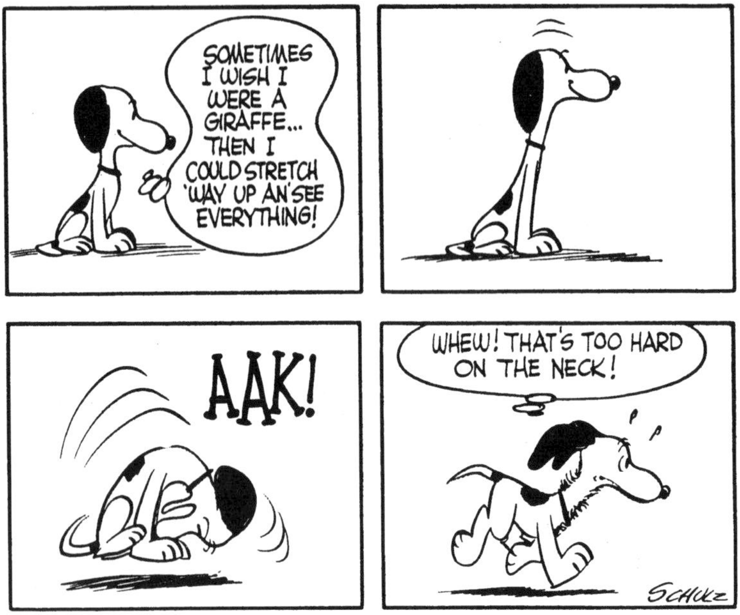
SOMETIMES I WISH I WERE A GIRAFFE... THEN I COULD STRETCH 'WAY UP AN'SEE EVERYTHING!
AAK!
WHEW! THAT'S TOO HARD ON THE NECK!
SCHULZ

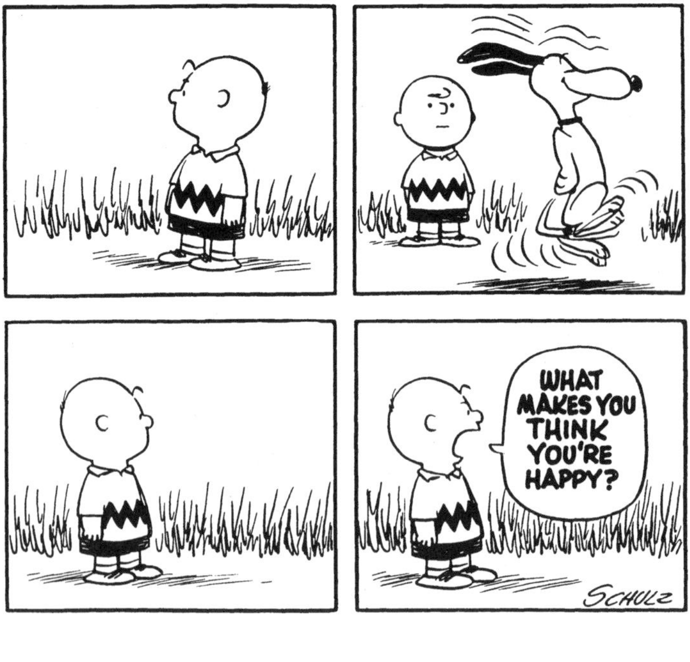
WHAT MAKES YOU THINK YOU'RE HAPPY?
SCHULZ

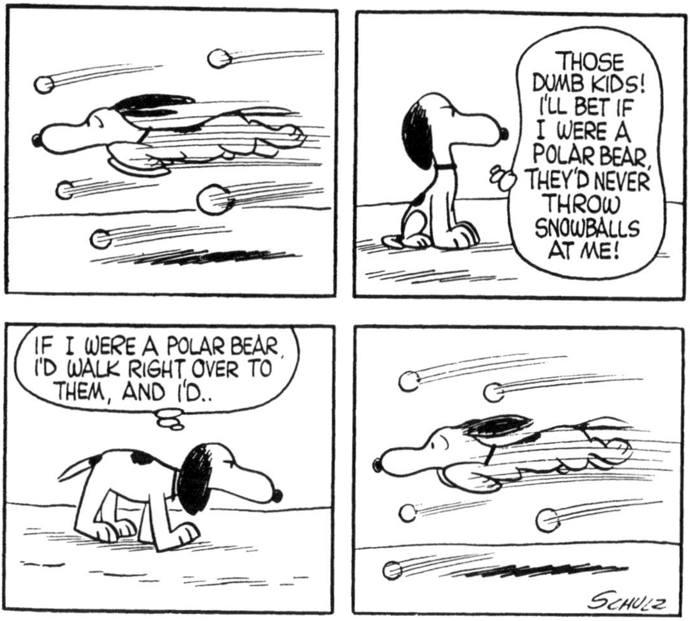
THOSE DUMB KIDS! I'LL BET IF I WERE A POLAR BEAR, THEY'D NEVER THROW SNOWBALLS AT ME!
IF I WERE A POLAR BEAR, I'D WALK RIGHT OVER TO THEM, AND I'D..
SCHULZ

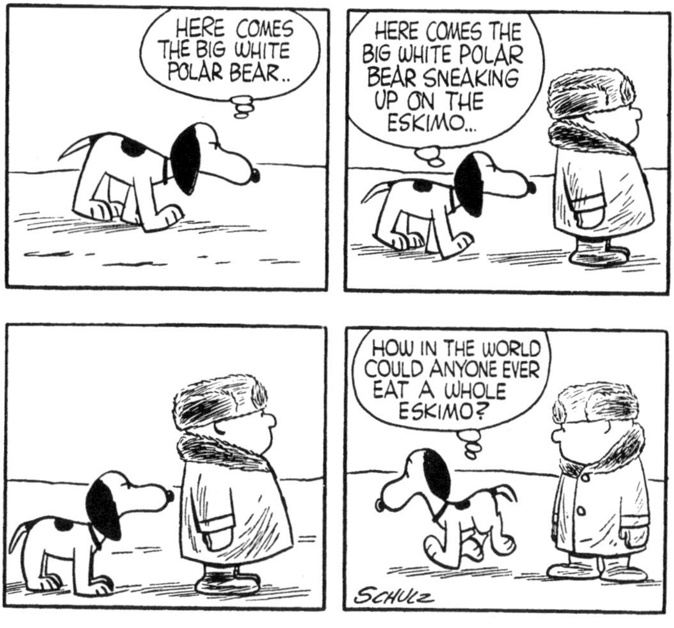
HERE COMES THE BIG WHITE POLAR BEAR..
HERE COMES THE BIG WHITE POLAR BEAR SNEAKING UP ON THE ESKIMO...
HOW IN THE WORLD COULD ANYONE EVER EAT A WHOLE ESKIMO?
SCHULZ

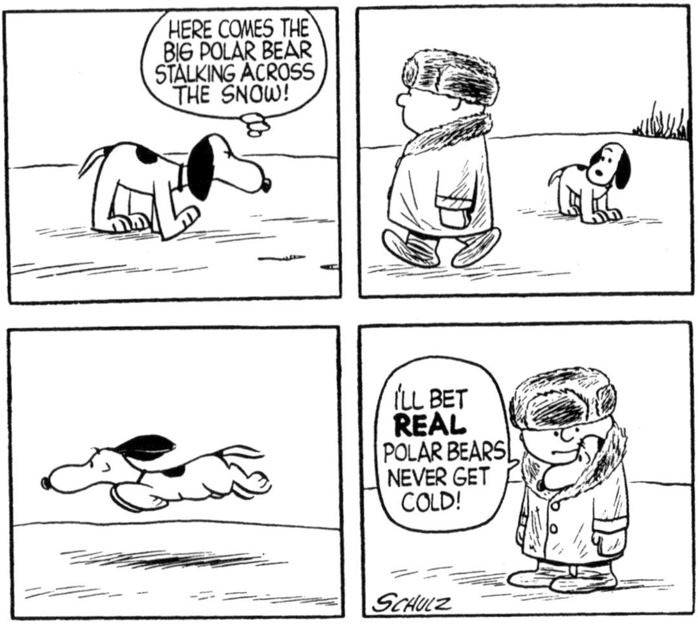
HERE COMES THE BIG POLAR BEAR STALKING ACROSS THE SNOW!
I'LL BET REAL POLAR BEARS NEVER GET COLD!
SCHULZ

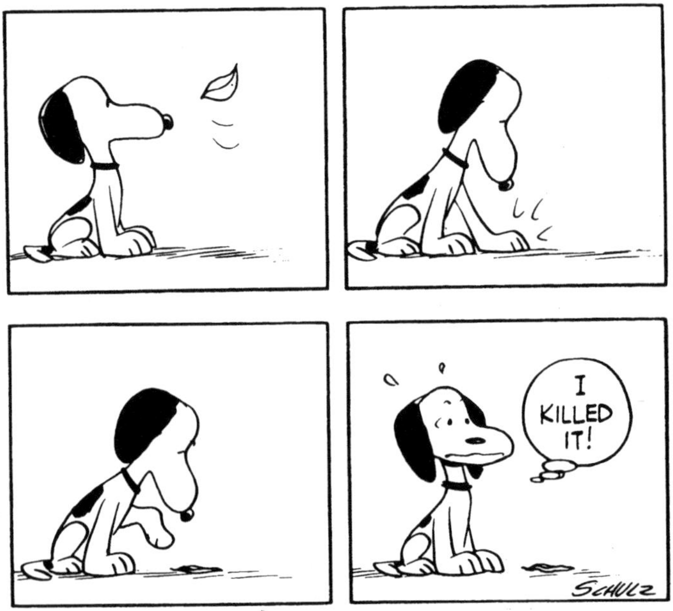
I KILLED IT!
SCHULZ

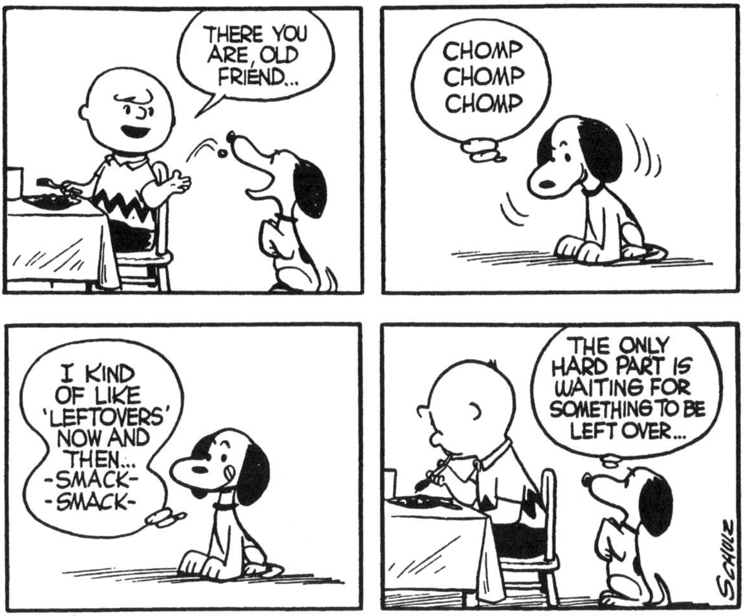
THERE YOU ARE, OLD FRIEND...
CHOMP CHOMP CHOMP
I KIND OF LIKE 'LEFTOVERS' NOW AND THEN... -SMACK- -SMACK-
THE ONLY HARD PART IS WAITING FOR SOMETHING TO BE LEFT OVER...
SCHULZ

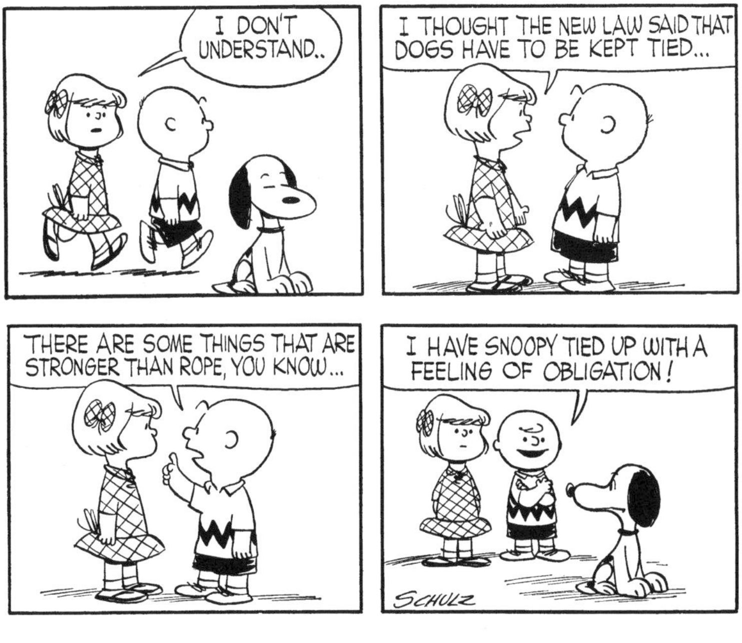
I DON'T UNDERSTAND..
I THOUGHT THE NEW LAW SAID THAT DOGS HAVE TO BE KEPT TIED...
THERE ARE SOME THINGS THAT ARE STRONGER THAN ROPE, YOU KNOW...
I HAVE SNOOPY TIED UP WITH A FEELING OF OBLIGATION!
SCHULZ

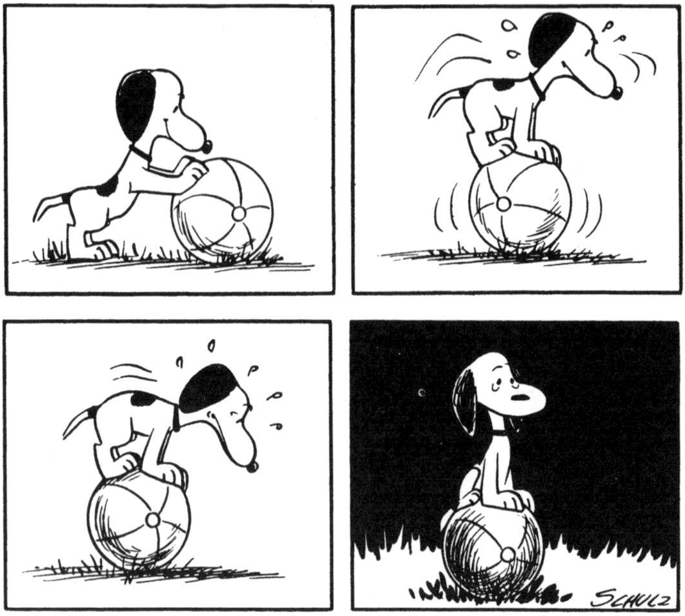
SCHULZ

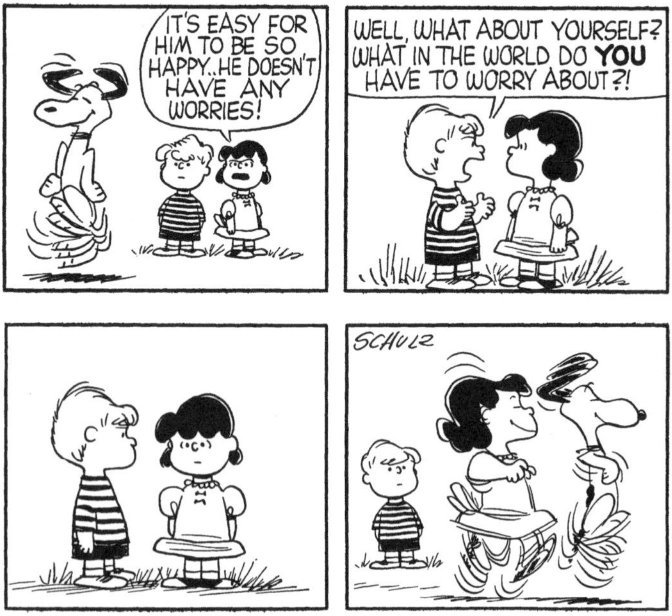
IT'S EASY FOR HIM TO BE SO HAPPY..HE DOESN'T HAVE ANY WORRIES!
WELL, WHAT ABOUT YOURSELF? WHAT IN THE WORLD DO YOU HAVE TO WORRY ABOUT?!
SCHULZ

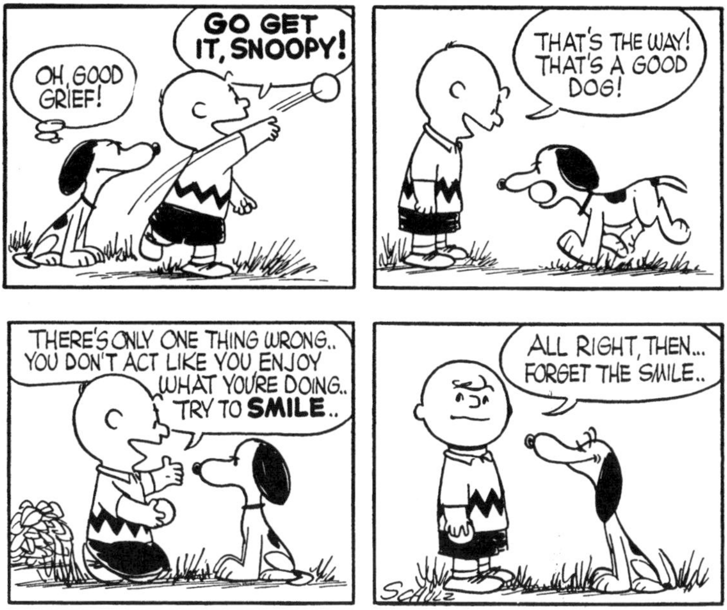
GO GET IT, SNOOPY!
OH, GOOD GRIEF!
THAT'S THE WAY! THAT'S A GOOD DOG!
THERE'S ONLY ONE THING WRONG.. YOU DON'T ACT LIKE YOU ENJOY WHAT YOU'RE DOING.. TRY TO SMILE..
ALL RIGHT, THEN... FORGET THE SMILE..
SCHULZ

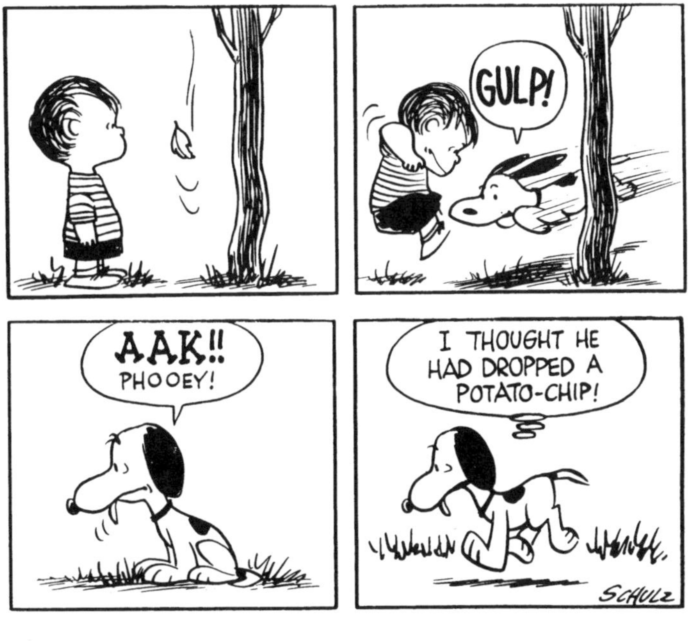
GULP!
AAK!! PHOOEY!
I THOUGHT HE HAD DROPPED A POTATO-CHIP!
SCHULZ

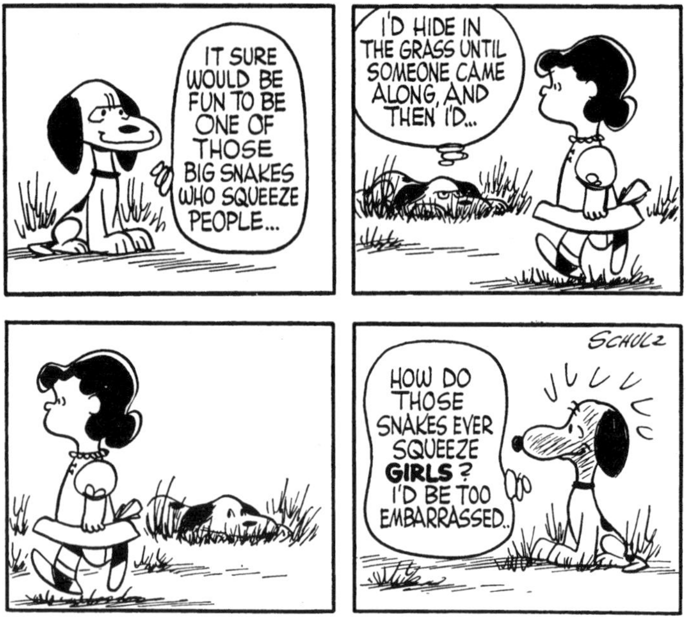
IT SURE WOULD BE FUN TO BE ONE OF THOSE BIG SNAKES WHO SQUEEZE PEOPLE...
I'D HIDE IN THE GRASS UNTIL SOMEONE CAME ALONG, AND THEN I'D...
SCHULZ
HOW DO THOSE SNAKES EVER SQUEEZE **GIRLS**? I'D BE TOO EMBARRASSED..

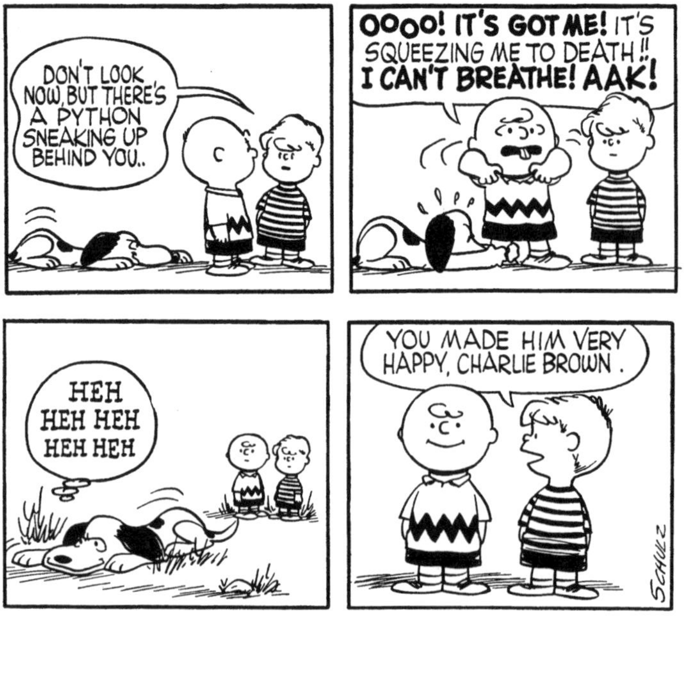
DON'T LOOK NOW, BUT THERE'S A PYTHON SNEAKING UP BEHIND YOU..
OOOO! IT'S GOT ME! IT'S SQUEEZING ME TO DEATH!! **I CAN'T BREATHE! AAK!**
HEH HEH HEH HEH HEH
YOU MADE HIM VERY HAPPY, CHARLIE BROWN.
SCHULZ

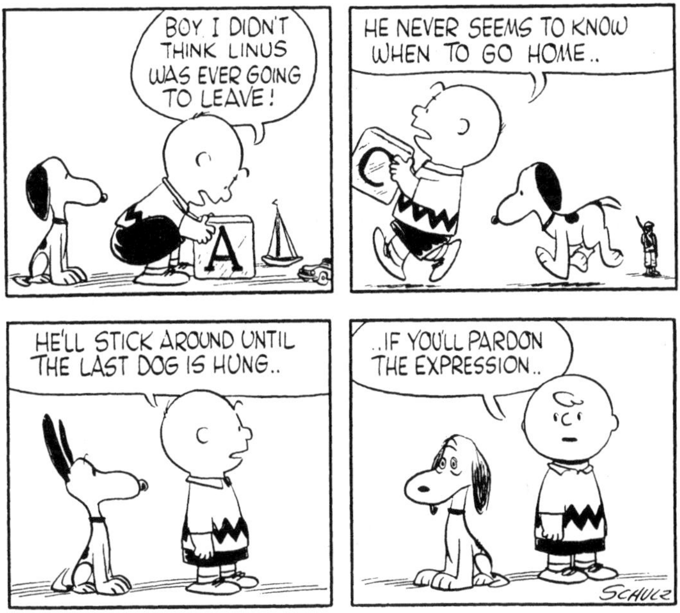
BOY, I DIDN'T THINK LINUS WAS EVER GOING TO LEAVE!
HE NEVER SEEMS TO KNOW WHEN TO GO HOME..
HE'LL STICK AROUND UNTIL THE LAST DOG IS HUNG..
..IF YOU'LL PARDON THE EXPRESSION..
SCHULZ

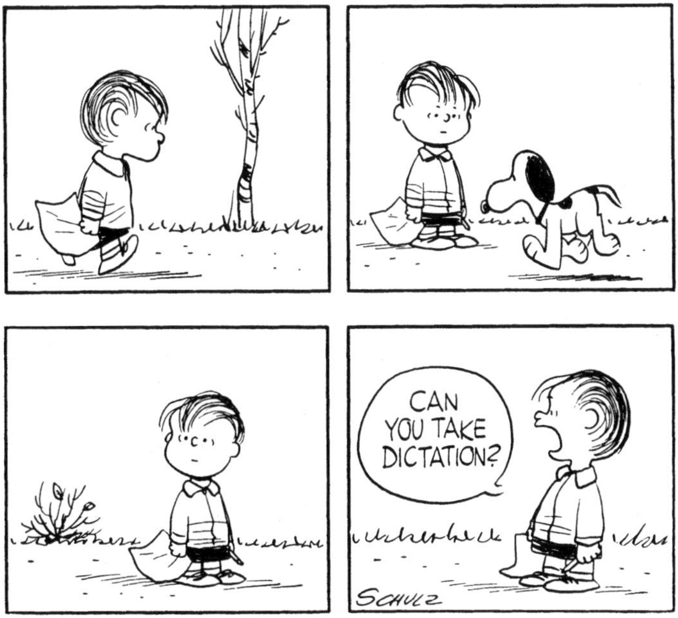
CAN YOU TAKE DICTATION?
SCHULZ

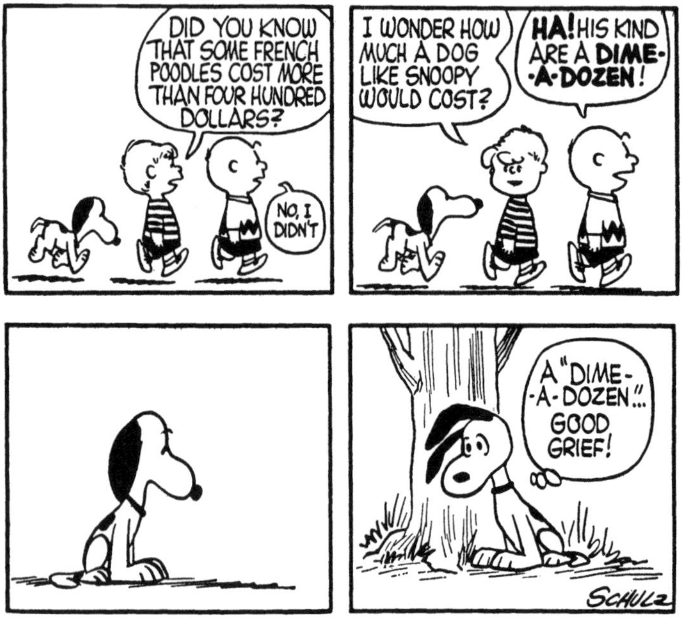
DID YOU KNOW THAT SOME FRENCH POODLES COST MORE THAN FOUR HUNDRED DOLLARS?
NO, I DIDN'T
I WONDER HOW MUCH A DOG LIKE SNOOPY WOULD COST?
HA! HIS KIND ARE A DIME-A-DOZEN!
A "DIME-A-DOZEN"!... GOOD GRIEF!
SCHULZ

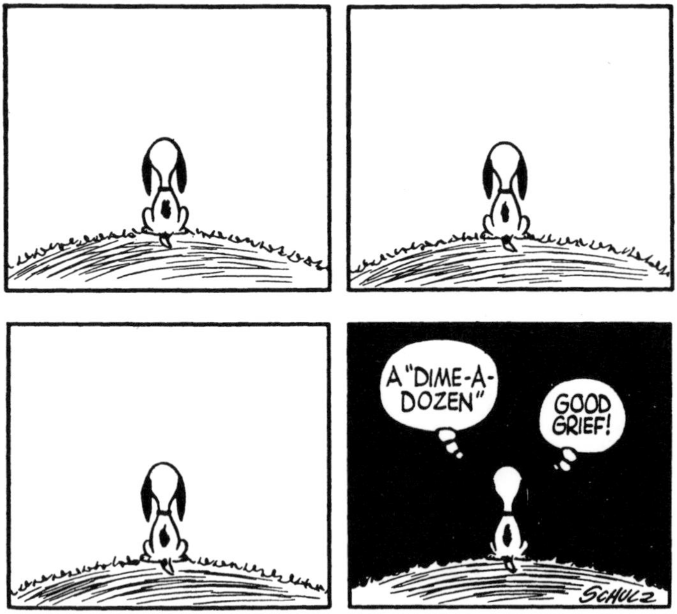
A "DIME-A-DOZEN"
GOOD GRIEF!
SCHULZ

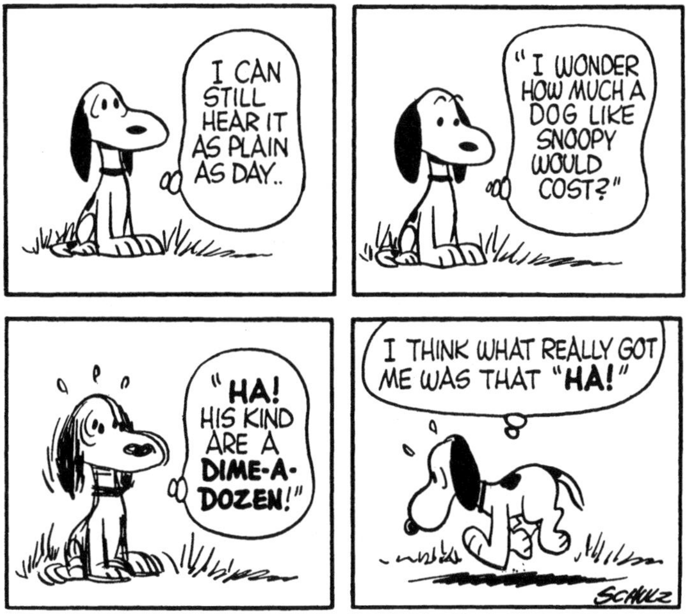
I CAN STILL HEAR IT AS PLAIN AS DAY..
"I WONDER HOW MUCH A DOG LIKE SNOOPY WOULD COST?"
"HA! HIS KIND ARE A DIME-A-DOZEN!"
I THINK WHAT REALLY GOT ME WAS THAT "HA!"
SCHULZ

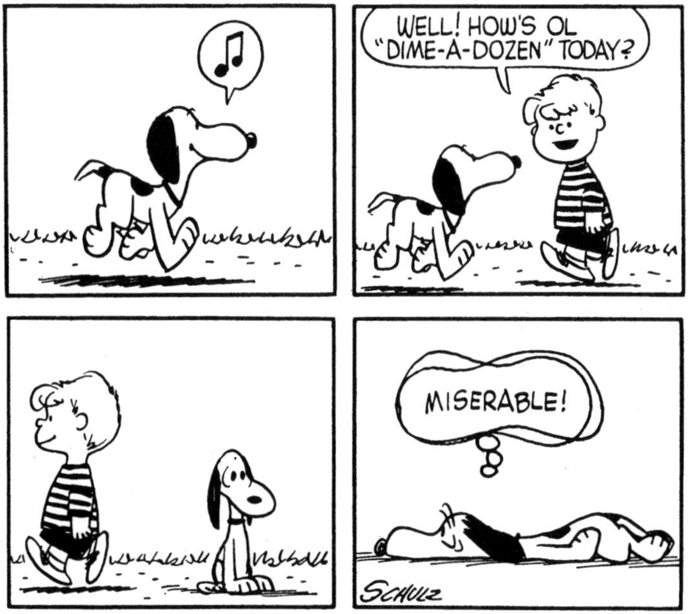
WELL! HOW'S OL "DIME-A-DOZEN" TODAY?
MISERABLE!
SCHULZ

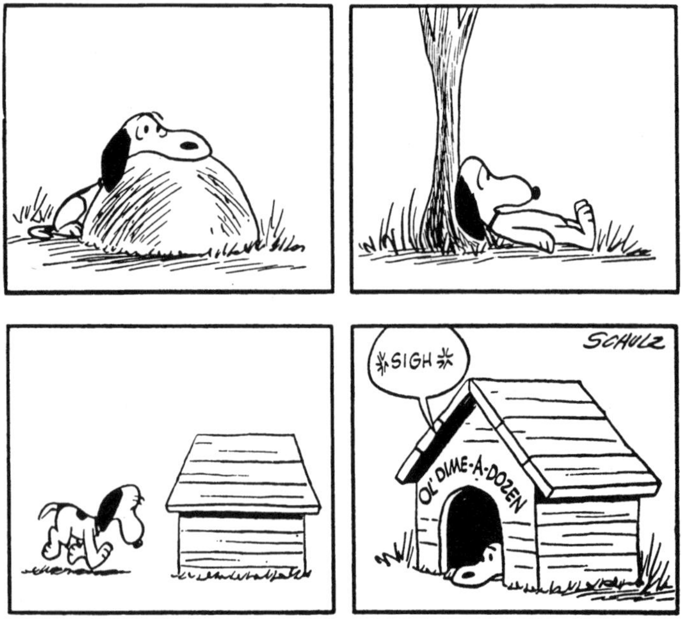
SCHULZ
SIGH
OL' DIME-A-DOZEN

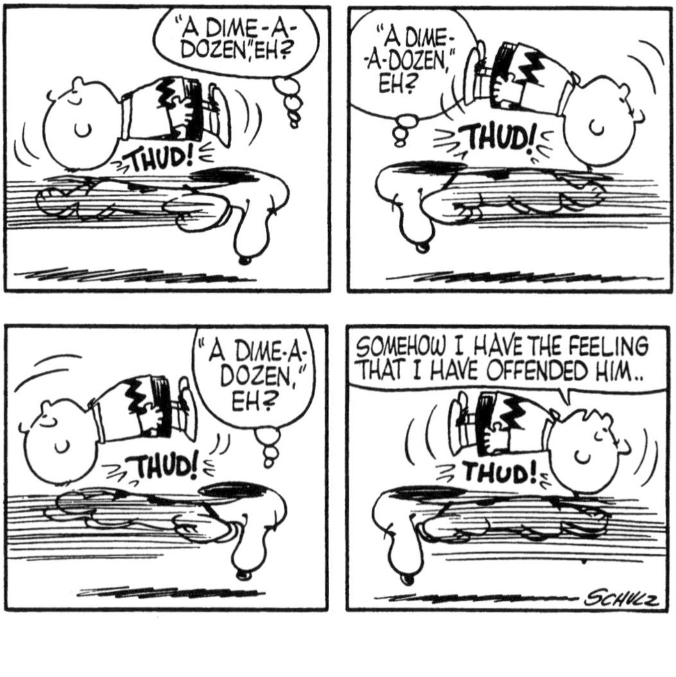
"A DIME-A-DOZEN," EH?
THUD!
"A DIME-A-DOZEN," EH?
THUD!
"A DIME-A-DOZEN," EH?
THUD!
SOMEHOW I HAVE THE FEELING THAT I HAVE OFFENDED HIM..
THUD!
SCHULZ

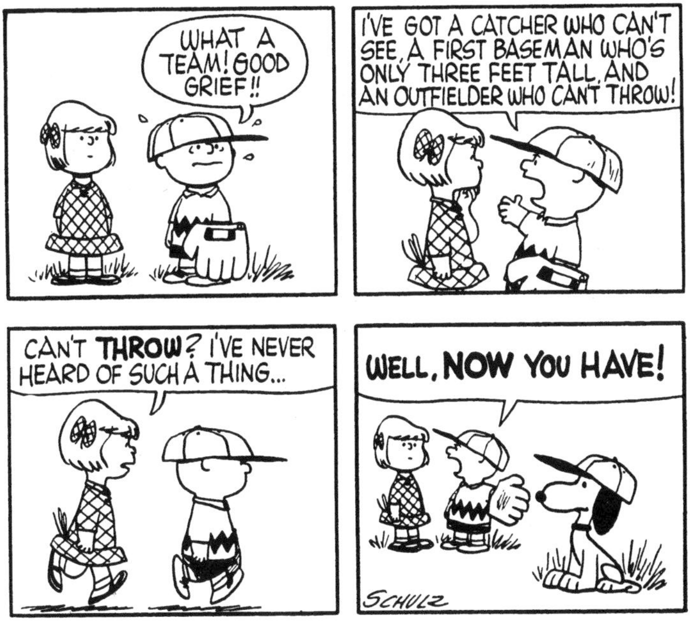
WHAT A TEAM! GOOD GRIEF!!
I'VE GOT A CATCHER WHO CAN'T SEE, A FIRST BASEMAN WHO'S ONLY THREE FEET TALL, AND AN OUTFIELDER WHO CAN'T THROW!
CAN'T **THROW**? I'VE NEVER HEARD OF SUCH A THING...
WELL, NOW YOU HAVE!
SCHULZ

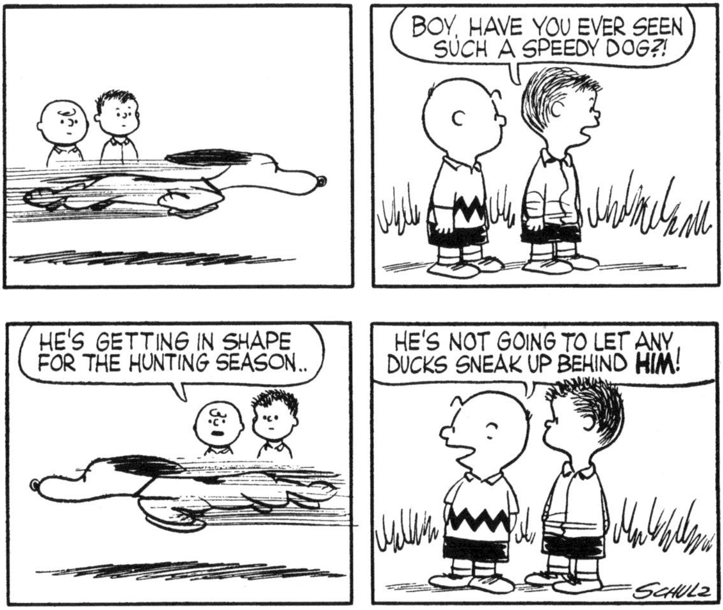
BOY, HAVE YOU EVER SEEN SUCH A SPEEDY DOG?!
HE'S GETTING IN SHAPE FOR THE HUNTING SEASON..
HE'S NOT GOING TO LET ANY DUCKS SNEAK UP BEHIND **HIM**!
SCHULZ

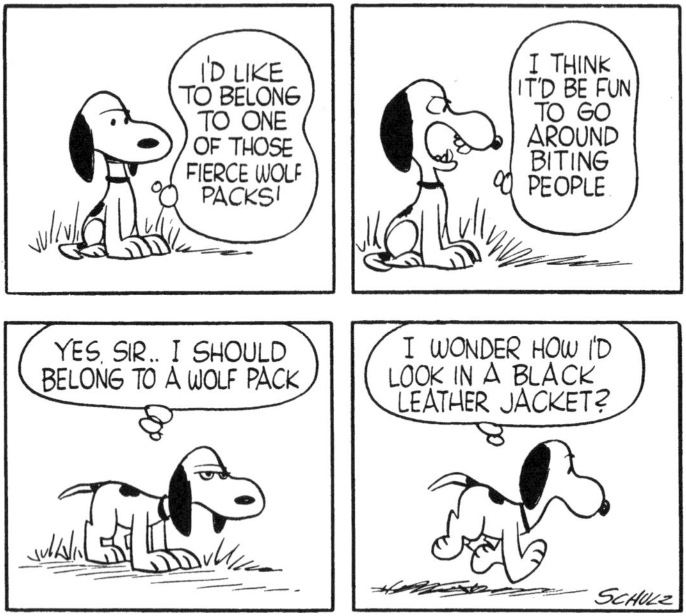
I'D LIKE TO BELONG TO ONE OF THOSE FIERCE WOLF PACKS!
I THINK IT'D BE FUN TO GO AROUND BITING PEOPLE
YES, SIR.. I SHOULD BELONG TO A WOLF PACK
I WONDER HOW I'D LOOK IN A BLACK LEATHER JACKET?
SCHULZ

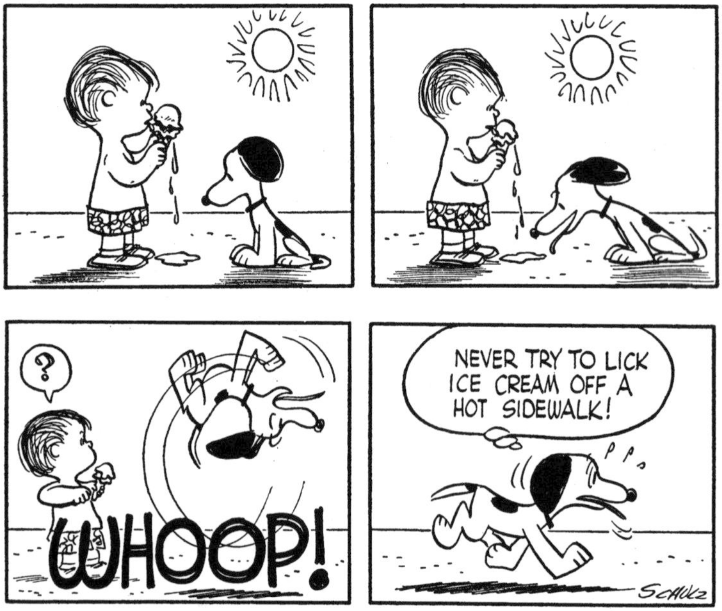
?
WHOOP!
NEVER TRY TO LICK ICE CREAM OFF A HOT SIDEWALK!
SCHULZ

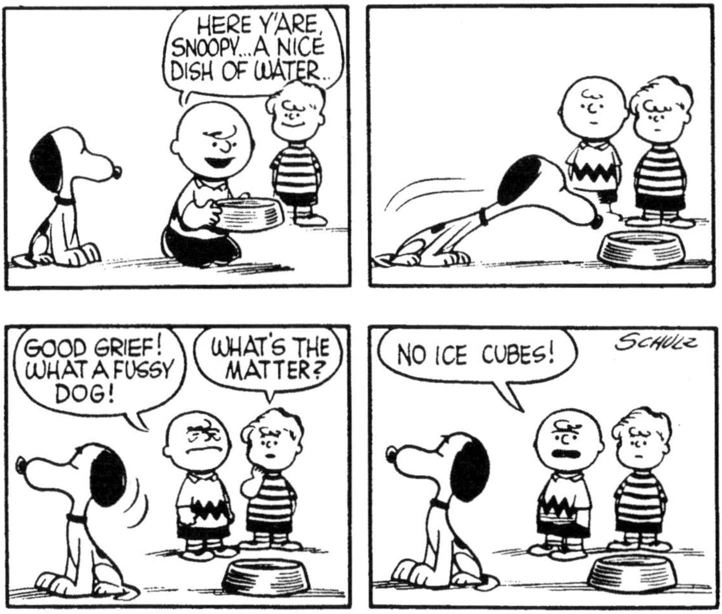
HERE Y'ARE, SNOOPY...A NICE DISH OF WATER..
GOOD GRIEF! WHAT A FUSSY DOG!
WHAT'S THE MATTER?
NO ICE CUBES!
SCHULZ

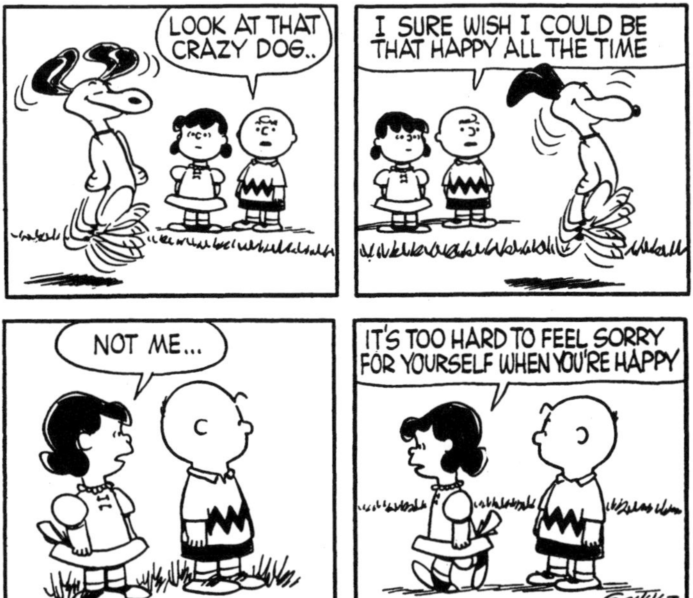
LOOK AT THAT CRAZY DOG..
I SURE WISH I COULD BE THAT HAPPY ALL THE TIME
NOT ME...
IT'S TOO HARD TO FEEL SORRY FOR YOURSELF WHEN YOU'RE HAPPY
SCHULZ

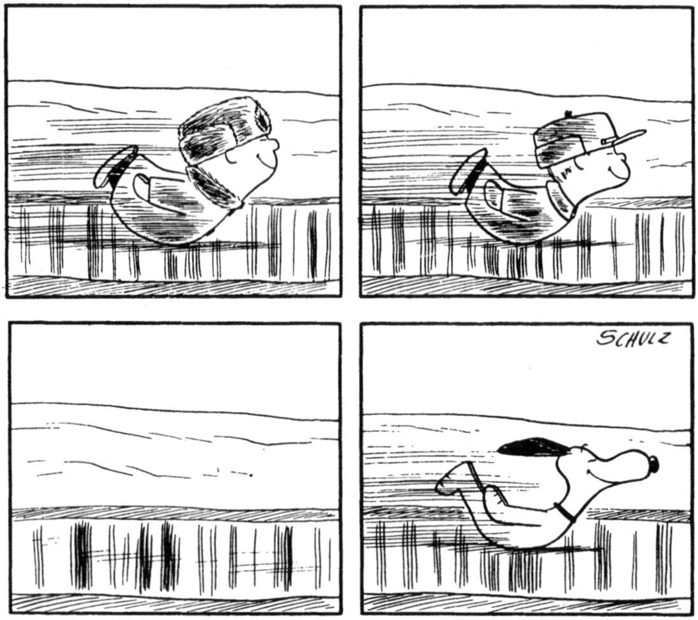
SCHULZ

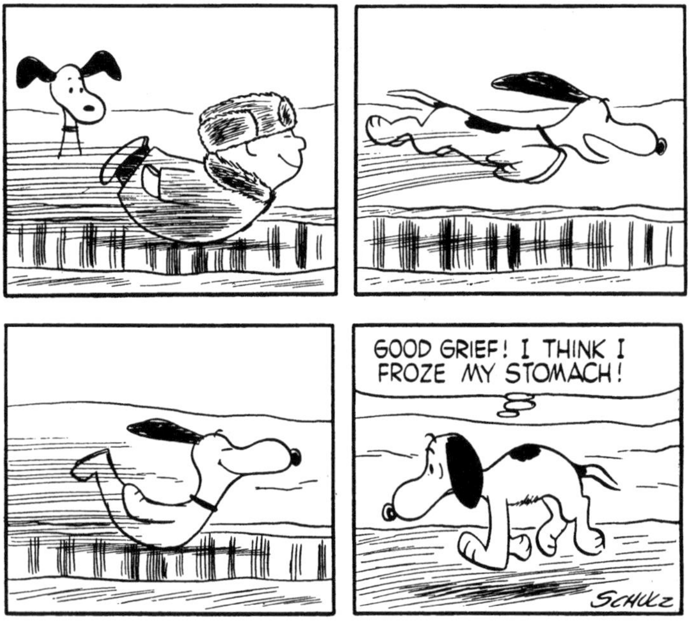
GOOD GRIEF! I THINK I FROZE MY STOMACH!
SCHULZ

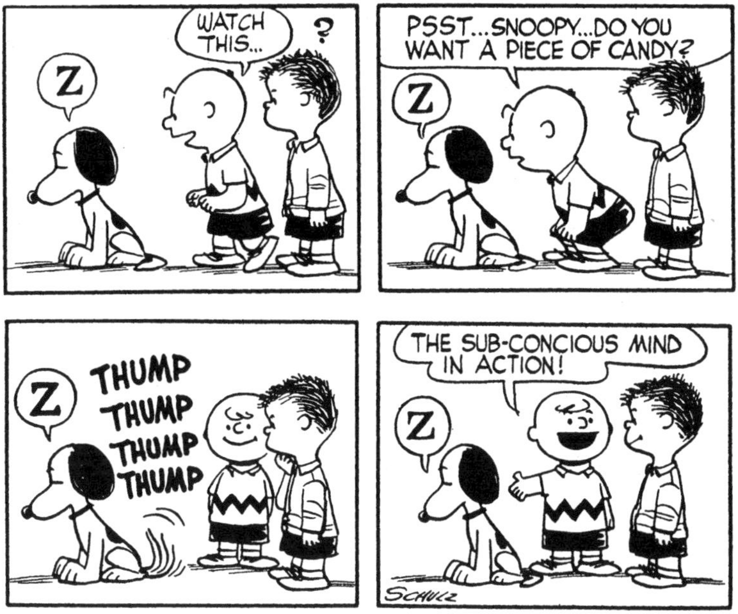
Z
WATCH THIS...
?
PSST...SNOOPY...DO YOU WANT A PIECE OF CANDY?
Z
Z
THUMP
THUMP
THUMP
THUMP
THE SUB-CONCIOUS MIND IN ACTION!
Z
SCHULZ

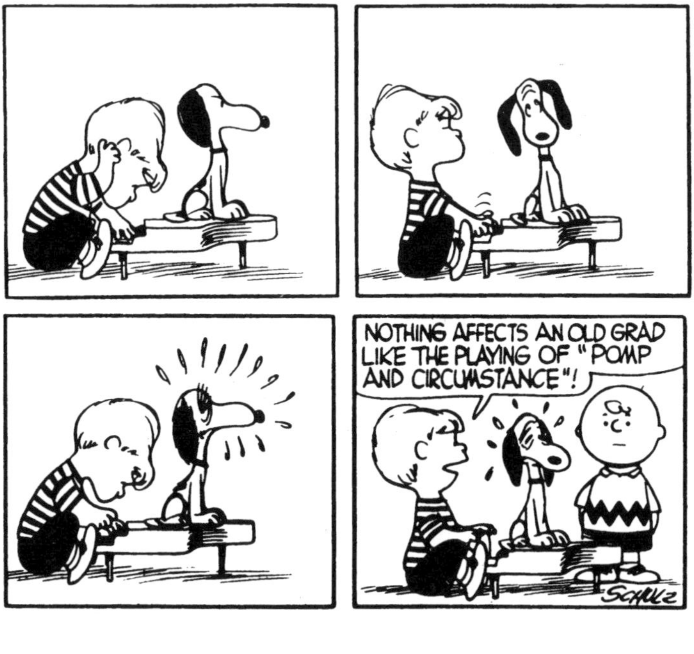
NOTHING AFFECTS AN OLD GRAD LIKE THE PLAYING OF "POMP AND CIRCUMSTANCE"!
SCHULZ

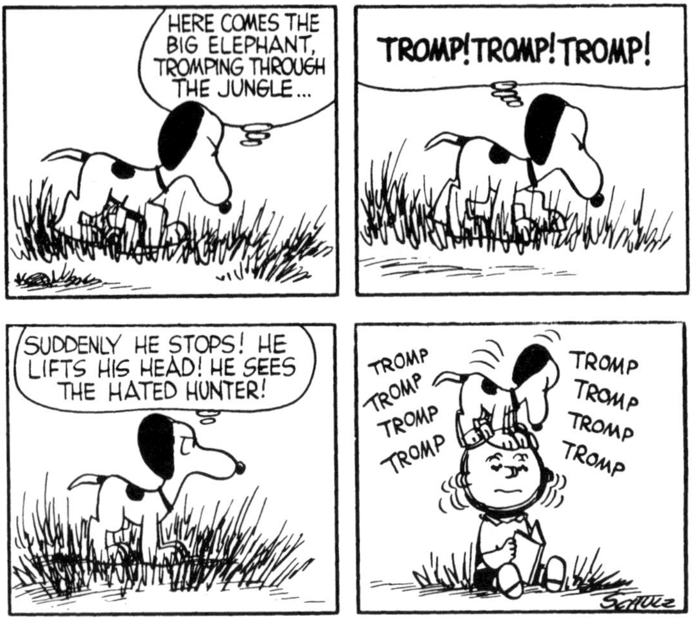
HERE COMES THE BIG ELEPHANT, TROMPING THROUGH THE JUNGLE...
TROMP! TROMP! TROMP!
SUDDENLY HE STOPS! HE LIFTS HIS HEAD! HE SEES THE HATED HUNTER!
TROMP TROMP TROMP TROMP
TROMP TROMP TROMP TROMP
SCHULZ

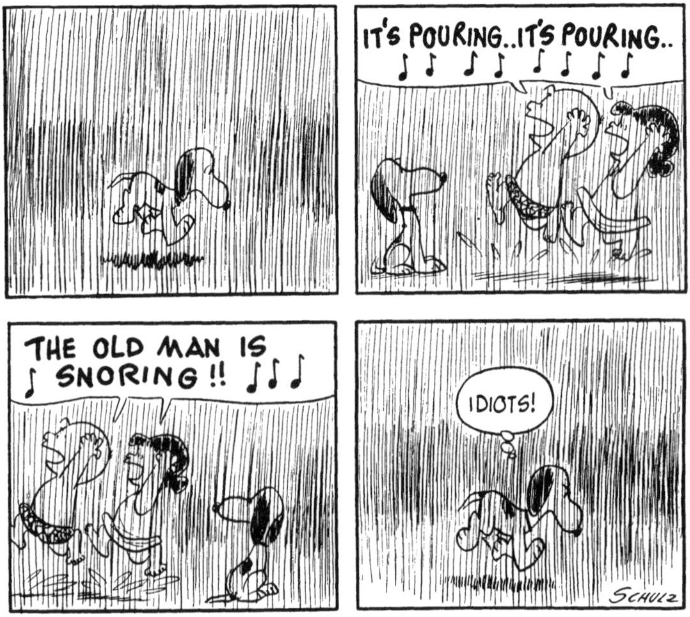
IT'S POURING..IT'S POURING..
THE OLD MAN IS SNORING!!
IDIOTS!
SCHULZ

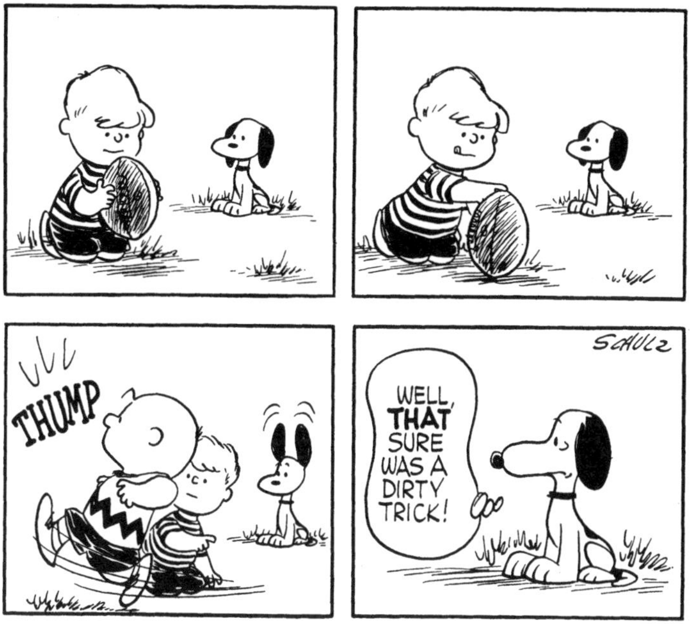
THUMP
SCHULZ
WELL, THAT SURE WAS A DIRTY TRICK!

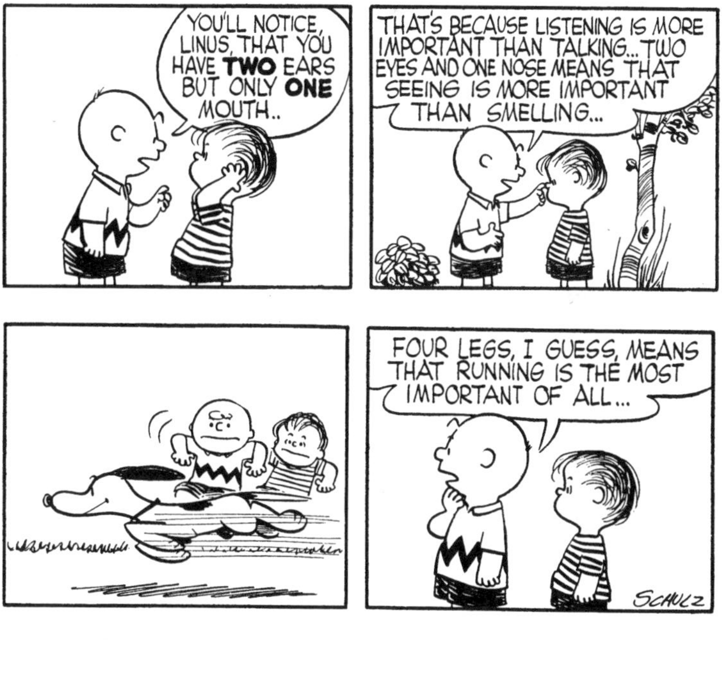
YOU'LL NOTICE, LINUS, THAT YOU HAVE TWO EARS BUT ONLY ONE MOUTH..
THAT'S BECAUSE LISTENING IS MORE IMPORTANT THAN TALKING...TWO EYES AND ONE NOSE MEANS THAT SEEING IS MORE IMPORTANT THAN SMELLING...
FOUR LEGS, I GUESS, MEANS THAT RUNNING IS THE MOST IMPORTANT OF ALL...
SCHULZ

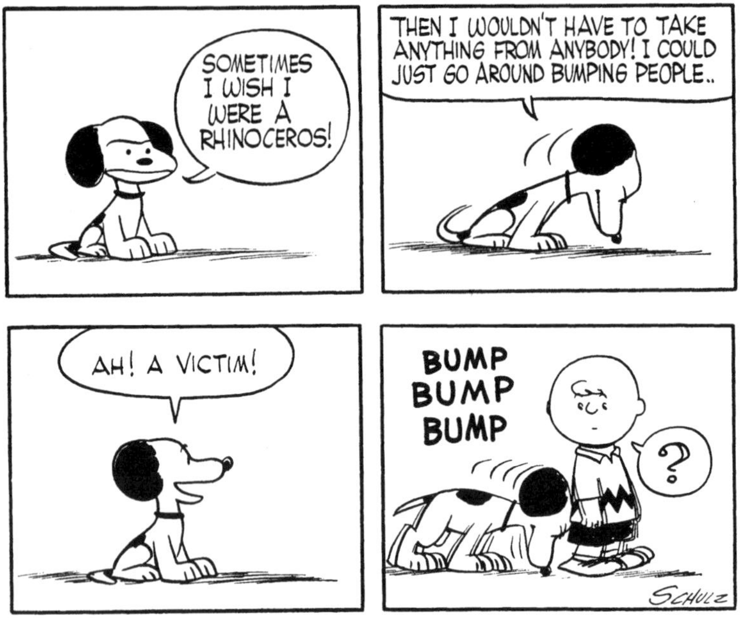
SOMETIMES I WISH I WERE A RHINOCEROS!
THEN I WOULDN'T HAVE TO TAKE ANYTHING FROM ANYBODY! I COULD JUST GO AROUND BUMPING PEOPLE..
AH! A VICTIM!
BUMP
BUMP
BUMP
?
SCHULZ

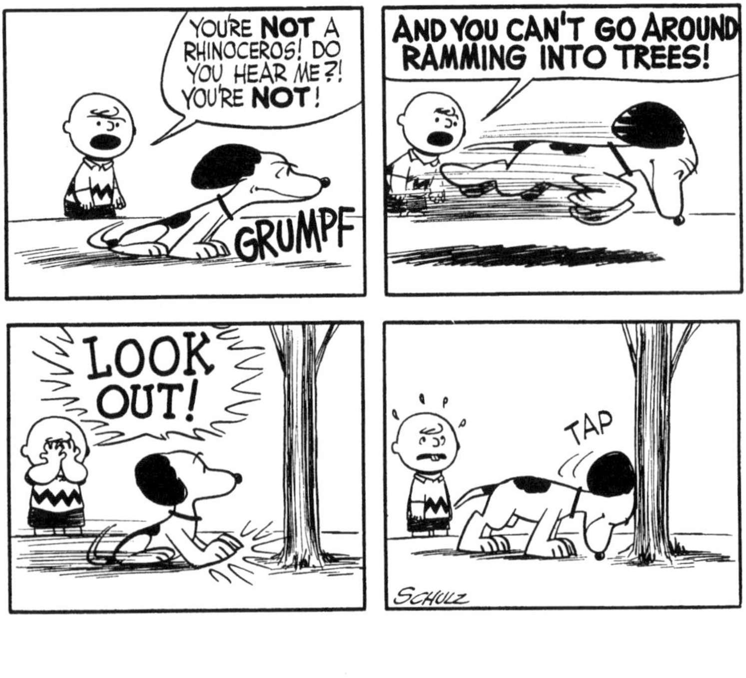
YOU'RE **NOT** A RHINOCEROS! DO YOU HEAR ME?! YOU'RE **NOT**!
GRUMPF
AND YOU CAN'T GO AROUND RAMMING INTO TREES!
LOOK OUT!
TAP
SCHULZ

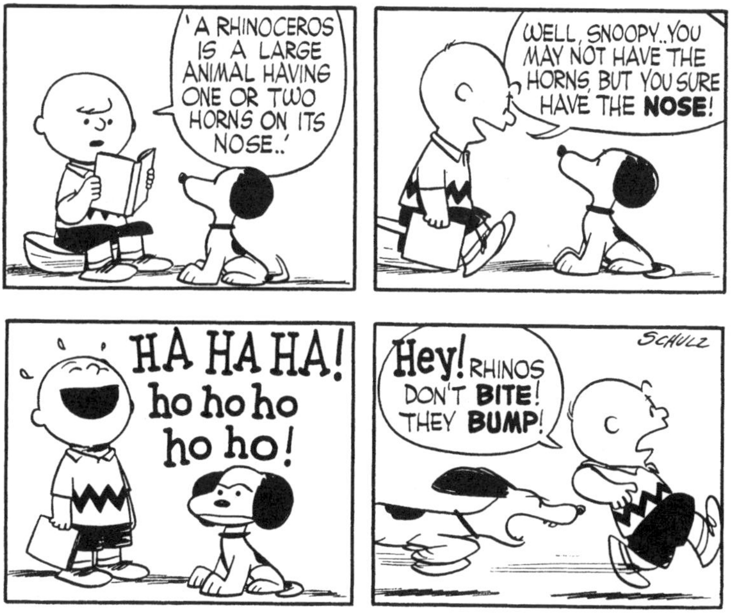
'A RHINOCEROS IS A LARGE ANIMAL HAVING ONE OR TWO HORNS ON ITS NOSE..'
WELL, SNOOPY..YOU MAY NOT HAVE THE HORNS, BUT YOU SURE HAVE THE **NOSE**!
HA HA HA HA! ho ho ho ho ho!
SCHULZ
Hey! RHINOS DON'T **BITE**! THEY **BUMP**!

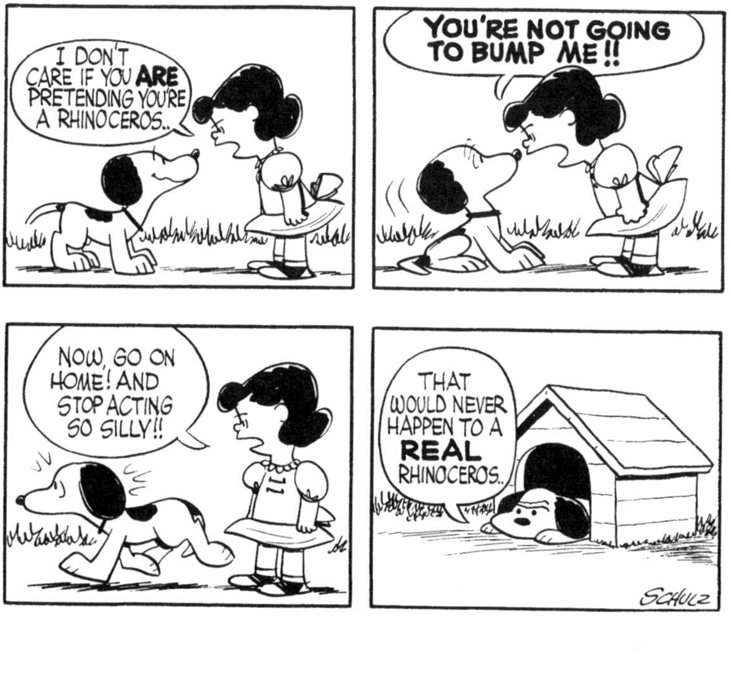
I DON'T CARE IF YOU **ARE** PRETENDING YOU'RE A RHINOCEROS..
YOU'RE NOT GOING TO BUMP ME!!
NOW, GO ON HOME! AND STOP ACTING SO SILLY!!
THAT WOULD NEVER HAPPEN TO A **REAL** RHINOCEROS..
SCHULZ

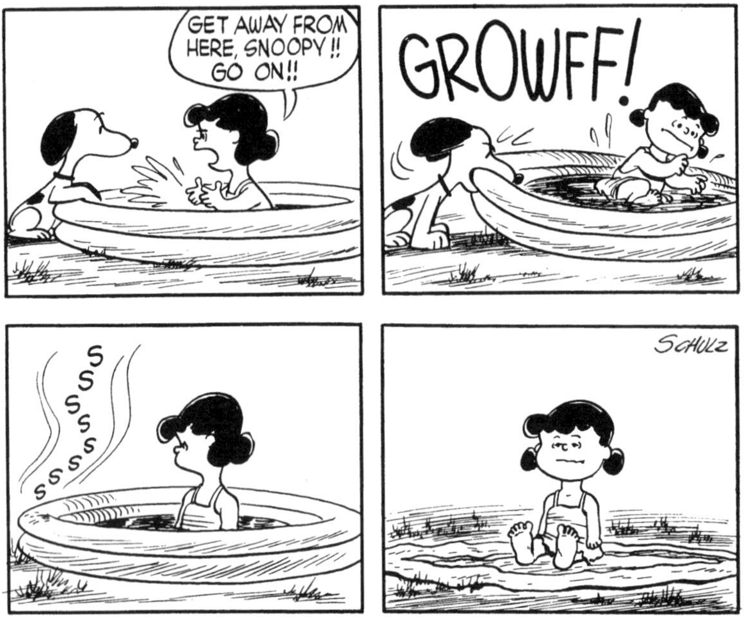
GET AWAY FROM HERE, SNOOPY !! GO ON!!
GROWFF!
SCHULZ

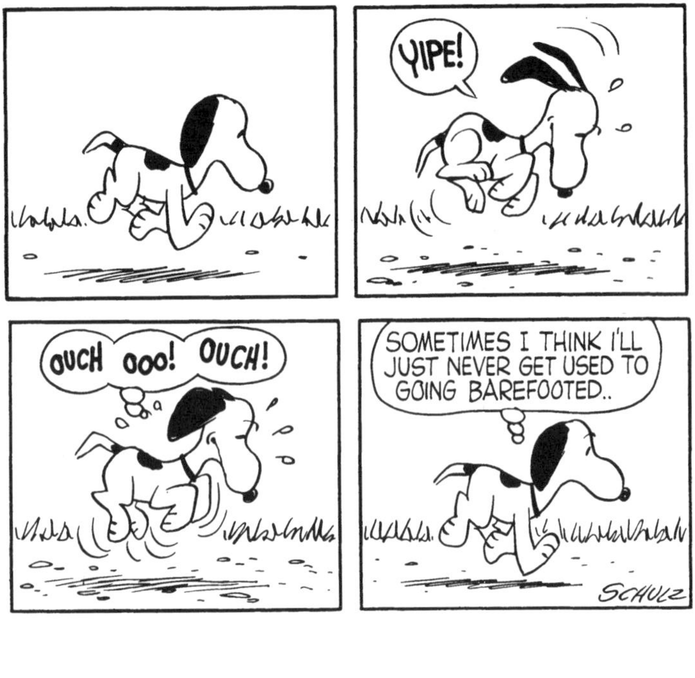
YIPE!
OUCH OOO! OUCH!
SOMETIMES I THINK I'LL JUST NEVER GET USED TO GOING BAREFOOTED..
SCHULZ

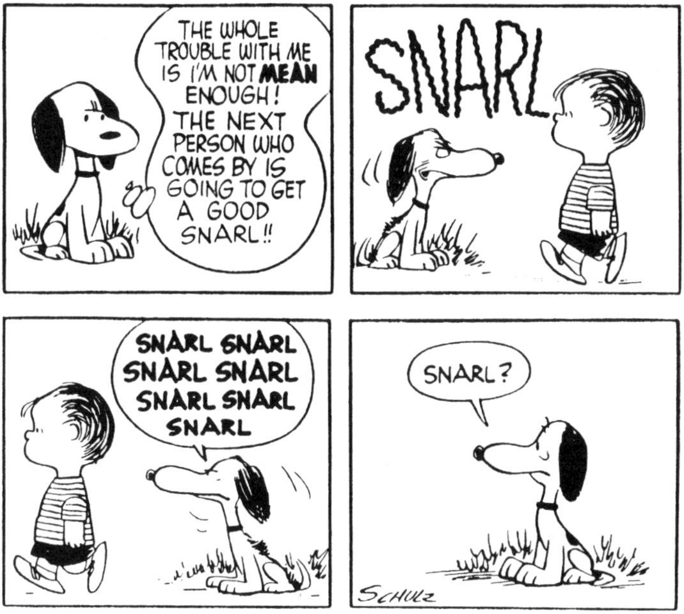
THE WHOLE TROUBLE WITH ME IS I'M NOT **MEAN** ENOUGH! THE NEXT PERSON WHO COMES BY IS GOING TO GET A GOOD SNARL!!
SNARL
SNARL SNARL SNARL SNARL SNARL SNARL SNARL
SNARL?
SCHULZ

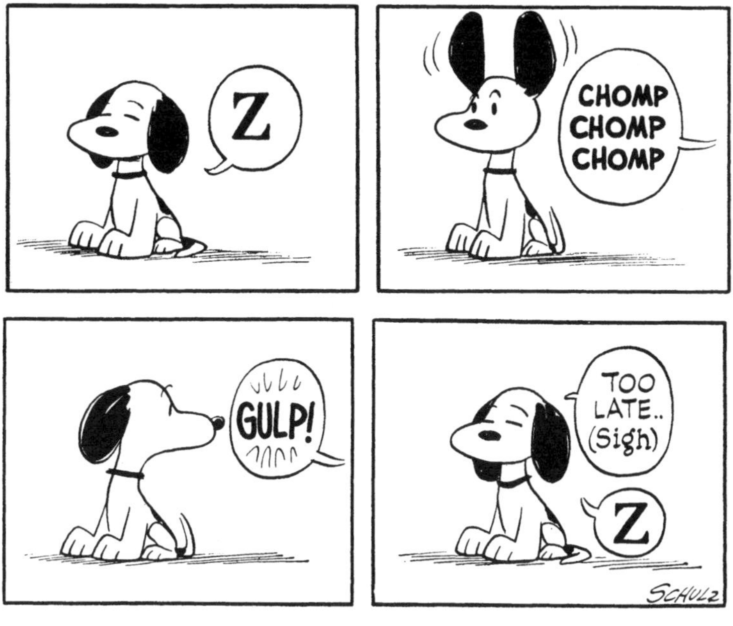
Z
CHOMP CHOMP CHOMP
GULP!
TOO LATE.. (Sigh)
Z
SCHULZ

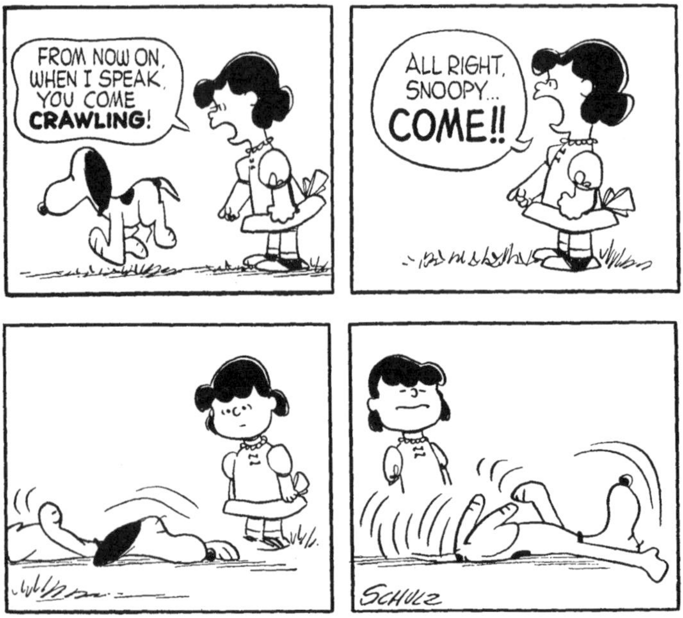
FROM NOW ON, WHEN I SPEAK, YOU COME **CRAWLING**!
ALL RIGHT, SNOOPY... COME!!
SCHULZ

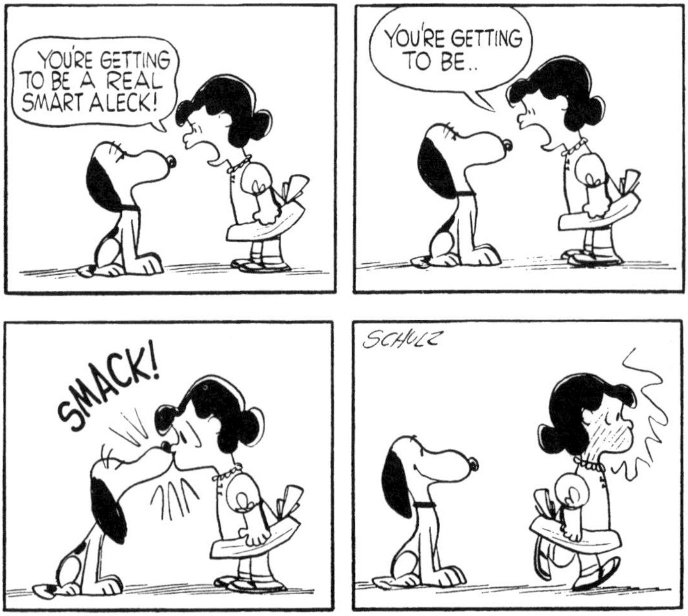
YOU'RE GETTING TO BE A REAL SMART ALECK!
YOU'RE GETTING TO BE..
SMACK!
SCHULZ

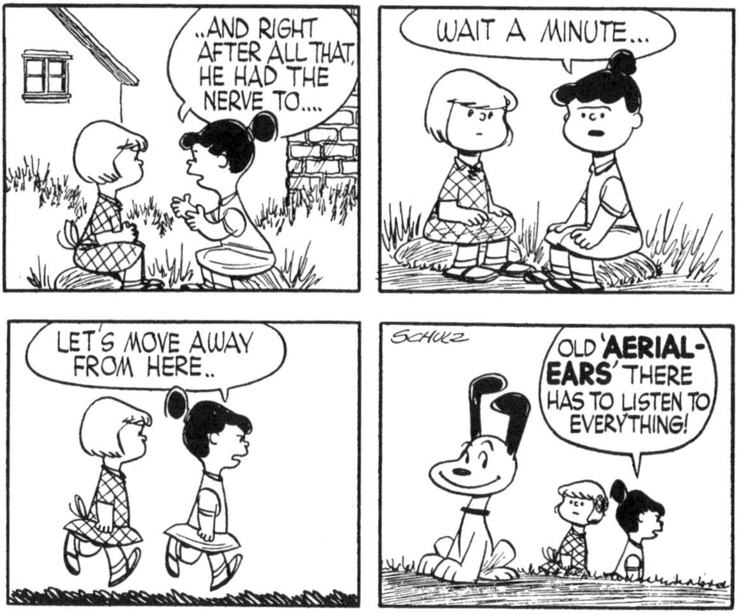
..AND RIGHT AFTER ALL THAT, HE HAD THE NERVE TO....
WAIT A MINUTE...
LET'S MOVE AWAY FROM HERE..
SCHULZ
OLD 'AERIAL-EARS' THERE HAS TO LISTEN TO EVERYTHING!

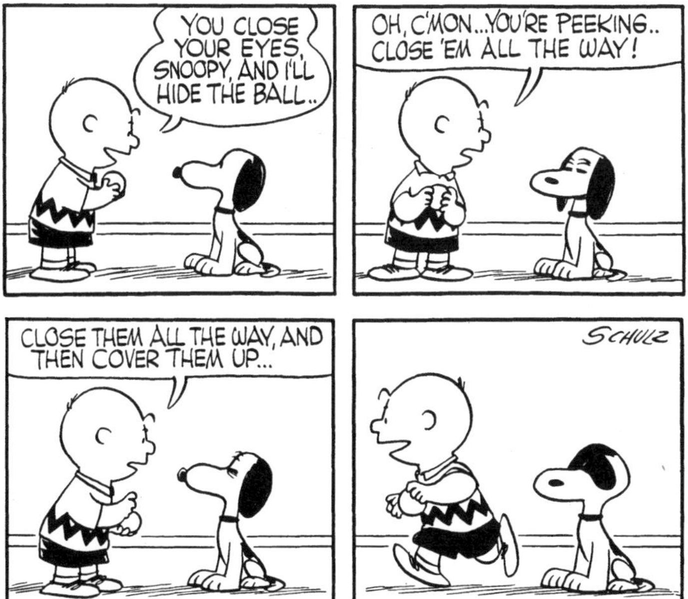
YOU CLOSE YOUR EYES, SNOOPY, AND I'LL HIDE THE BALL..
OH, C'MON...YOU'RE PEEKING.. CLOSE 'EM ALL THE WAY!
CLOSE THEM ALL THE WAY, AND THEN COVER THEM UP...
SCHULZ

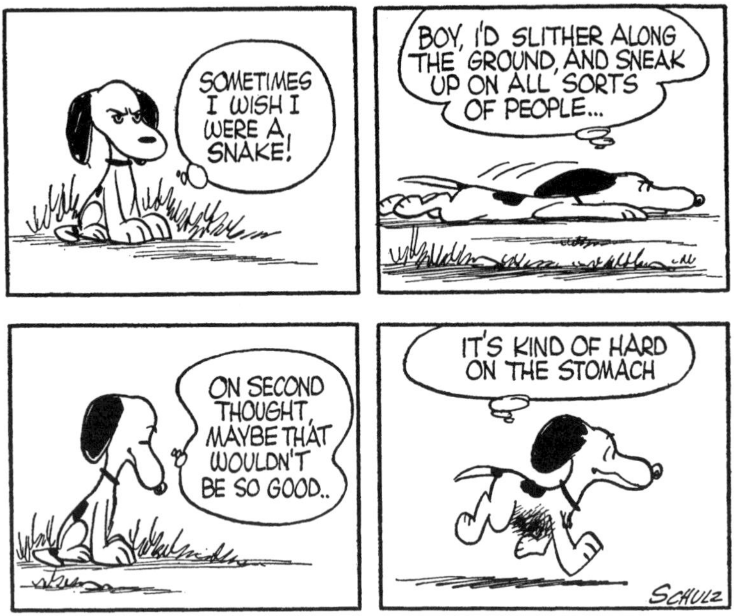
SOMETIMES I WISH I WERE A SNAKE!
BOY, I'D SLITHER ALONG THE GROUND, AND SNEAK UP ON ALL SORTS OF PEOPLE...
ON SECOND THOUGHT, MAYBE THAT WOULDN'T BE SO GOOD..
IT'S KIND OF HARD ON THE STOMACH
SCHULZ

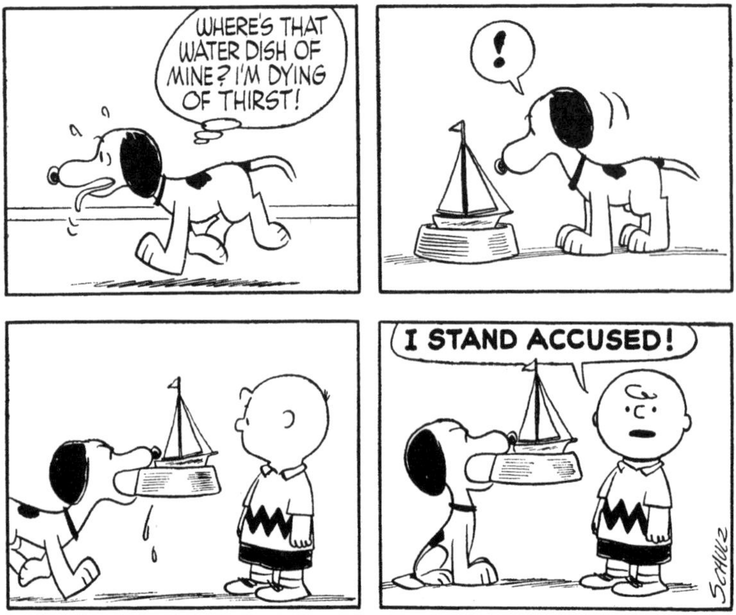
WHERE'S THAT WATER DISH OF MINE? I'M DYING OF THIRST!
!
I STAND ACCUSED!
SCHULZ

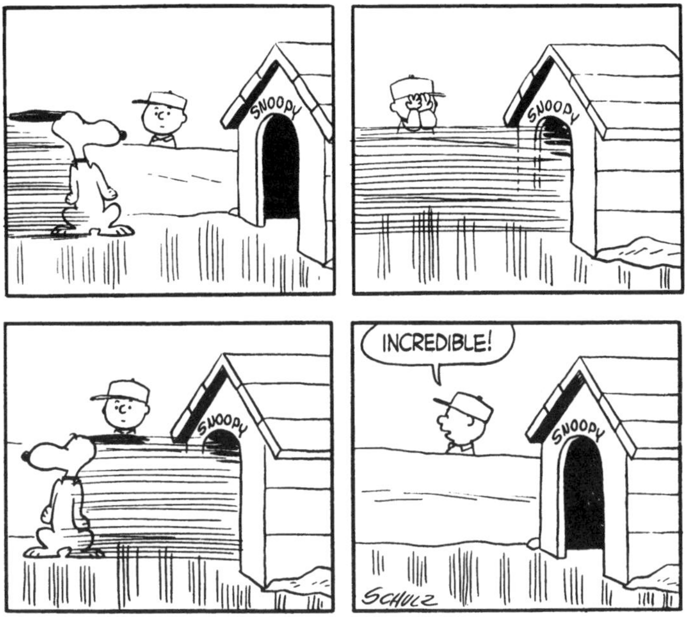
SNOOPY
SNOOPY
SNOOPY
INCREDIBLE!
SNOOPY
SCHULZ

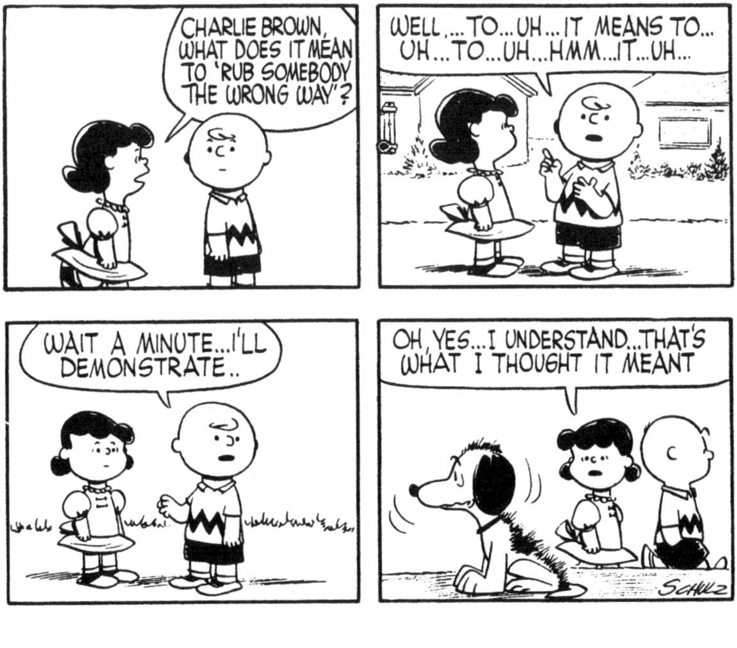
CHARLIE BROWN, WHAT DOES IT MEAN TO 'RUB SOMEBODY THE WRONG WAY'?
WELL,...TO...UH...IT MEANS TO... UH...TO...UH...HMM...IT...UH...
WAIT A MINUTE...I'LL DEMONSTRATE..
OH, YES...I UNDERSTAND...THAT'S WHAT I THOUGHT IT MEANT
SCHULZ

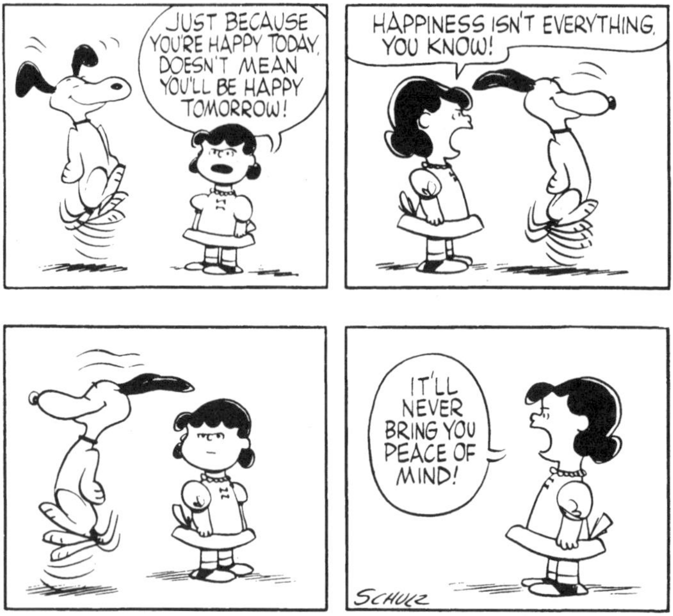
JUST BECAUSE YOU'RE HAPPY TODAY, DOESN'T MEAN YOU'LL BE HAPPY TOMORROW!
HAPPINESS ISN'T EVERYTHING, YOU KNOW!
IT'LL NEVER BRING YOU PEACE OF MIND!
SCHULZ

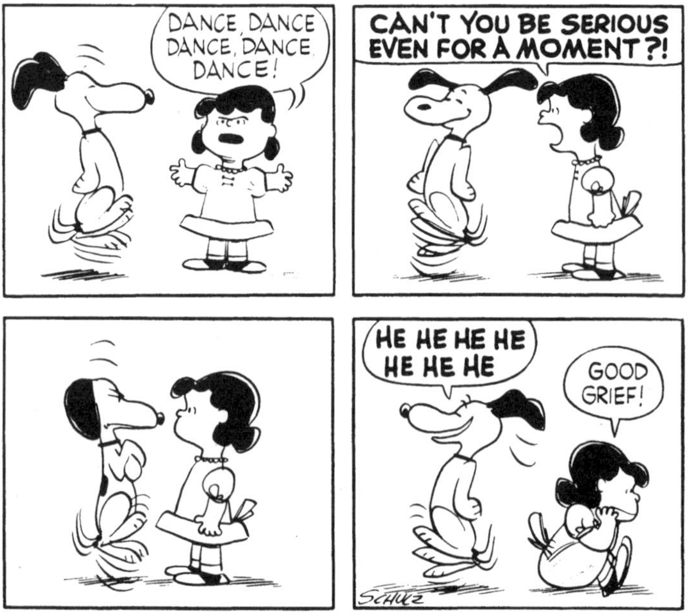
DANCE, DANCE DANCE, DANCE DANCE!
CAN'T YOU BE SERIOUS EVEN FOR A MOMENT?!
HE HE HE HE HE HE HE
GOOD GRIEF!
SCHULZ

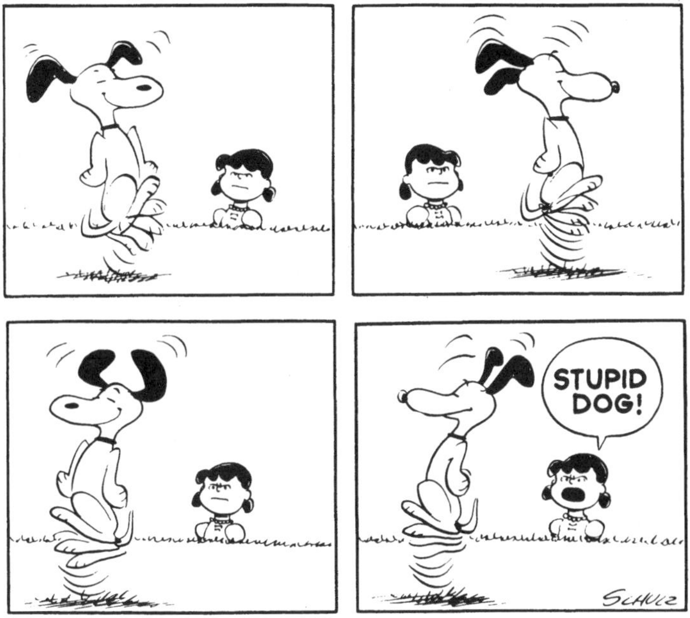
STUPID DOG!
SCHULZ

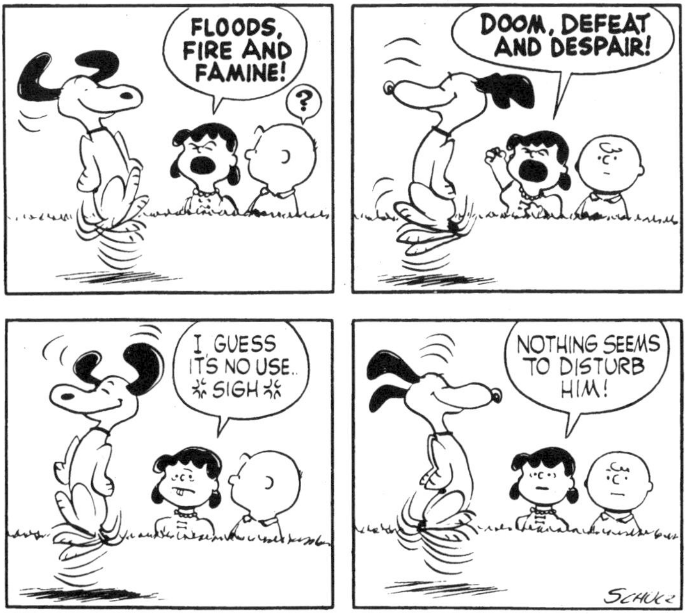
FLOODS, FIRE AND FAMINE!
?
DOOM, DEFEAT AND DESPAIR!
I GUESS IT'S NO USE.. SIGH
NOTHING SEEMS TO DISTURB HIM!
SCHULZ

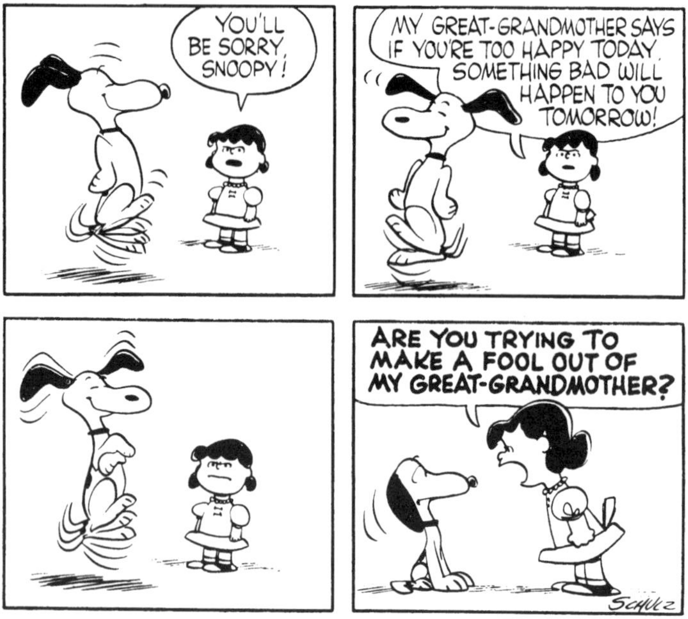
YOU'LL BE SORRY, SNOOPY!
MY GREAT-GRANDMOTHER SAYS IF YOU'RE TOO HAPPY TODAY, SOMETHING BAD WILL HAPPEN TO YOU TOMORROW!
ARE YOU TRYING TO MAKE A FOOL OUT OF MY GREAT-GRANDMOTHER?
SCHULZ

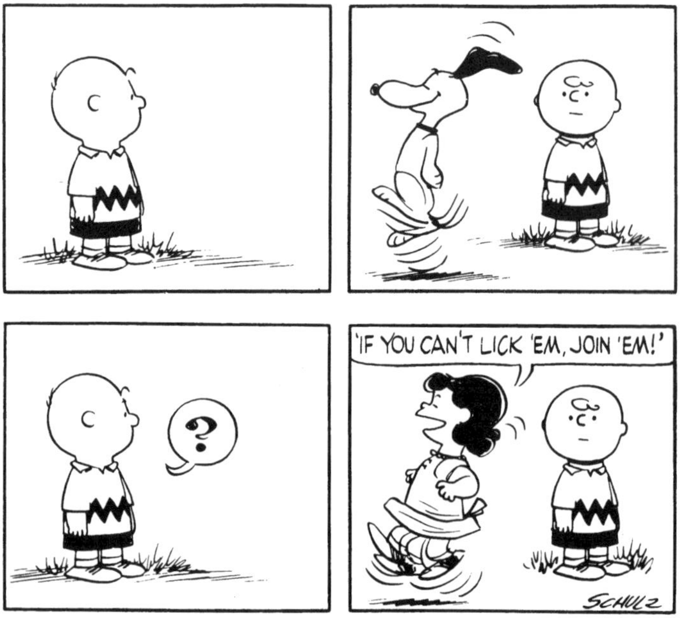
?
'IF YOU CAN'T LICK 'EM, JOIN 'EM!'
SCHULZ

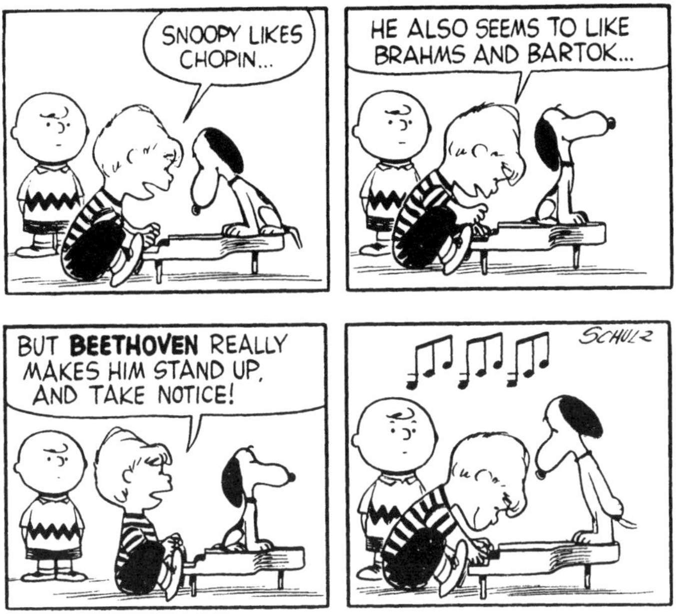
SNOOPY LIKES CHOPIN...
HE ALSO SEEMS TO LIKE BRAHMS AND BARTOK...
BUT **BEETHOVEN** REALLY MAKES HIM STAND UP, AND TAKE NOTICE!
SCHULZ

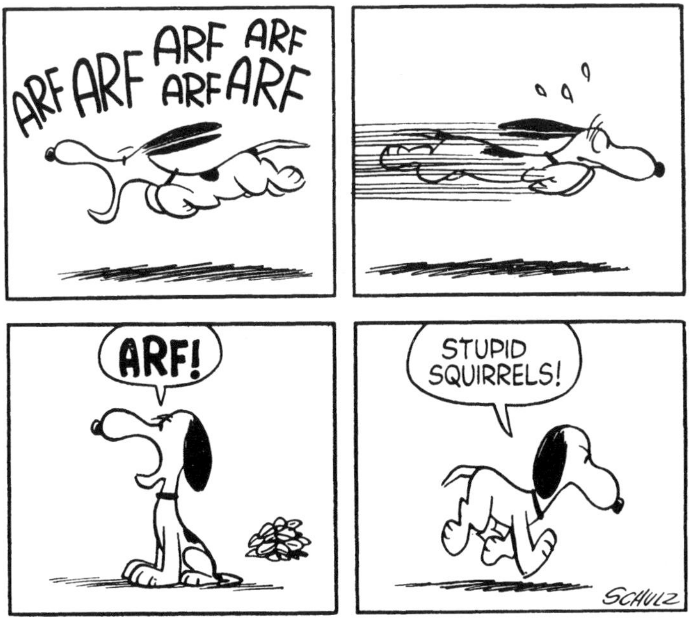
ARF ARF ARF ARF ARF ARF
ARF!
STUPID SQUIRRELS!
SCHULZ

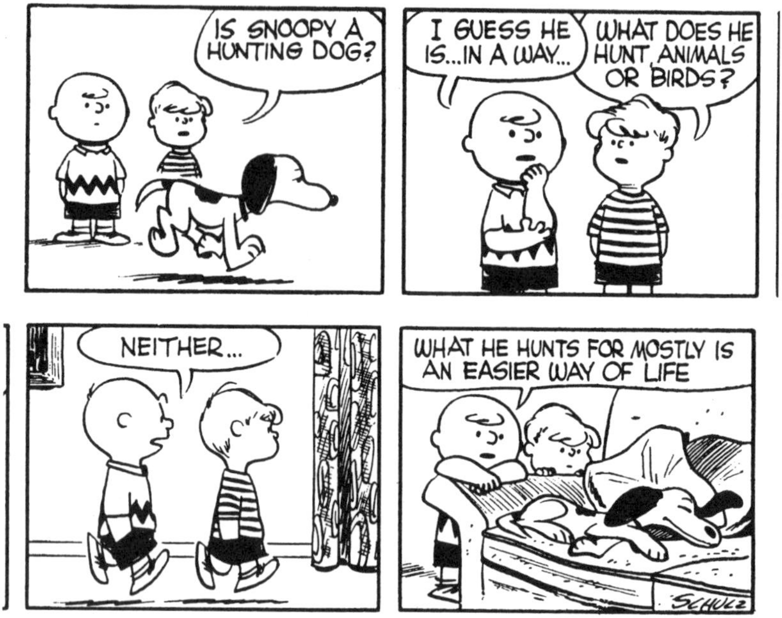
IS SNOOPY A HUNTING DOG?
I GUESS HE IS...IN A WAY...
WHAT DOES HE HUNT, ANIMALS OR BIRDS?
NEITHER...
WHAT HE HUNTS FOR MOSTLY IS AN EASIER WAY OF LIFE
SCHULZ

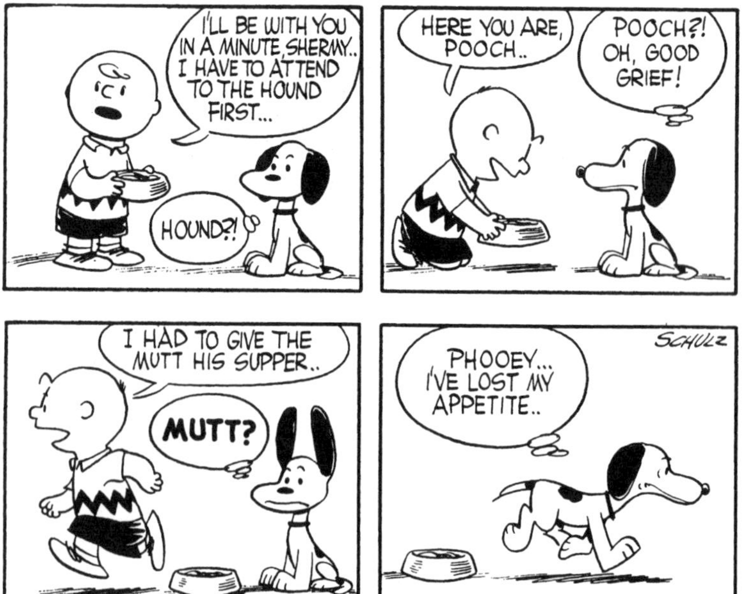
I'LL BE WITH YOU IN A MINUTE, SHERMY.. I HAVE TO ATTEND TO THE HOUND FIRST...
HOUND?!
HERE YOU ARE, POOCH..
POOCH?! OH, GOOD GRIEF!
I HAD TO GIVE THE MUTT HIS SUPPER..
MUTT?
SCHULZ
PHOOEY... I'VE LOST MY APPETITE..

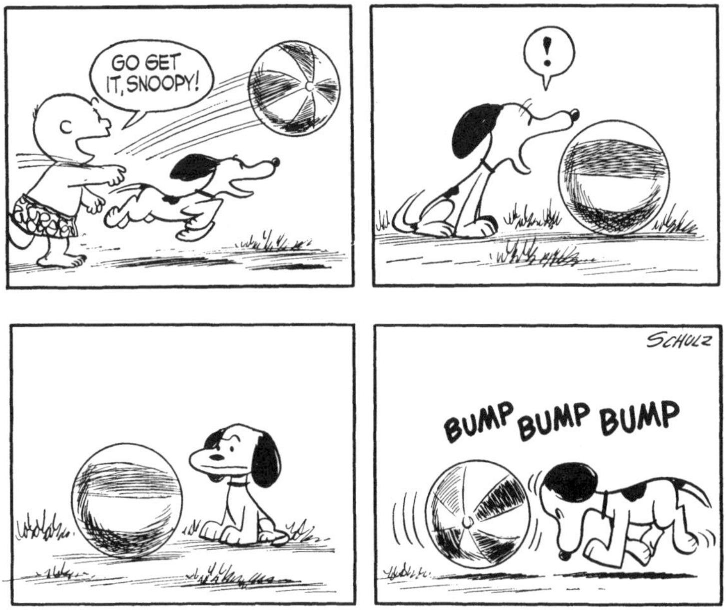
GO GET IT, SNOOPY!
!
SCHULZ
BUMP BUMP BUMP

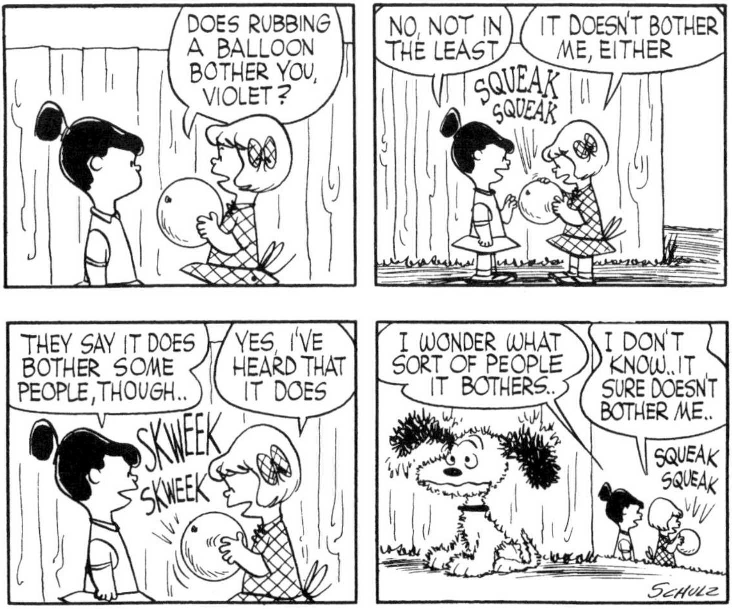
DOES RUBBING A BALLOON BOTHER YOU, VIOLET?
NO, NOT IN THE LEAST
IT DOESN'T BOTHER ME, EITHER
SQUEAK SQUEAK
THEY SAY IT DOES BOTHER SOME PEOPLE, THOUGH..
YES, I'VE HEARD THAT IT DOES
SKWEEK SKWEEK
I WONDER WHAT SORT OF PEOPLE IT BOTHERS..
I DON'T KNOW..IT SURE DOESN'T BOTHER ME..
SQUEAK SQUEAK
SCHULZ

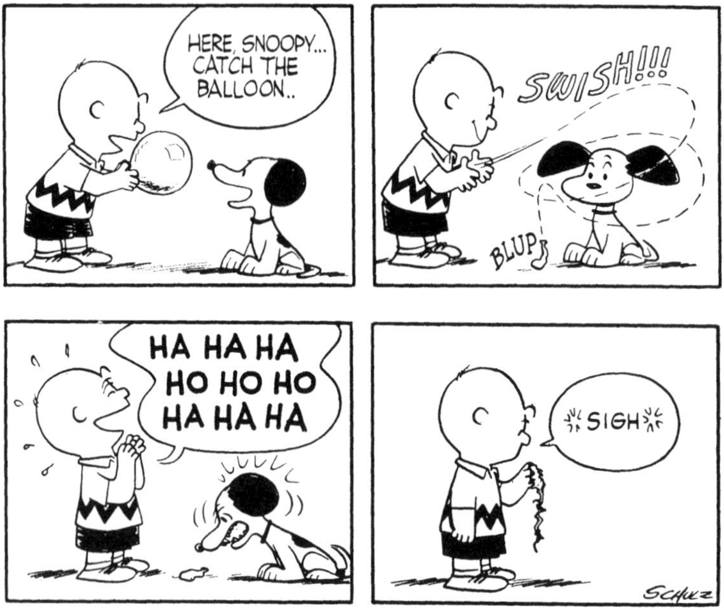
HERE, SNOOPY... CATCH THE BALLOON..
SWISH!!!
BLUP
HA HA HA HO HO HO HA HA HA
SIGH
SCHULZ

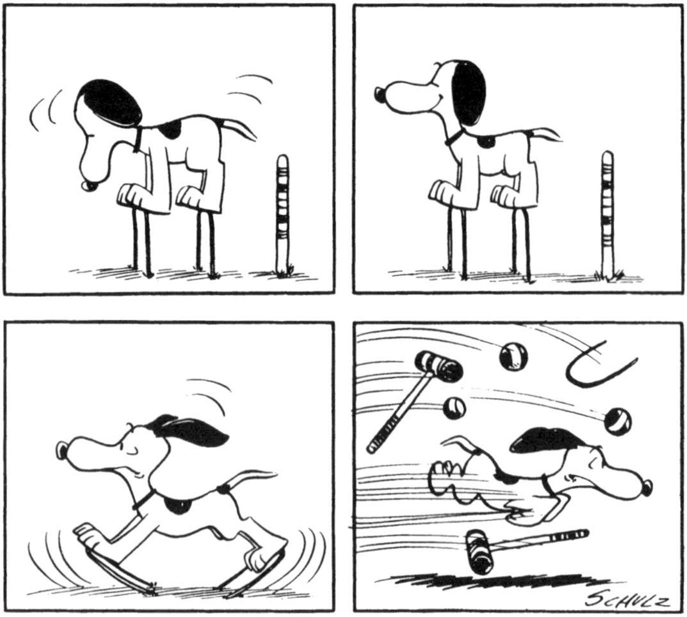
SCHULZ

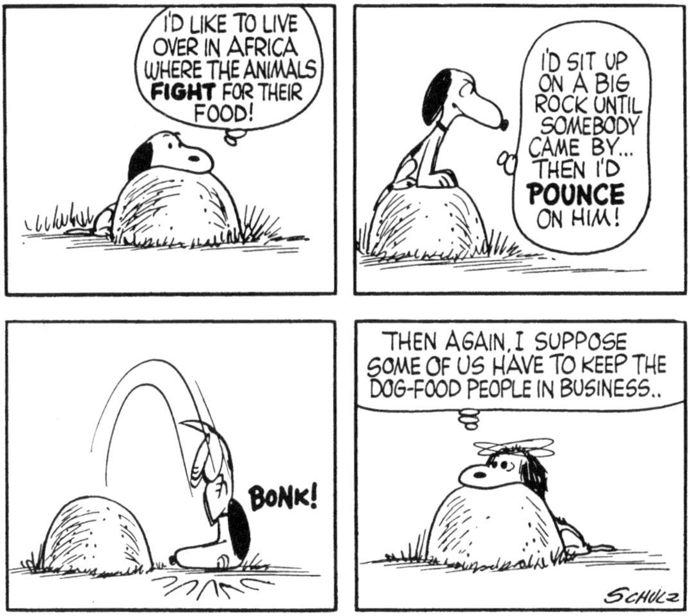
I'D LIKE TO LIVE OVER IN AFRICA WHERE THE ANIMALS **FIGHT** FOR THEIR FOOD!
I'D SIT UP ON A BIG ROCK UNTIL SOMEBODY CAME BY... THEN I'D **POUNCE** ON HIM!
BONK!
THEN AGAIN, I SUPPOSE SOME OF US HAVE TO KEEP THE DOG-FOOD PEOPLE IN BUSINESS..
SCHULZ

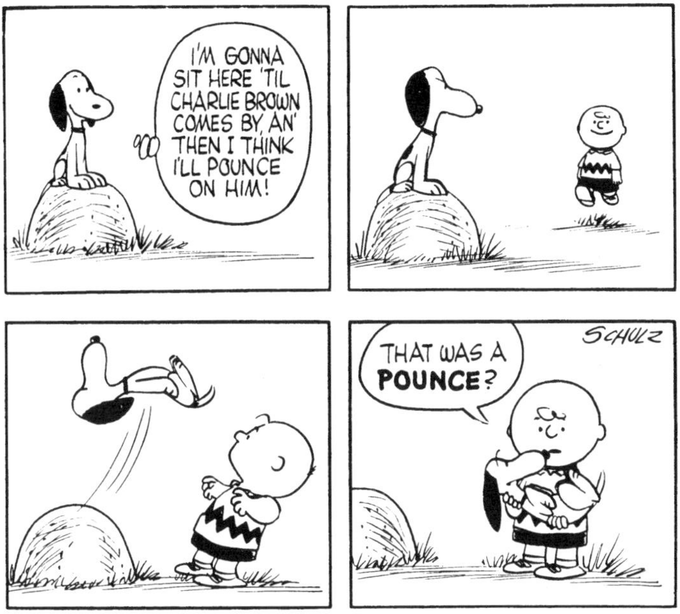
I'M GONNA SIT HERE 'TIL CHARLIE BROWN COMES BY, AN' THEN I THINK I'LL POUNCE ON HIM!
SCHULZ
THAT WAS A **POUNCE**?

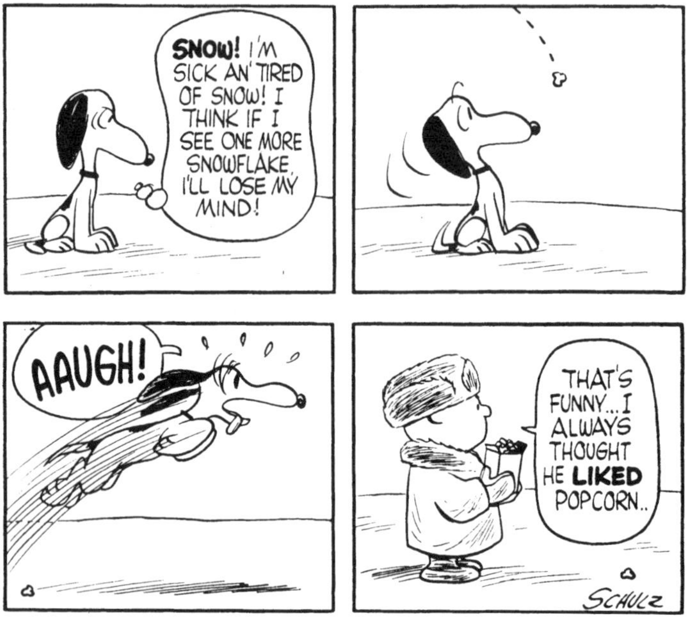
SNOW! I'M SICK AN' TIRED OF SNOW! I THINK IF I SEE ONE MORE SNOWFLAKE, I'LL LOSE MY MIND!
AAUGH!
THAT'S FUNNY... I ALWAYS THOUGHT HE LIKED POPCORN..
SCHULZ

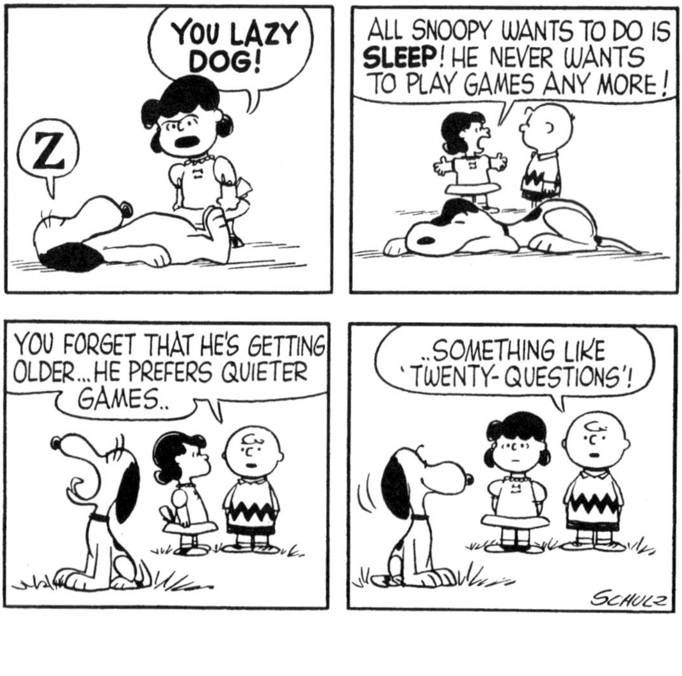
YOU LAZY DOG!
Z
ALL SNOOPY WANTS TO DO IS SLEEP! HE NEVER WANTS TO PLAY GAMES ANY MORE!
YOU FORGET THAT HE'S GETTING OLDER... HE PREFERS QUIETER GAMES..
..SOMETHING LIKE 'TWENTY-QUESTIONS'!
SCHULZ

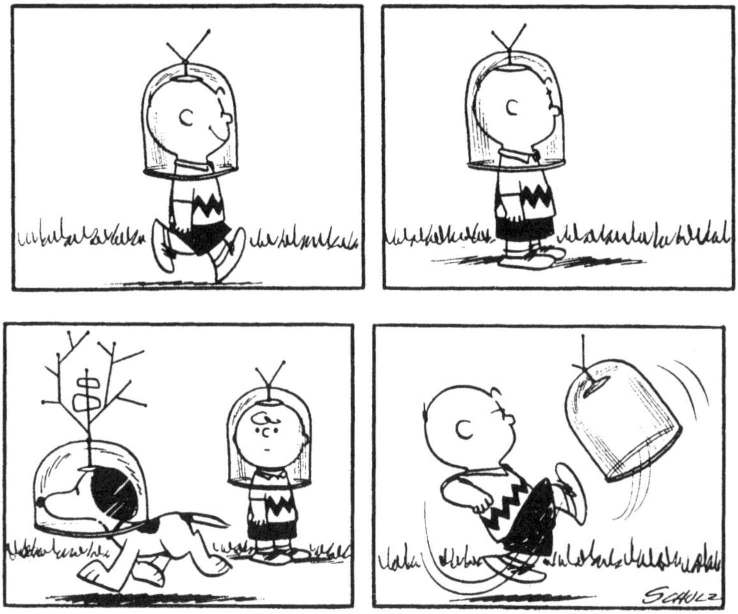
SCHULZ

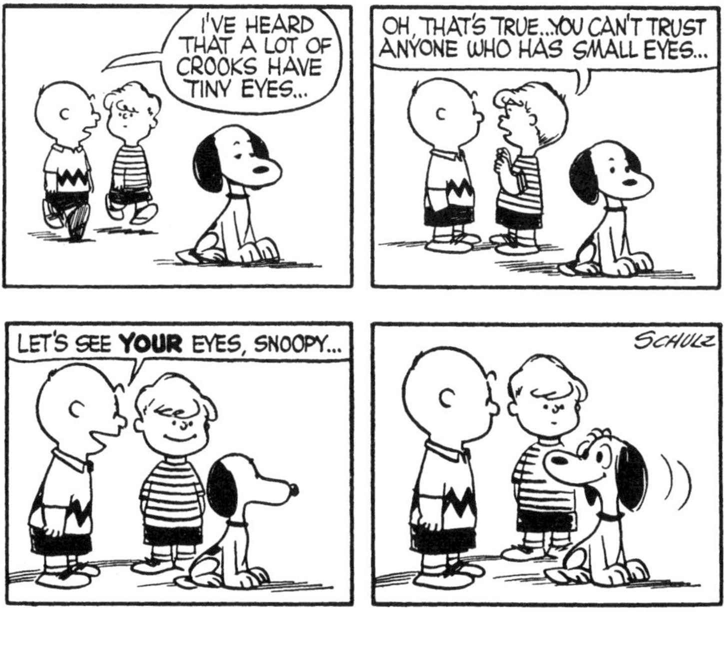
I'VE HEARD THAT A LOT OF CROOKS HAVE TINY EYES...
OH, THAT'S TRUE...YOU CAN'T TRUST ANYONE WHO HAS SMALL EYES...
LET'S SEE YOUR EYES, SNOOPY...
SCHULZ

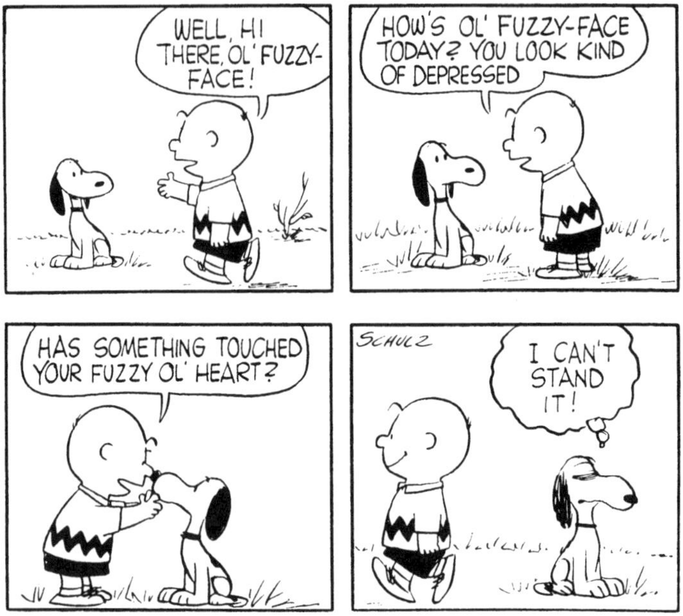
WELL, HI THERE, OL' FUZZY-FACE!
HOW'S OL' FUZZY-FACE TODAY? YOU LOOK KIND OF DEPRESSED
HAS SOMETHING TOUCHED YOUR FUZZY OL' HEART?
SCHULZ
I CAN'T STAND IT!

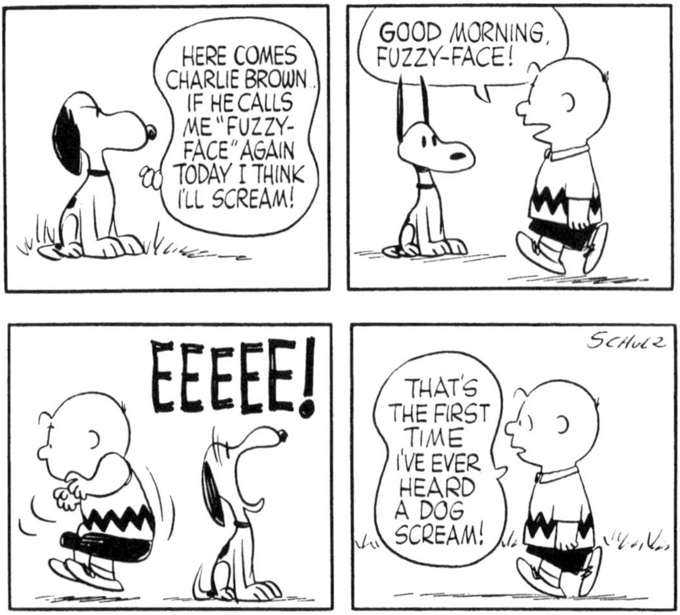
HERE COMES CHARLIE BROWN.. IF HE CALLS ME "FUZZY-FACE" AGAIN TODAY I THINK I'LL SCREAM!
GOOD MORNING, FUZZY-FACE!
EEEEE!
SCHULZ
THAT'S THE FIRST TIME I'VE EVER HEARD A DOG SCREAM!

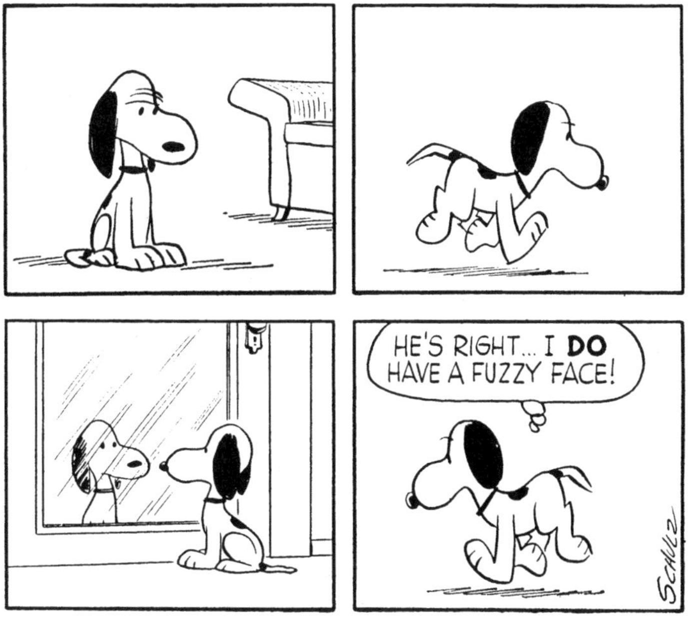
HE'S RIGHT... I **DO** HAVE A FUZZY FACE!
SCHULZ

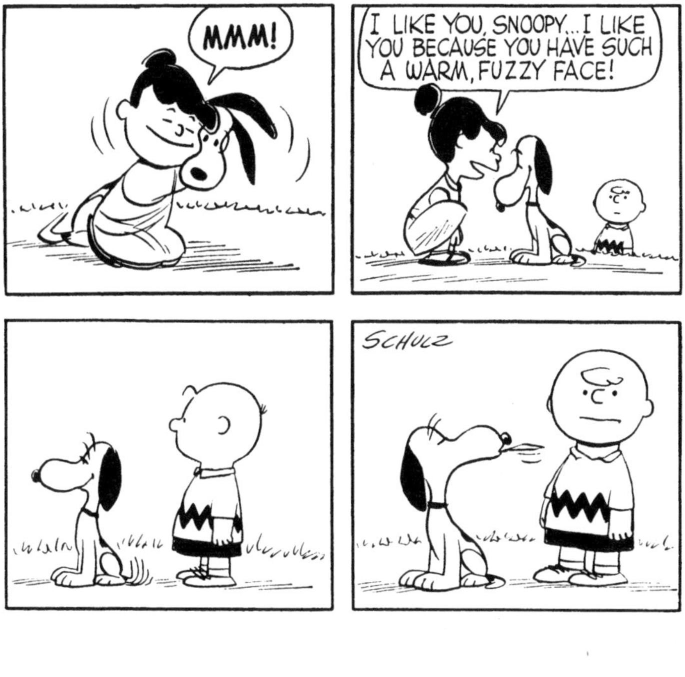
MMM!
I LIKE YOU, SNOOPY... I LIKE YOU BECAUSE YOU HAVE SUCH A WARM, FUZZY FACE!
SCHULZ

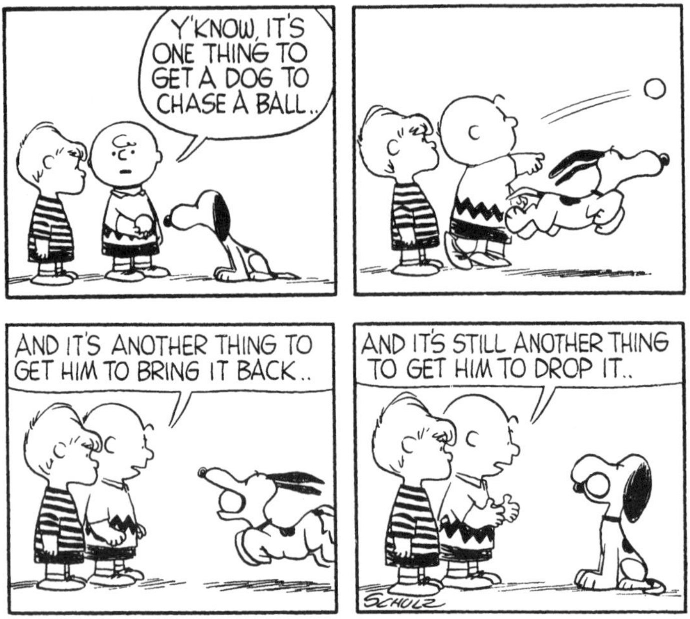
Y'KNOW, IT'S ONE THING TO GET A DOG TO CHASE A BALL..
AND IT'S ANOTHER THING TO GET HIM TO BRING IT BACK..
AND IT'S STILL ANOTHER THING TO GET HIM TO DROP IT..
SCHULZ

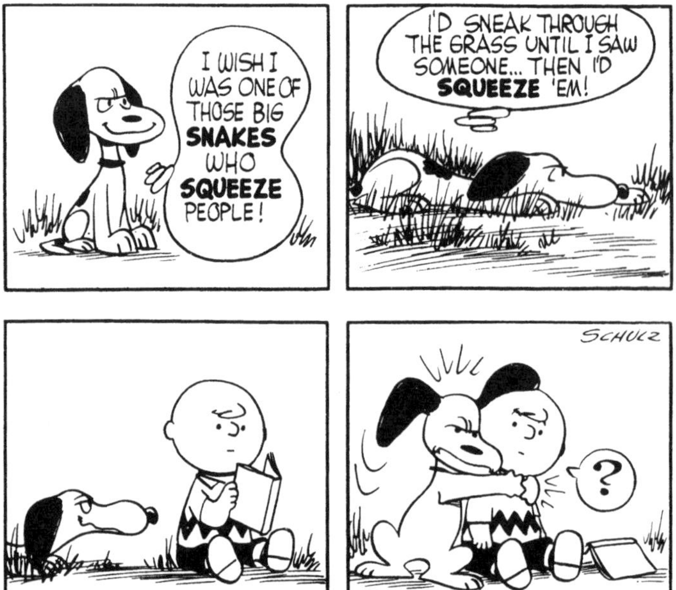
I WISH I WAS ONE OF THOSE BIG **SNAKES** WHO **SQUEEZE** PEOPLE!
I'D SNEAK THROUGH THE GRASS UNTIL I SAW SOMEONE... THEN I'D **SQUEEZE** 'EM!
SCHULZ
?

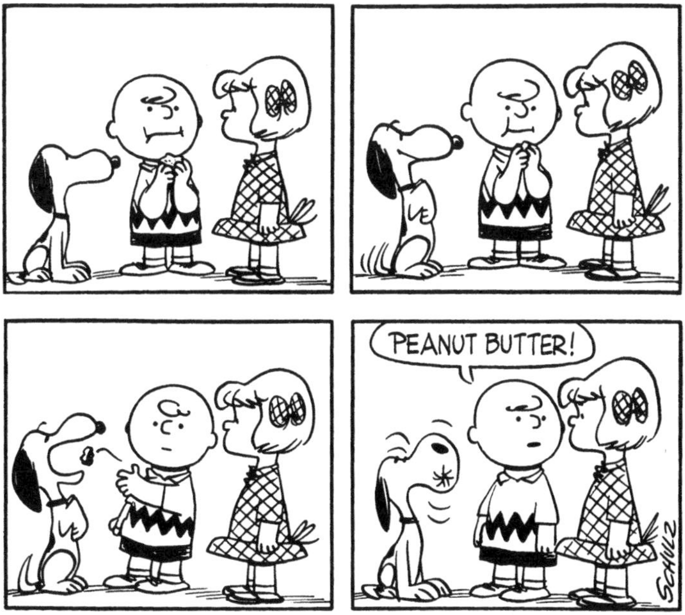
PEANUT BUTTER!
SCHULZ

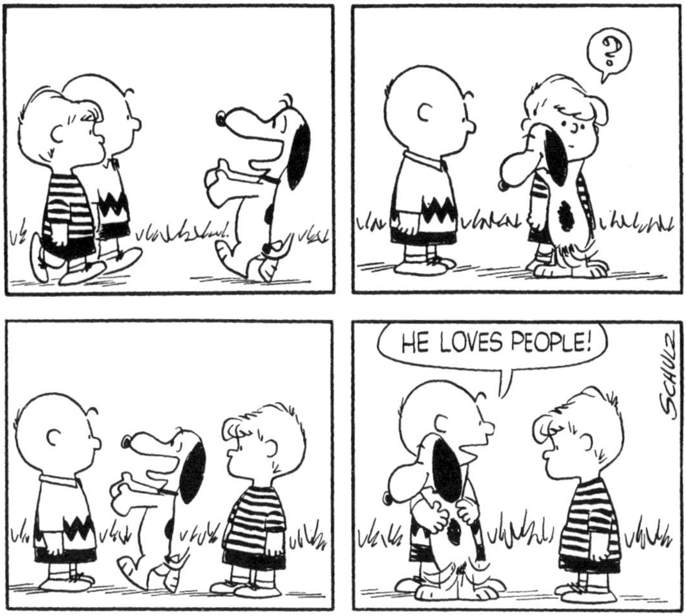
?
HE LOVES PEOPLE!
SCHULZ

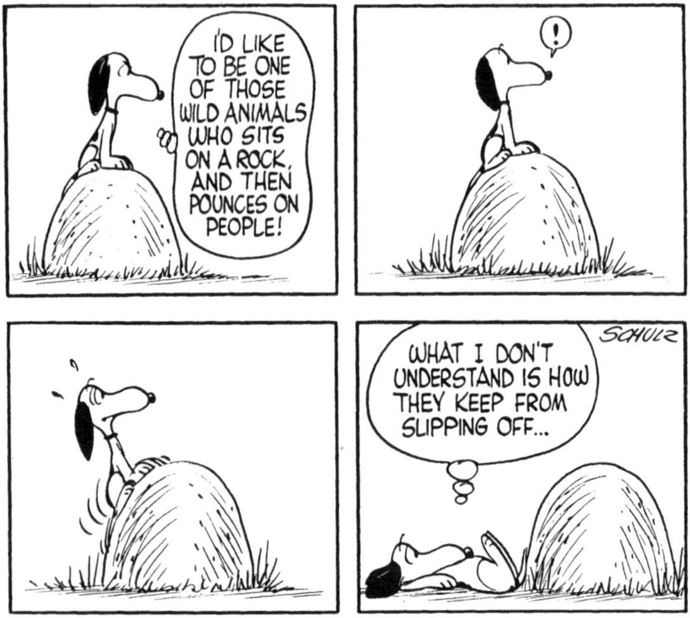
I'D LIKE TO BE ONE OF THOSE WILD ANIMALS WHO SITS ON A ROCK, AND THEN POUNCES ON PEOPLE!
!
SCHULZ
WHAT I DON'T UNDERSTAND IS HOW THEY KEEP FROM SLIPPING OFF...

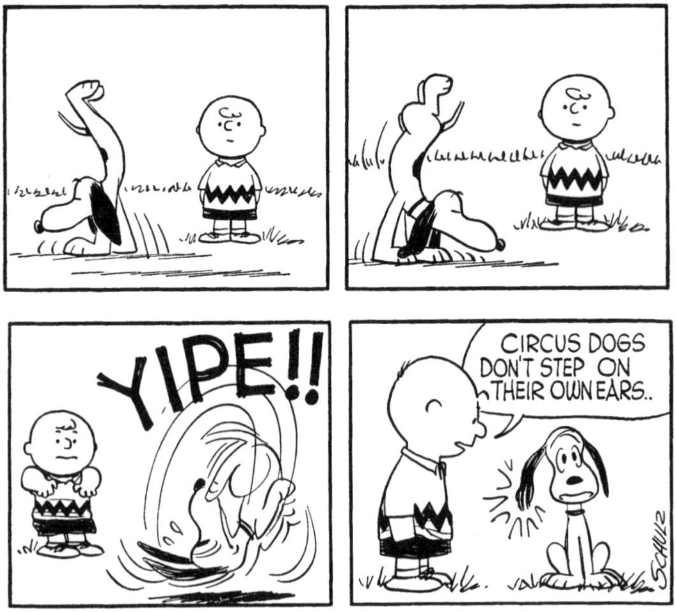
YIPE!!
CIRCUS DOGS DON'T STEP ON THEIR OWN EARS..
SCHULZ

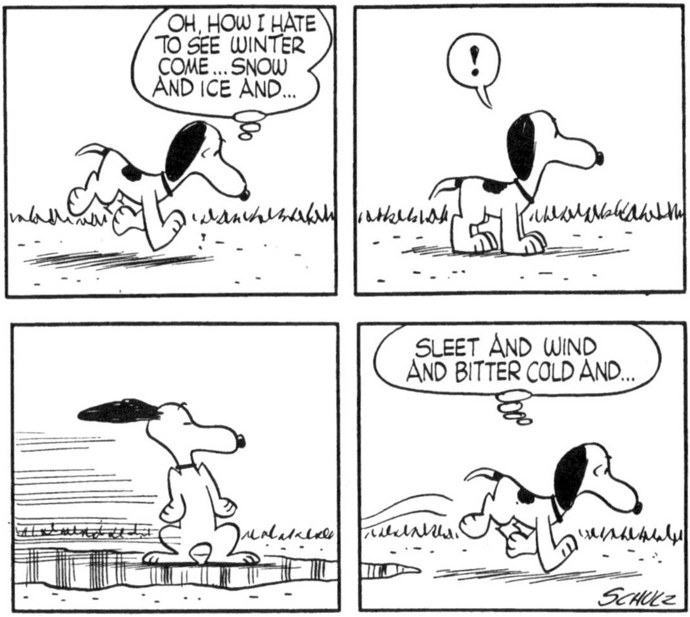
OH, HOW I HATE TO SEE WINTER COME... SNOW AND ICE AND...
!
SLEET AND WIND AND BITTER COLD AND...
SCHULZ

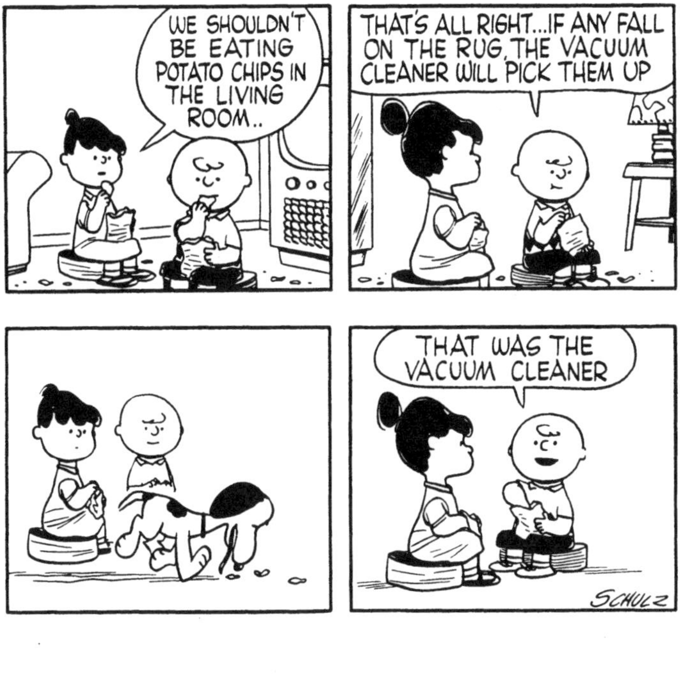
WE SHOULDN'T BE EATING POTATO CHIPS IN THE LIVING ROOM..
THAT'S ALL RIGHT...IF ANY FALL ON THE RUG, THE VACUUM CLEANER WILL PICK THEM UP
THAT WAS THE VACUUM CLEANER
SCHULZ

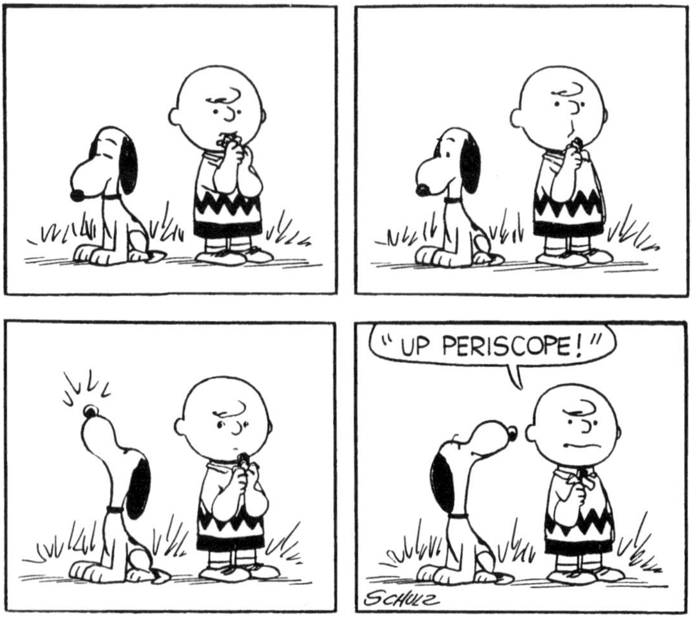
"UP PERISCOPE!"
SCHULZ

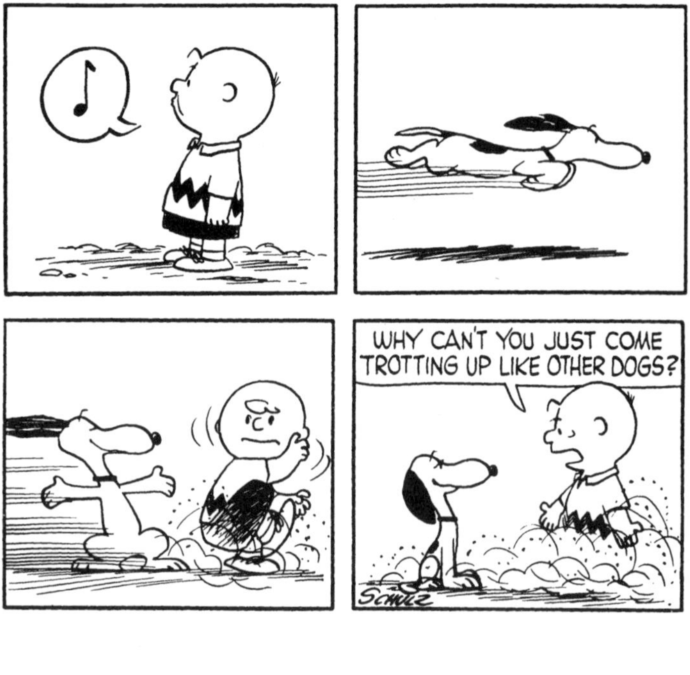
♪
WHY CAN'T YOU JUST COME TROTTING UP LIKE OTHER DOGS?
SCHULZ

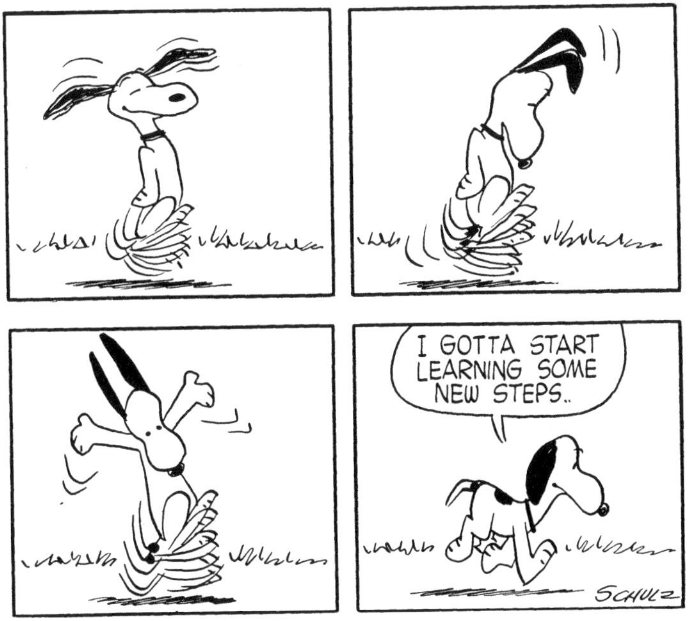
I GOTTA START LEARNING SOME NEW STEPS..
SCHULZ

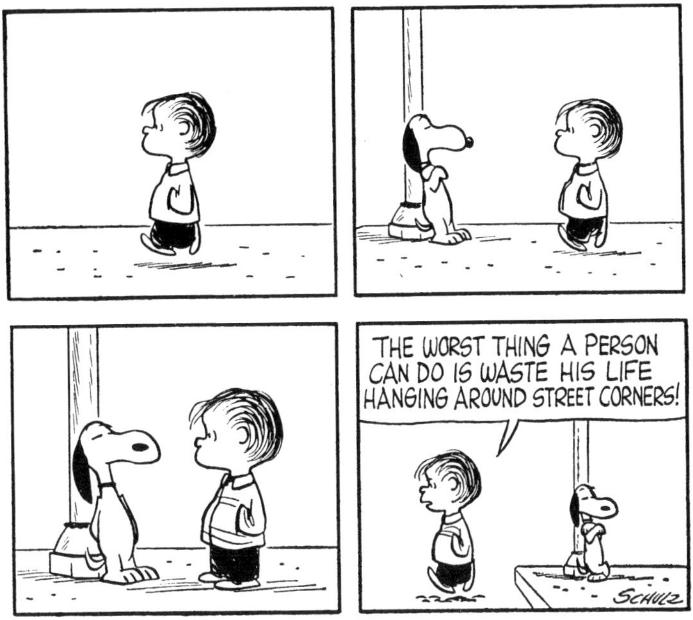
THE WORST THING A PERSON CAN DO IS WASTE HIS LIFE HANGING AROUND STREET CORNERS!
SCHULZ

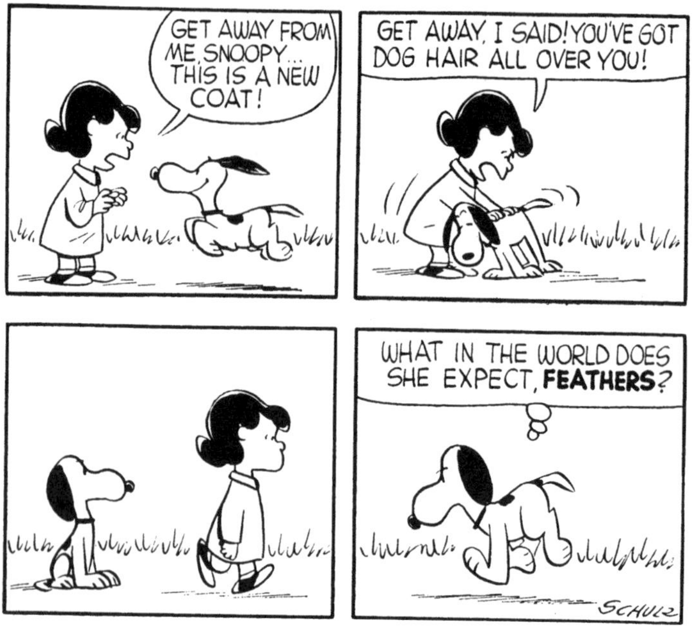
GET AWAY FROM ME, SNOOPY... THIS IS A NEW COAT!
GET AWAY, I SAID! YOU'VE GOT DOG HAIR ALL OVER YOU!
WHAT IN THE WORLD DOES SHE EXPECT, FEATHERS?
SCHULZ

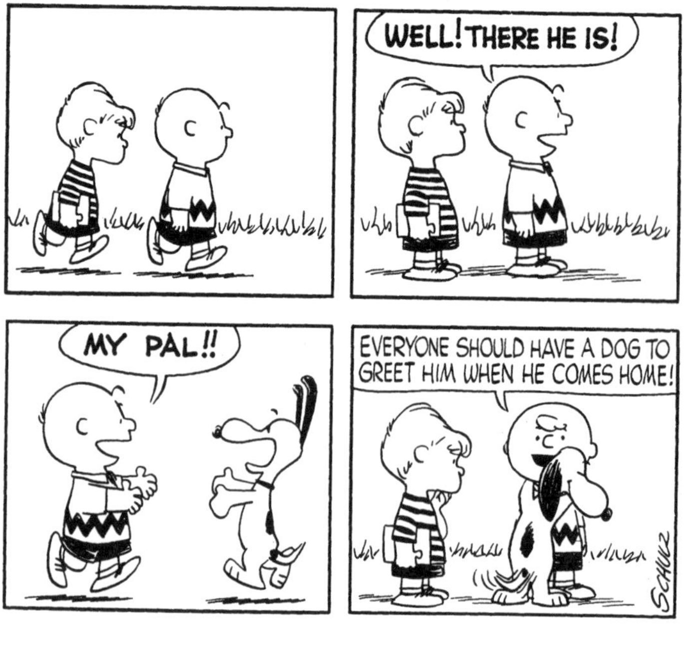
WELL! THERE HE IS!
MY PAL!!
EVERYONE SHOULD HAVE A DOG TO GREET HIM WHEN HE COMES HOME!
SCHULZ

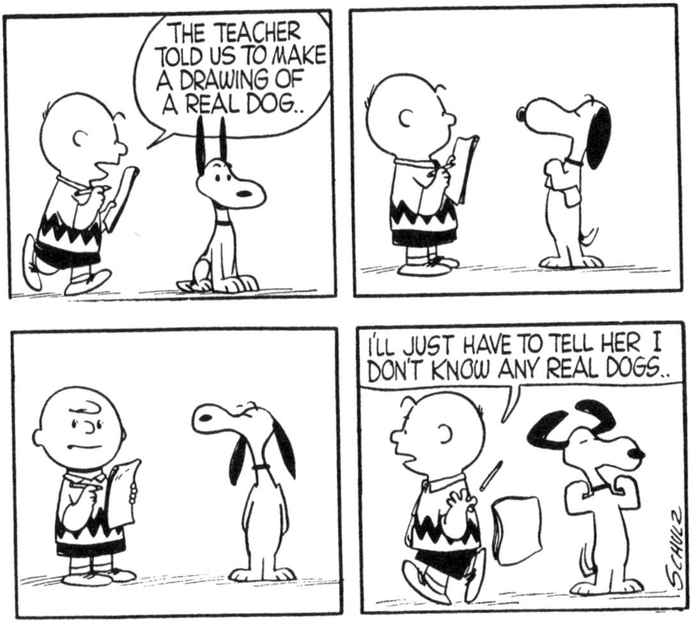
THE TEACHER TOLD US TO MAKE A DRAWING OF A REAL DOG..
I'LL JUST HAVE TO TELL HER I DON'T KNOW ANY REAL DOGS..
SCHULZ

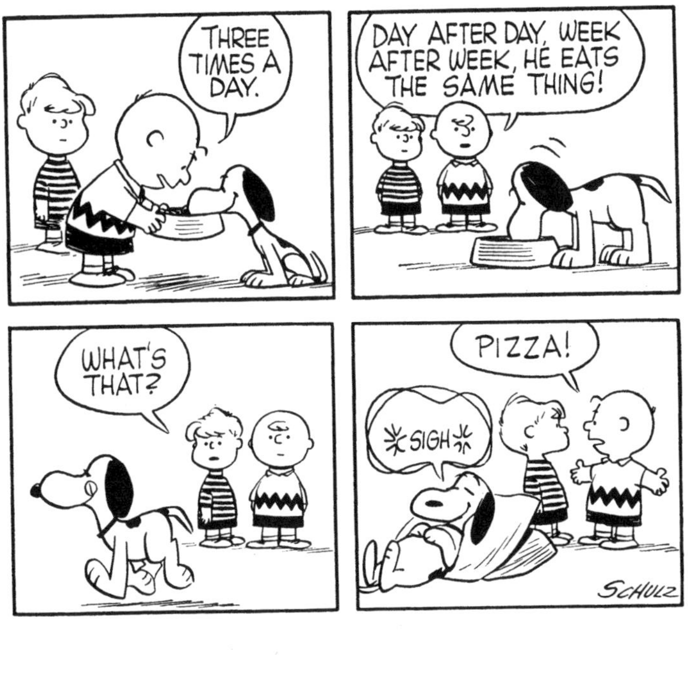
THREE TIMES A DAY.
DAY AFTER DAY, WEEK AFTER WEEK, HE EATS THE SAME THING!
WHAT'S THAT?
PIZZA!
SIGH
SCHULZ

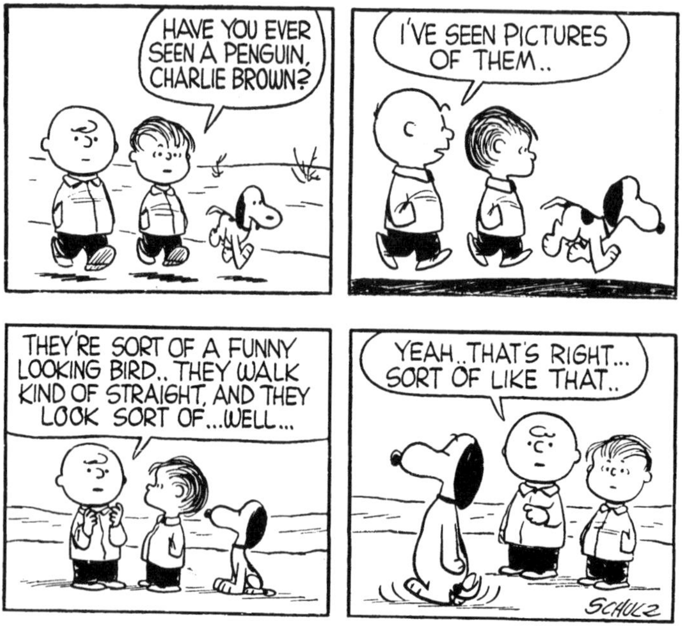
HAVE YOU EVER SEEN A PENGUIN, CHARLIE BROWN?
I'VE SEEN PICTURES OF THEM..
THEY'RE SORT OF A FUNNY LOOKING BIRD.. THEY WALK KIND OF STRAIGHT, AND THEY LOOK SORT OF...WELL...
YEAH..THAT'S RIGHT... SORT OF LIKE THAT..
SCHULZ

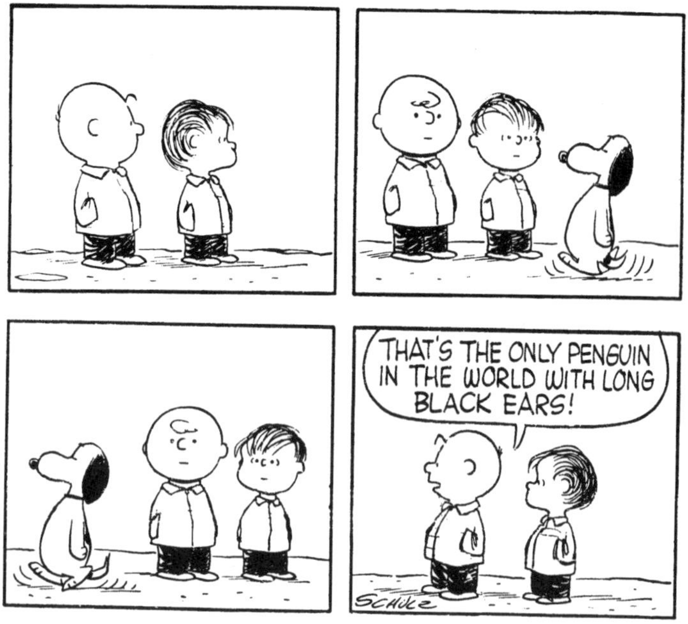
THAT'S THE ONLY PENGUIN IN THE WORLD WITH LONG BLACK EARS!
SCHULZ

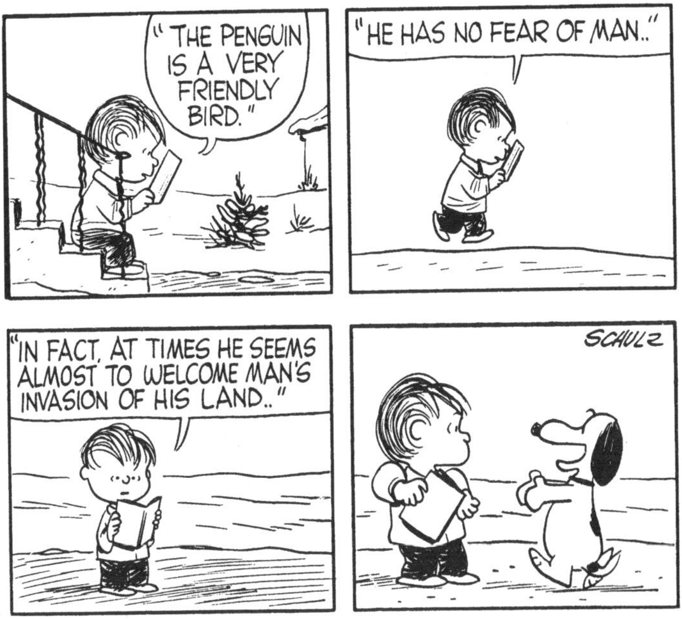
"THE PENGUIN IS A VERY FRIENDLY BIRD."
"HE HAS NO FEAR OF MAN.."
"IN FACT, AT TIMES HE SEEMS ALMOST TO WELCOME MAN'S INVASION OF HIS LAND.."
SCHULZ

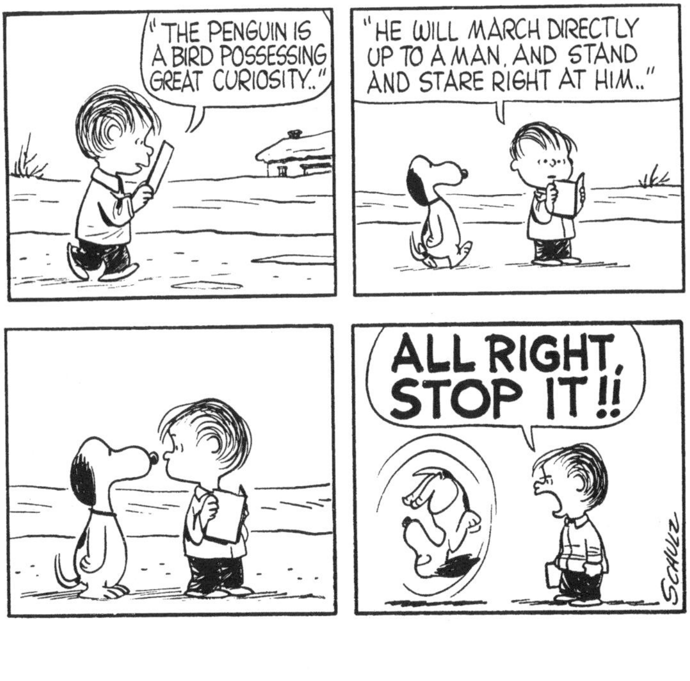
"THE PENGUIN IS A BIRD POSSESSING GREAT CURIOSITY.."
"HE WILL MARCH DIRECTLY UP TO A MAN, AND STAND AND STARE RIGHT AT HIM.."
ALL RIGHT, STOP IT!!
SCHULZ

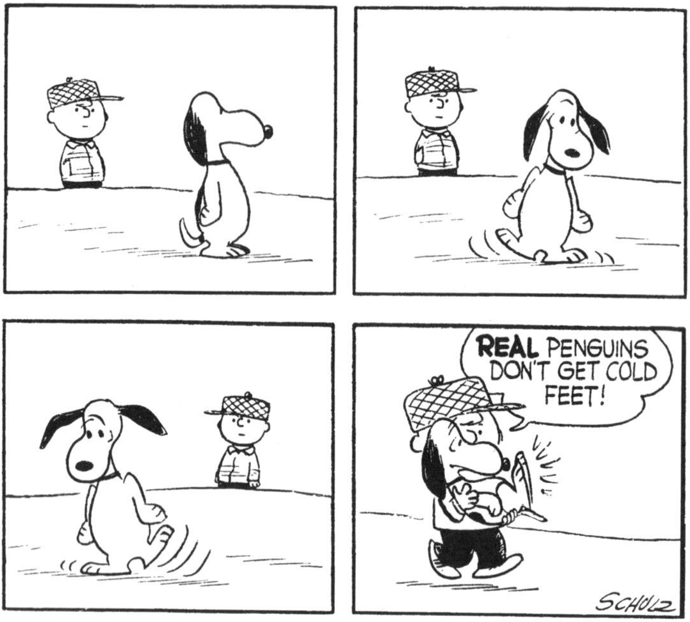
REAL PENGUINS DON'T GET COLD FEET!
SCHULZ

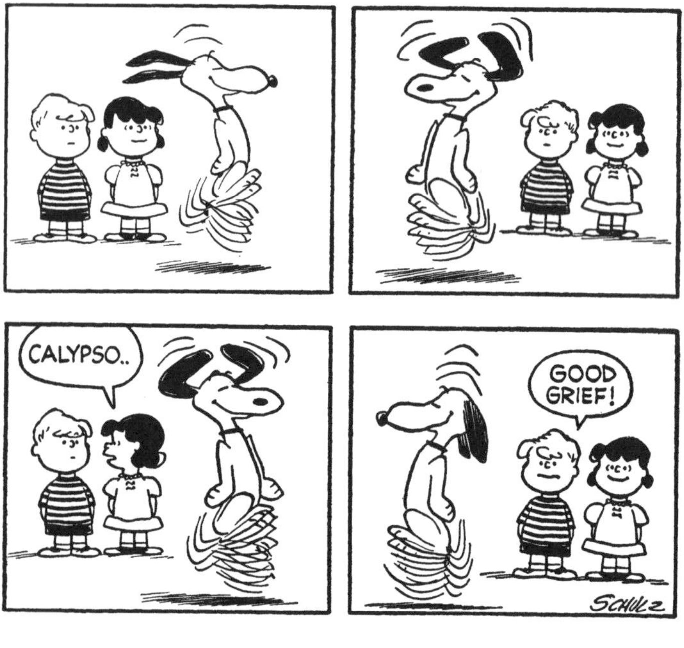
CALYPSO..
GOOD GRIEF!
SCHULZ

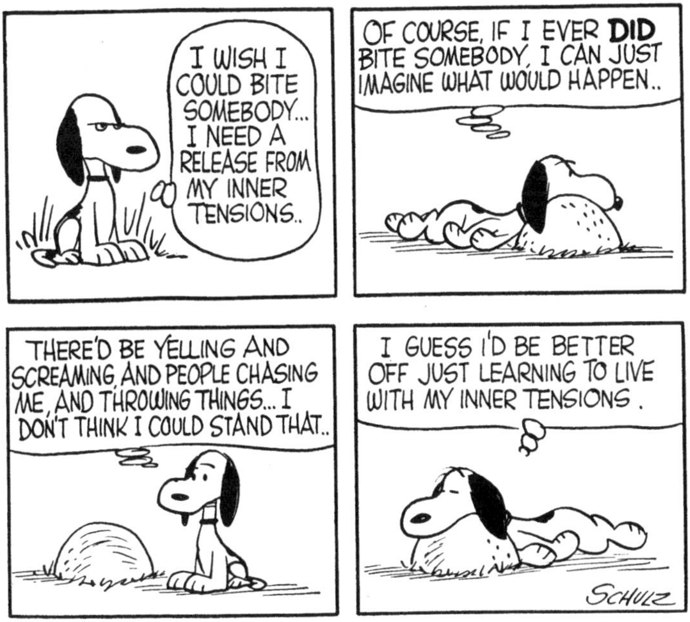
I WISH I COULD BITE SOMEBODY... I NEED A RELEASE FROM MY INNER TENSIONS..
OF COURSE, IF I EVER **DID** BITE SOMEBODY, I CAN JUST IMAGINE WHAT WOULD HAPPEN..
THERE'D BE YELLING AND SCREAMING, AND PEOPLE CHASING ME, AND THROWING THINGS... I DON'T THINK I COULD STAND THAT..
I GUESS I'D BE BETTER OFF JUST LEARNING TO LIVE WITH MY INNER TENSIONS.
SCHULZ

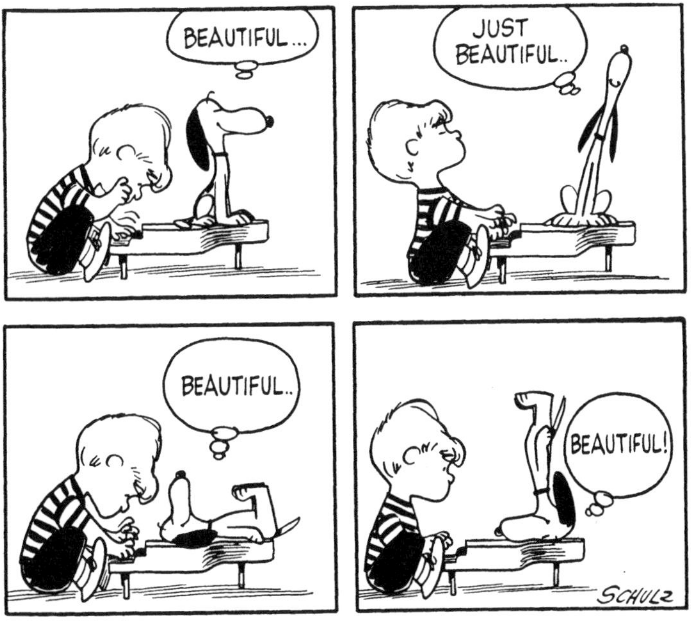
BEAUTIFUL...
JUST BEAUTIFUL..
BEAUTIFUL..
BEAUTIFUL!
SCHULZ

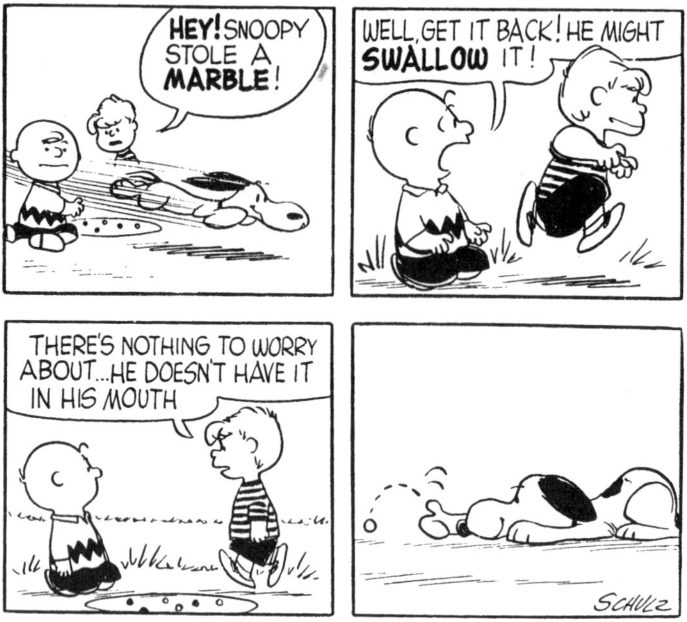
HEY! SNOOPY STOLE A MARBLE!
WELL, GET IT BACK! HE MIGHT SWALLOW IT!
THERE'S NOTHING TO WORRY ABOUT...HE DOESN'T HAVE IT IN HIS MOUTH
SCHULZ

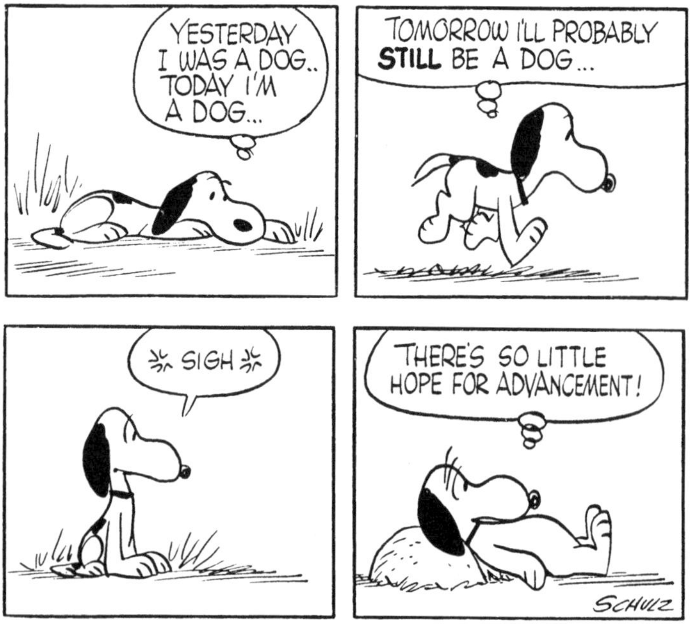
YESTERDAY I WAS A DOG.. TODAY I'M A DOG...
TOMORROW I'LL PROBABLY STILL BE A DOG...
SIGH
THERE'S SO LITTLE HOPE FOR ADVANCEMENT!
SCHULZ